❈ SUFI WISDOM SERIES

VOLUME 2

PEARLS AND CORAL
SECRETS OF THE SUFI WAY

BY
SHAYKH MUHAMMAD HISHAM KABBANI

Discourses delivered by permission of his master
Mawlana Shaykh Muhammad Nazim Adil Al-Haqqani,
World Leader of the Most Distinguished
Naqshbandi Sufi Order

December 1991-January 1993
Ann Arbor, Detroit, London, Los Altos, Montreal, New York
City, Oakland, Washington, Woodstock

ISLAMIC SUPREME COUNCIL OF AMERICA

© Copyright 2006 by the Islamic Supreme Council of America.
All rights reserved.
ISBN: 1-930409-08-7
No part of this book may be reproduced, stored in a retrieval system, or transmitted in any form, or by any means, electronic, mechanical, photocopying, or otherwise, without the written permission of the Islamic Supreme Council of America.

Library of Congress Cataloging-in-Publication Data
Kabbani, Shaykh Muhammad Hisham.
   Pearls and coral : secrets of the sufi way : discourses of Shaykh Muhammad Hisham Kabbani delivered by permission of his master Shaykh Muhammad Nazim Adil Al-Haqqani, world leader of the most distinguished Naqshbandi sufi order, December 1991-January 1993, Ann Arbor, Detroit, London, Los Altos, Montreal, New York City, Oakland, Washington, Woodstock.
   p. cm. -- (Sufi wisdom series)

1. Naqshabandīyah--Doctrines. 2. Sufism--Doctrines. I. Naqshbandi, Muhammad Nazim
Adil al-Haqqani, 1922- . II. Title. III. Series.
BP189.7.N35K336 2005
297.4--dc22
                                        2005009441

Published and Distributed by:
Islamic Supreme Council of America
17195 Silver Parkway, #201 Fenton, MI 48430
USA
Tel: (888) 278-6624
Fax:(810) 815-0518
Email: staff@islamicsupremecouncil.org
Web: http://www.islamicsupremecouncil.org

Shaykh Muhammad Nazim Adil al-Haqqani (right), world leader of the most distinguished Naqshbandi-Haqqani Sufi Order, with his representative, and author of this book, Shaykh Muhammad Hisham Kabbani.

**From them come forth
the pearls and the coral.**
Holy Qur'an: Ar-Rahman, 55:22

TABLE OF CONTENTS

Publisher's Notes	ix
About the Author	11
Foreword	13
The Equality of God's Servants	15
Bombard Your Ego With All Kinds Of Weapons	16
Knowledge Is Revelation According to Station	17
Stop Running From God	20
God Created You Regardless of Religion	22
Treat Everyone as Jesus, Moses, and Buddha Treated Everyone	23
God Made Everything the Fruit of Unity	29
Leave the Religion That Does Not Make You Holy	32
Surrender! He Will Provide	32
Return from Annihilation to Real Existence	34
Surrender of a Corpse is Rejected	39
Seclusion	41
Belief is in the Unseen	43
Five Heart Levels	44
The Loveliest Title is 'Servant'	47
Powerful Intentions Work Miracles	48
Hide Others' Mistakes	49
Respect Everyone	52
A Hindu Shows Miraculous Power	54
The Smell of the Naqshbandiyyah	58
Where to Hide?	59
Who Can be Called 'Naqshbandi'?	61
Eat Simple Food and Welcome Guests	64
Honor Your Guests	64
Rumi was Muslim	66
The Second Era of Ignorance and the Coming of Mahdi	67
The Coming Golden Age	72
Keep Account of Yourself	74
Love is the Key	75
Sufism in not Idolatry or Innovation	77
The Accusations of the Ignorant	80
The Perfect Listener	80

Avoid Suspicion	81
How Did God Sit on the Throne?	82

The Power of Shaykh Nazim's Advice — 85

States — 87

- Jealousy and Pride are the Cause of Fighting — 89
- Grandshaykh Lowers Himself — 90
- Keep a Stone in Your Mouth — 92

Faith in the Shaykh — 93

- Mawlana Speaks from the Heart of the Prophet — 94
- The Worst Sin — 95
- Are You Mistake-Free? — 97
- No Salvation Except Prophet Muhammad — 98

Cover People's Faults — 100

- The Holy Stone of Abu Bakr as-Siddiq — 100
- Look Under Your Own Turban — 101
- Don't Stir up Waste — 102

On Surat Al-Kahf 28-31 — 106

- The Atheists and Sayyidina 'Ali — 107
- Association to Combat the Ego's Tricks — 109
- A Lady Corrects the Caliph — 110

Be Merciful — 112

- Adam was Forgiven for the Sake of Muhammad — 112
- God Tests Abraham Severely — 113
- The Fire of Love — 116
- Two Wings Are Needed to Fly — 117

Migrating to Good Manners — 120

- All Prophets Suffered — 121
- Be Patient with Difficulty — 122
- The Prophet's Favorite Name — 123

Do Not Use Mind in *Tariqah* but Love — 126

- Everything Depends on Love — .126
- Leave Behind Your Mind — 128
- How Imam Ghazali Became a Saint — 131
- Visit to a Cemetery — 133
- Who is Considered Responsible in Tariqah? — 134

Use the *Miswak* — 137

The Meaning of Religion — 138

- Accept All of God's Messengers — 139

Tariqah in the Qur'an — 146

- Degrees in Religion — 147
- Discover Qur'an's Secrets — 148

God's Messengers Bring You to Perfect Happiness — 150

The Worthless Century — 158

World Filled with Tyrants	160
Sincere Ones Treated as Criminals	164
Awaiting Mahdi	167
Praise the Prophet for He Hears You	169
Khidr and Moses	172
Listen Humbly to Advice	175
Scholars Must Open Their Minds	177
Do Not be the Judge	179
The Ignorant Trust-Bearer	180
The Limits of God's Mercy	181
The Prayer of Salvation	183
Don't Arrogate Yourself	184
Holy Diamonds	187
The Cursing of the Shaykh	189
Don't Let Your Love Shake	192
Submit to Your Heart	196
Hearts Are All-Important	197
The Purpose of Martial Arts	198
Carry Servants' Difficulties	200
Knowledge of Allah's Names	204
Saints' Ranks are on the Knowledg of Divine Names	205
The Power of Saints	205
Die Before You Die	208
Overwhelming Consciousness	212
There Is Only One Main Station	214
We Are Images of Our Lord in This World	215
The Seven Powers of the Perfect Saint	216
The Seven Foremost Names of God	221
The Duality of Creation and Knowledge	225
Passing of the World through the Needle's Eye	231
Power of the Shaykh	232
The Last Seven Breaths	234
Earth, Moon and Sun	235
"He Is Closer to You than Your Jugular Vein"	239
The Three Stations of Certainty (*Yaqeen*)	243
Obedience Is the Test of Love	245
The Precious Knowledge	253
Everyone is a Worshipper	261
Endnotes	263

Publisher's Notes

This book is specifically designed for laypersons and readers unfamiliar with Sufi terms. As such, we have often replaced Arabic terminology with English translations, except in instances where Arabic terms are crucial to the tone and substance of the text. In such instances, we have included transliterations or footnoted explanations.

As the source material is an oral transmission, its language was revised for a written format, and references have been added as appropriate; however, we have tried our best to retain the essence of the author's original talks. We ask the reader's forgiveness for any omissions in this final text.

For those who are familiar with Arabic and Islamic teachings, we apologize for the simplified transliterations. Our experience is that unfamiliar symbols and diacritical marks make for difficult reading by laypersons; as such, please indulge this compromise between accuracy and accessibility.

Qur'anic quotes are centered, highlighted in bold and italics and footnoted, citing chapter name, number and verse. The Holy Traditions of Prophet Muhammad ﷺ (known as *hadith*) are offset, italicized and footnoted referencing the book(s) in which they are cited.

Where gender-specific pronouns such as "he" and "him" are applied in a general sense, it has been solely for the flow of text, and no discrimination is intended towards female readers.

Universally Recognized Symbols

The following Arabic symbols connote sacredness and are universally recognized by Sufi Muslims:

The symbol ﷻ represents *subhanahu wa ta'ala*, a high form of praise reserved for God alone, which is customarily recited after reading or pronouncing the common name Allah, and any of the ninety-nine Islamic Holy Names of God.

The symbol ﷺ represents *sall-allahu 'alayhi wa sallam* (God's blessings and greetings of peace be upon the Prophet), which is customarily recited after reading or pronouncing the holy name of Prophet Muhammad.

The symbol عليه السلام represents *'alayhi 's-salam* (peace be upon him/her), which is customarily recited after reading or pronouncing the sanctified names of prophets, Prophet Muhammad's family members, and the angels.

The symbol ﵁ represents *radi-allahu 'anh/'anha* (may God be pleased with him/her), which is customarily recited after reading or pronouncing the holy names of Prophet Muhammad's Companions.

The symbol ق represents *qaddas-allahu sirrah* (may God sanctify his or her secret), which is customarily recited after reading or pronouncing the name of a saint.

ABOUT THE AUTHOR

Shaykh Muhammad Hisham Kabbani is a world-renowned author and religious scholar. He has devoted his life to the promotion of the traditional Islamic principles of peace, tolerance, love, compassion and brotherhood, while opposing extremism in all its forms. The shaykh is a member of a respected family of traditional Islamic scholars, which includes the former head of the Association of Muslim Scholars of Lebanon and the present Grand Mufti[1] of Lebanon.

In the U.S., Shaykh Kabbani serves as Chairman, Islamic Supreme Council of America; Founder, Naqshbandi Sufi Order of America; Advisor, World Organization for Resource Development and Education; Chairman, As-Sunnah Foundation of America; Chairman, Kamilat Muslim Women's Organization; and, Founder and President, The Muslim Magazine.

Shaykh Kabbani is highly trained, both as a Western scientist and as a classical Islamic scholar. He received a bachelor's degree in chemistry and studied medicine. In addition, he also holds a degree in Islamic Divine Law, and under the tutelage of Shaykh 'Abd Allah Daghestani ق, license to teach, guide and counsel religious students in Islamic spirituality from Shaykh Muhammad Nazim 'Adil al-Qubrusi al-Haqqani an-Naqshbandi ق, the world leader of the Naqshbandi-Haqqani Sufi Order.

His books include: *A Spiritual Commentary on the Chapter of Sincerity* (2006), *Sufi Science of Self-Realization* (Fons Vitae, 2005),

---

[1] The highest Islamic religious authority in the country.

Keys to the Divine Kingdom (2005); *Classical Islam and the Naqshbandi Sufi Order* (2004); *The Naqshbandi Sufi Tradition Guidebook* (2004); *The Approach of Armageddon? An Islamic Perspective* (2003); *Encyclopedia of Muhammad's Women Companions and the Traditions They Related* (1998, with Dr. Laleh Bakhtiar); *Encyclopedia of Islamic Doctrine* (7 vols. 1998); *Angels Unveiled* (1996); *The Naqshbandi Sufi Way* (1995); *Remembrance of God Liturgy of the Sufi Naqshbandi Masters* (1994).

In his long-standing endeavor to promote better understanding of classical Islam, Shaykh Kabbani has hosted two international conferences in the United States, both of which drew scholars from throughout the Muslim world. As a resounding voice for traditional Islam, his counsel is sought by journalists, academics and government leaders.

Foreword

Our praise and thanks be to God, and our salutations on his beloved Prophet Muhammad and on all sincere servants of the Lord. I am most happy that my son-in-law and deputy, Shaykh Hisham Kabbani has been able to publish this second volume of talks from the teachings of our Grandshaykh Mawlana Shaykh 'Abd Allah al-Fa'iz ad-Daghestani ق.

Our Grandshaykh's teachings are to love God, appreciate His Divine favors, and strive in His service. The greatest Sufi teaching is that there is no higher station than serving the Lord Almighty and serving God's creation, human beings.

The teachings of our Grandshaykh are such that with patience and strong aspiration, those who follow them may reach perfected levels and attain the stations that saints in earlier times were unable to. Just as an average citizen today has capabilities at his hands that far surpass those available even to kings and queens in earlier times, so too does the "average" seeker of the Way have access to extraordinary levels of spiritual attainment – not due to their cleverness or excellent aspects of their worship, but due to the times in which we live.

These lessons are designed to overcome fear, doubt and negativity that bind one to the physical world, thereby opening the heart to spiritual blessings. At the same time extremism and terrorism stand condemned by every moral and spiritual person as one of today's most terrible evils.

Shaykh Hisham is coming to you and bringing you Sufi teachings. Shaykh Hisham has been blessed by our Grandshaykh and from me also. He and his brother Shaykh Adnan did their best for our Grandshaykh when they were young and up until today we are observing their work and seeing that they are constant on right path. He belongs to me and I am sending to him to speak and give advice to our brothers everywhere and anywhere. He calls you to Allah and to his beloved Prophet ﷺ and to saints. He is not calling you to the worldly life. I am not calling you to the worldly life, *dunya,* and he is also never calling you to the worldly life.

He did his best also for me from his early childhood up to today and he is, as you know, my son-in-law. For perhaps 35 years or more he has been working and establishing the Naqshbandi Way. I am happy with him. If he is coming and speaking to you, give your respect and accept his advice and try to be with him, attending his association. Love him and respect him; he should be happy and he has been blessed by our Grandshaykh also.

People do not know about Shaykh Hisham. Shaykh Hisham is one of the saints and he is doing his best for people, not to build their worldly life but in the hope of reaching to the time of Sayyidina Mahdi ؏. And we are asking Allah Almighty to make the readers of this blessed volume under the flag of Mahdi ؏ and to reach the time of Prophet Jesus ؏. Pray for me also, to have good health for reaching the days of Mahdi ؏ *insha-Allah* and to see him and the Prophet Jesus ؏. Keep the right path, be with true ones, and you should be happy here and hereafter.

I would like to particularly thank my daughter, Hajjah Nazihe Adil, and those who labored hard with Shaykh Hisham to bring this second volume to print.

Shaykh Muhammad Nazim Adil al-Haqqani
Lefke, Cyprus
26 Dhu'l-Hijjah, 1426
25 December, 2006

THE EQUALITY OF GOD'S SERVANTS

If your students make mistakes, correct them and try to make them feel happy by giving them a higher grade. Don't give them a failing grade. If you fail them, God will fail you in the Judgment Day, so be careful!

God loves everyone as the mother loves her child. He loves us because we are His servants, by which I mean we are His creation. He created us from His light. If God opens the light which He put in your heart, that light will make the light of the sun seem as nothing. Allah, God, put that secret in everyone's heart—not in special people but in everyone! In God's eye there is no discrimination. He has created everyone from the same origin and the same source. At that time there is no "bad" nor "good." All of them are the same.

The Prophet ﷺ gave an excellent, concise example of that similarity:

People are the same, like the teeth of the comb.[2]

People are equal—he said "people," not "Muslims," "Christians," or "Jews," but "human beings"—as the teeth of the comb are equal. No one is higher, no one is lower. In God's Eyes no one is higher or lower; it is in our eyes that we are "higher" and "lower." Everyone thinks himself high, and the rest are low. No one accepts advice. Advise even a young boy and what will he say? "No; I am right and you are wrong." This is human nature. Put toddlers here and give them a toy: after five minutes they will be fighting. Who taught them to do that?

---

[2] Narrated from Sahl bin Sa'd. Al-Khatib and ad-Dulabi reported it.

The nature of human beings is the ego. The ego never accepts, even in a child, except that everything be for himself alone and not for others. If this is true of young children, what about us? We are worse. We have to teach this fact to our egos. When our ego knows this reality, at that time you can control it. If you control your ego, you surrender to God. If you cannot control your ego, you will never surrender.

Bombard Your Ego With All Kinds of Weapons

Why do they bombard different countries with all kinds of weapons? To force the ruling tryant to surrender, because he is a tyrant. Tyranny never surrenders. The ego never surrenders. You have to bombard your ego with all kinds of weapons that you can muster, in order for it to surrender. When it surrenders, you are finally in the Divine Presence.

Allah has sent all the prophets and all the saints to teach us how to surrender to Him. That is why He said:

I did not create human beings and other creatures except to worship Me.[3]

Or it could be interpreted to remember Me, to come to Me, to be happy with Me. But instead, I am seeing them running away, following their ego.

You can come to your Lord in any way you like. Everyone has a way in his heart. Find that way and go to your Lord. Your Lord will accept you. He is merciful. If He is merciful, He loves everyone.

May our Lord give us control over our ego, because by ourselves it is difficult. One saint said, "O my Lord, you have created prophets, and they never sin because you are protecting

---

[3] Suratu 'dh-Dhariyat, 51:56.

them. Angels are created from your light and they too never sin. You have created us and you imposed ego over us. It is not our fault, therefore, that we sin, so forgive us!"

You have to control your ego. Once you control it, you control yourself. May Allah control us and control our ego. In this way we can surrender completely.

What can we say? He is the powerful One and we are weak. May He send us of His light to our hearts and make our hearts enlightened with His light, His knowledge, His wisdom. As much as you know, you cannot know everything—therefore you are ignorant. And everyone in this world is ignorant! As much as you try to study, you will only know something, for you cannot know everything. This means that you are ignorant. Did not Allah say, **"Above every knower there is a greater knower"**?[4] How then are we proud of ourselves? Because we can read the alphabet? Is this knowledge?

Knowledge Is Revelation According to Station

Knowledge is the state in which you connect your heart with your Lord in the Divine Presence, and revelation comes to your heart according to the station you are in at that time. Whatever station you are in, you receive knowledge different from that of another station. This is what we call knowledge. It is perceived without connecting yourself to a book. Books are limited. Books are words. Read the Holy Qur'an; others read the Holy Bible. What do they understand? They read words, sentences. You and I read it and give the same meaning: is this knowledge of the Holy Bible? Is this knowledge of the holy Qur'an? No. This is ignorance of the Holy Bible, of the Holy Qur'an, of the Holy Torah.

---

[4] Surah Yusuf, 12:76.

When you read a verse, that verse must take you to a station, or *manzil* in Arabic, because God's revelation comes down stations, one from another. As you rise in stations, leaving one to go to another, the meaning of that verse changes. The meanings will be completely different according to the station. This is what reading of holy books means. This is the knowledge God wants us to have; not scriptural knowledge as one reads literature, understanding only literal meanings. There are no limits to Allah's words.

Rumi, one of the greatest saints, wrote poems with which everyone is so pleased! Why? Because there are so many meanings and inspirations to be found there. What about the holy books? Is no one wondering whether Rumi's words are better or God's? People run after these saints: we respect them deeply, because we know that they are saints, and are connected, but they would not have been able to write these words had they not been been able to understand God's word. Unfortunately, nowadays, people are taking the poems of saints and leaving God's word, which is in the holy books we have mentioned.

If you want to read, you will find deeper knowledge in reading these poems as pathways to the source of their knowledge. Reading as one reads mere stories, therefore, is not going to lead you to an understanding of the holy books. Saints took every verse they read from a different station of revelation, and that revelation gave a different meaning, every time, of the same verse. Saints are able to take, from one verse, 12,000 oceans of knowledge. What I mean by "ocean of knowledge" is a complete school of thought for one verse because of these changes in revelation. This is what saints are after. They are not after bookish knowledge, but after stations—*manazil*—where they can alight and pick up the meanings of these verses.

Moses ﷺ did not read and write. Where did he get these teachings from? His pocket? Some books he read? No, but through revelation. God taught him, and taught Jesus ﷺ, and taught Muhammad ﷺ. Saints, therefore, are in no need of books. When revelation comes, it fills their hearts and comes to their mouth. Sit with them and you will see that what they say today is different from what they say tomorrow. That is because they go to another station. The definition they gave you today about a given object may be superseded the next day by another explanation of the same object. At that time they are at a different station. My shaykh said "If I repeat a story 1,000 times it will have 1,000 different meanings." More meanings come every time.

May Allah give us of this knowledge. This is the important knowledge that we need. This you cannot learn at school, nor find in universities. You cannot find it anywhere, except through your heart, by surrendering. Surrender is the key to that knowledge and the secret of getting that knowledge. Pay that price and you will reach that knowledge. Don't pay the price and you will never reach that knowledge. And may Allah bless all listeners everywhere. The Prophet ﷺ said:

The hearts of human beings are between two fingers of the Merciful: He changes them as He likes.[5]

If He wants them to change this way, do not ask why. He changes them for the best. Don't let your ego say, "No." This is surrender: submitting to God's will.

How to submit? You cannot submit to God directly. It is difficult. You need someone to train you to submit. If you find in someone acceptance and light, and believe that he is a holy man and a saint, hold on to him and ask him, "Show me the way." Without guidance you cannot go that way. It is full of thorns and mines. You need an expert to take you around. If you do not take a guide, you will be fed up after the first or second step and

---

[5] Muslim, Ahmad, at-Tirmidhi, Ibn Majah from Anas ﷺ.

cannot continue. If your heart tells you, "That one is going to show you the way," then surrender to his will. He will take you to God quickly. If you are not satisfied yet, then wait until the sign comes for it is difficult to surrender immediately.

May Allah show us that one who will direct us to surrender to God's will. How long are we going to live? We are near our grave:

No one knows in what land he is going to die.[6]

Some of you [He causes to] die earlier -: and [all this He ordains] so that you might reach a term set [by Him],[7]

Someone might die after one second. What are you preparing for that moment? How are you going to face that One who has created you?

He is going to face you with love, but as for you, you are going to feel shy at that time, and you are going to sweat for shame. Do not be in a shameful position for it will hurt you and burn you.

Stop Running From God

God is coming to you running, and you are running away from Him. In the end, there is no more running. You come and can no longer run away when He takes away the soul from you—that spirit, that secret. At that time what is going to happen? What are you going to say? Has anyone thought about that? With what am I going to face my Lord and what am I going to tell Him? "O my Lord, I was happy in my life on earth, eating, drinking, sleeping, raising my children..." and He will say, "You

---

[6] Surah Luqman, 31:34.
[7] Surah Ghafir, 40:67.

remembered your children with the love I put in your heart for them: did you remember Me one day with that kind of love?" What are we going to say then?

Let us at least take the lowest station and come to our Lord every night repenting, sitting by our beds and saying, "O our Lord, please forgive us; we are sinners and we are weak." At least remember Him once a day. Do not go to sleep in your beds like dumb beasts, without remembering Him. Sit by yourself and meditate ten or fifteen minutes. Say, "O my Lord, please forgive me. I am coming to You; to whom else can I go? No one. I am coming to You: forgive me." Allah is forgiving. Because He loves us, He forgives us. Just as we forgive our children when they make mistakes: because we love them. May Allah grant us that love for Him, and grant us to love each other, as He loves us: all equally and the same, without any discrimination and without differences. And may He accept our association and bless this gathering.

GOD CREATED YOU REGARDLESS OF RELIGION

In any assembly, the speaker must know the reality of his weakness. He must know that he, first of all, is in need of advice. After that, the listeners in the audience are going to benefit. The speaker cannot raise himself above the others. He must know that he is under everyone. If those listeners were not present, the main source of his inspiration would cease. Inspiration is given for the sake of the listeners.

You must not be a lecturer. In our understanding, lecturers are people who prepare their speeches. When you prepare a speech, you are preparing it with ego. Philosophers, scholars, professors are introduced and summed up by their degrees. Who gave them those degrees? Other human beings.

There is a power over all powers. If you wish to call Him God, call Him God; Allah, call Him Allah; Superpower, call Him Superpower. But know that that Power has created everything out of absolute nothingness. We are appearing in this life according to this Power of creation.

The shape in which we appear in this life is not important. We are appearing here as reflections. Our reality is in the presence of that Superpower, never leaving Him. We are with Him always. We here are but shadows. A day is coming, therefore, when these bodies will finish. They are unimportant. What is important is the original Reality that causes these bodies to move. If you find that reality, you will be Ever-Living. If you don't find that reality, you are going to spend seventy or eighty years and then find no place to go.

Remember where you are going. Lecturers must not, therefore, be proud of their degrees and Ph.Ds. They have earned them through studying, accumulating limited amounts of knowledge. Whatever they are learning, however, is limited. No one can learn everything. There are limitations to your knowledge. Understand that if we are going to run after degrees and lecturers, that will be our plight: to be limited in our knowledge. But if we run after the inspirations of the heart, our knowledge is never going to be limited. It will always be raising from one station to another.

Treat Everyone as Jesus, Moses, and Buddha Treated Everyone

In any one of the main religions that people are following, from the beginning to the end, who taught these prophets? They learned nothing from books, but Allah the Creator taught them. Look at the wisdom of Chinese and Indian philosophers and monks, Hindus and Buddhists. They did not get their knowledge by reading books, but through their hearts. They were giving their hearts to their Creator.

God has created us with His love and He said, "O My servant, I created you, and I am giving you free will. Go and do whatever you like. But never come to Me having broken the heart of another person." One of the Attributes of God is Love, and He never likes for someone to break the heart of people. Because of this attribute of love, many Sufi lovers, when they wrote poems, described God with feminine attributes; sometimes they even used the metaphor of woman to represent this aspect of our Lord. From the beginning, therefore, woman was held in the highmost respect.

God said, *"I was a hidden treasure and I wanted to be known, so I created human beings."* When God created human beings, what was the religion? Was there Judaism, Christianity, Islam,

Buddhism or Hinduism? There was God and human beings, His servants. Why are we changing our respect to each other based on one's religion? Why do Jews say, "We are going to Paradise, the rest are going to Hell." Christians, "We are going to Paradise, the rest are going to Hell." Muslims, "We are going to Paradise, the rest are going to Hell"? Why does each think that they are right and the others are wrong?

God has given everyone's heart a secret, and He is reaching you wherever you go. Jewish, Christian, Muslim, Buddhist, Hinduist, or be an atheist: you are still the Lord's creation. Therefore we human beings have to respect each other as our Lord's creation. We change our God's name but that Superpower never changes. Does any religion admit that God can be changed?

Our mistake is that we made differences between the messages of Moses, of Jesus, of Muhammad, peace be on them all. Those who followed them were all called "believers." God has moulded our spirit with His love. If He did not love us He would never have created us. He loved us, and He created everyone because of this love.

A perfect human being, a perfect person will be dressed by God in such a way that everyone is attracted: this is the dress of God's Attributes. God is bringing to every person a different light and a different secret in the heart. You appear by virtue of this light. What He gave X He did not give Y, and what He gave me He did not give you. You cannot exist by yourself; you exist through His existence. And if you exist through His existence, how dare I look at you in a negative way? I must consider that God has put that light in your heart and I must respect it.

Human beings are carrying the manifesttions of God's Attributes. That is why Sufi masters say, following the Prophet ﷺ, that God has created Adam ﷺ in His form. We are honored because we represent God on this planet.

Allah said:

And when thy Lord said unto the angels: Lo! I am about to place a viceroy in the earth. [8]

And this planet is not the only planet on which people are living. There are endless numbers of planets such as our planet. If God gave the eyes of the heart power to be opened, you would see planets with Divine light on them as there is Divine light on this one.

What God has given to human hearts no one can understand. He is the Creator of continuous creation. The Lord did not create once and for all and then stopped. In some traditions they say that God created everything in six days and then "rested." Why rest? If He is tired, this is not perfection. The Creator does not even need the recourse of creating by saying "Be," and it will be. This power has been granted to prophets and saints. But God never stops creating and creation never ends. As soon as it appears in Him, it is reflected in creation.

Sufi saints say that in this world we are blind. We see when we pass away. At that time we can free our spirit from its prison. Do you think that there is death? "Death" is for blind people. As you are changing your clothes when they are dirty, God is changing your body when it deteriorates. It is going to be moved to another station, then another station, then another. Just as there is no end for God, there is no end for you. You are there as long as God is there: no end, everlasting, and ever-living. When you gain that power, then you can reach the Divine Presence.

We spoke previously of that famous orientalist who went everywhere asking questions, never satisfied with the world

---

[8] Suratu 'l-Baqara, 2:30.

religions that he had studied. He came to my Master and said, "I feel as if I am catching air. I find myself knowing more than the rabbis and priests and Islamic scholars that I questioned. I am finally coming to you and ask you for an answer. If you do not give it to me, I am going to remain without belief for the rest of my life." And he said, "Show me God."

My teacher said:

O my son, why do you feel that you are only catching air? If you take the seed of a fruit and plant it and water it, you will find a green sprout coming out after thirty or forty days, and if you look for the original seed in the ground you will not find it anymore. If you come back after thirty years, you will find a large tree giving fruit to everyone. If you put an egg under a chicken for twenty-one days, the inner egg disappears, only a shell remains, and a chick will come out. The sperm that Allah allows to nest in the mother's womb, a holy place, undergoes a similar seclusion for a period of nine months to disappear completely and come out as a new generation.

God has chosen a sacred place to send His first light to humanity: the mother's womb. For that reason women are highly honored by God. He chose them, not men, to carry that light. Love in women, therefore, is ninety-nine times stronger than in the hearts of men. If women bring only one more part of love in their heart, women vanish in the love of God. They have been more honored than men because they carry God's Light in their womb. Yet they suffer tyranny and oppression everywhere in this life, but Allah never accepts that women be mistreated. He loves them more for it and the first people to go to paradise are women. This is Allah's Will from the beginning.

Grandshaykh then said:

My son, nothing depends on external knowledge. Unfortunately, all religions are today showing only external knowledge. None of the rabbis or priests or Islamic scholars are showing the inner side of religion, which is the spiritual side. That is why they are disappointing people and causing people to run away. They are only imposing obligations and formalities on people. God has freed you from everything but He is saying to you: Come to Me with love, and that is enough.

Someone came to the Prophet Muhammad once. All the Companions were sitting inside and worshipping, but that person only came to the door and asked, "O Muhammad! When is Judgment Day?" The Prophet did not answer. A second time he asked, "O Muhammad! When is Judgment Day?" Again, the Prophet did not answer, until the Holy Spirit, the angel Gabriel, came to him and said, "God instructs you to answer."

When a saint reaches the Divine Presence, he can never speak any more except by permission. If there is no permission, you cannot force him to speak.

The Prophet said to the man, "It is a long journey; have you prepared anything for that journey?"

People are awaiting Judgment Day, but every second there is a Judgment Day, because God is the Creator. There is not only one last day, as people think. Every person has a Judgment Day through the heart, and every second there is a Judgment Day—by repenting and coming to your Lord, saying, "Forgive me, my Lord. That ego made me weak. Take it away, and I will be powerful."

> *The Prophet ﷺ said, "That journey is full of thorns. What have you prepared?" He said: Love of God and the Prophet!*[9]
> *The Prophet ﷺ cried and said to him, "It is enough. You will be with the ones you love." Then that person did not enter and pray with them, but continued on his way.*

When you have such love for God, it means that you have love for His creation. If you don't have love for God, it means you don't have love for His creation.

You must treat everyone as Jesus ؑ treated everyone: with love and humbleness. You must treat everyone as Moses ؑ treated everyone. You must treat everyone as the Prophet Muhammad ﷺ treated everyone. You must treat everyone as saints, holy men, treat everyone. Saints understand, but the common people do not understand. That is why we don't appreciate our brothers and sisters, and always try to set ourselves higher than them. Know yourself and lower yourself. It is good enough for us to have the status of dust on a shoe! As much as you can lower yourself, do it, and God will raise you. Don't try to raise yourself. Let God give you that title. Don't get your title from universities. You don't need it. You need God to give you that title. Universities will only give you ego.

Everything depends on the inner reality. The body is disappearing. The inner reality is a seed which, in order to grow, must sever all connection with the material life. Grandshaykh continued:

> My son, there was no connection between the seed and the material life. It hid itself from the material life for a period of time, training itself to be alone in complete darkness, in complete emptiness, reaching absolute nothingness by telling itself: I am nothing; lowering itself until it

---

[9] Muslim and Al-Bukhari with slightly different wording.

vanished. When you vanish, you exist, when you refuse to vanish, you don't yet exist but your ego pretends to exist. By vanishing, that seed gave a green plant. That plant of good manners grew and grew until it gave a tree which gave fruit. You must let your ego vanish, and when you do that, you will be a fruit-bearing tree and people will come to you and benefit. If you do not do that you will never be happy, despite all the religions which you are studying, because you are still racked by ego and have not studied to empty yourself. Empty your heart and your life from all connections by meditating. Connect your heart with your Creator.

God Made Everything the Fruit of Unity

Grandshaykh continued:

When a man and a woman love teach other and come together, they become one. If you are still two, it mean that you are still saying "he" and "she." Each one is still saying, "I" and "you," which means "I am God," and "you are God," which means, "I am not accepting you, I am still claiming existence for myself before you." This cannot work if they are to become one. And this is the secret of creation: God made everything the fruit of unity, not partnership. If there is partnership, there is still a show of egoism. Out of the unity of husband and wife a new baby comes, the fruit of the highest perfection of unity.

In reality, therefore, there is no difference between Muslims' beliefs and the beliefs of Christians and Jews. If Christians say that Jesus ﷺ is God, it is acceptable. There is unity: we don't accept partnership, but unity we accept. When there is unity, there is one appearing, and the light of God is appearing in everyone. If you say, "He carries God's Light," you can say of anyone, including yourself,

"He carries the light of God." It would be true, because you are appearing with God's Existence. When you reach that station of perfection, at that time, there is no difference between source and the reflection: you are a reflection of the source, and the reflection always follows the source.

Out of such unity, God has made creation. In everything in creation there must be unity. When people sit together in unity, the energy in their hearts is passed to the one sitting next to them. When that happens, God sends knowledge and wisdom into hearts.

O my son, if you enter into seclusion, vanishing from this life, not existing anymore, at that time, you will be holding the Rope of God, you will no longer be catching air. At that time you can hope to see the manifestation of your Lord. With these limited eyes you can never see your Lord. When you vanish, you can find light in your heart and with that light you can reach your Lord. The light which God gave us is a Divine light.

May Allah send that light into our hearts and let it appear more and more. We are asking our Lord to make us see more and more with the eyes of the heart and let us visualize that light more and more. The first step in Sufism is love. From love we go to the second stage which is presence. At that time God is always present in your heart and you are present in His Divine Presence. The third stage is to vanish in His Existence. When you vanish in His Existence, at that time you will see everything.

Buddhists also teach that route, because everything is connected together in some way. We are giving different names to various groups, but in reality it is not like that. Everything is connected to the main center as God said:

each swimming in its own orbit. [10]

You have to know what is your orbit. Our orbit is the circumference of a circle. The center is the Creator, and that center is reaching every point on the circumference at the same time and within the same distance. Some people are feeling and some not, because they are veiling themselves with their ego and bad manners. If we free ourselves from bad manners, everyone on that circle will see each other.

Every creation, therefore, is going to find itself swimming in the same orbit in the end. There is no difference in God's Eyes. We are all His creation, His weak servants. The mother changes her baby's diapers every time. And our sins are enough for very big "diapers." We hope God will change our sins into good deeds!

We ask Allah to take away our ego and to break the boundaries we have made between each other and the boundaries between us and Him.

---

[10] Surah Ya Sin, 36:40.

LEAVE THE RELIGION THAT DOES NOT MAKE YOU HOLY

Allah provides even a mosquito with its food. When you say God is the Provider, it means He cannot but provide everyone. You cannot say that God is a provider and yet accept that he leave one unprovided for in all His creation.

> *I have created spiritual beings and human beings to worship and remember me. I do not want anything from them, and I do not want them to feed me. Allah is the One who will provide them and send them whatever they need without asking. He is the Lord of unbreakable might*[11]

Surrender! He Will Provide

Allah provides his creation without being asked. Maryam, the Virgin Mary was being visited by her uncle the Prophet Zakariyya who checked on her during her seclusion. She never went outside and he was responsible for her provision.

> *Whenever Zakariyya came to her temple, he saw provision*[12] *there and asked her, "From where did you get this?" She would answer him, "(Don't*

---

[11] Suratu 'dh-Dhariyat, 51:56:58.

[12] According to the classical commentaries the "provision" was fruit which was out of season.

ask!) Allah provides everyone as He likes, He is the provider!" [13]

If it did not rain, there would be no crops, and life would be threatened. Do not, therefore, think that God cannot provide people. God is the Provider. If we correct ourselves and we come to Him by returning some of the love He gave to us, God is going to provide everyone on this earth. He provides animals. Do you see animals starving? Why are human beings starving and not animals? There must be a reason. Human beings, if they don't work, cannot find provision for themselves, but not animals: God provides them. This is because animals submit and surrender to God.

Surrender to your Lord and you also will provide everyone. But we are not surrendering. We are not submitting. Animals are submitting. They know that their Creator is going to give them something. They don't work. They go to the streets to find where there is food and eat. See whether even an ant is missing her provision. According to some, "instinct" drives her to food; we ask: who sent her the inspiration that some call her instinct? Why are animals not worried? All animals eat and none is starving. This is because all animals are surrendering to God's will. Surrender to your Lord. He gave you will to make you free. Say

"O my Lord, you made me free. I am very thankful, and I believe in you." This is what He wants. And if you make mistakes, never mind, you come back and say: 'Forgive me.'"

Submit to God's Will. Surrender. Break that barrier between you and your Lord. If you don't break it, you cannot surrender. The barrier is "You" and "Me." You are saying to your Lord, "You," and you are saying to yourself, "Me." You must not

---

[13] Surat Ali 'Imran, 3:37.

say "Me. "You must say "You" every time. There is no "Me" in the act of surrendering and submitting to God's will. If there is a "Me," it means that you are not surrendering to God. You need to fight and struggle with your ego until your ego says, "I am no longer existing." When you reach that point, Allah is going to show Himself to you.

One of the great saints said, "I saw my Lord with the eyes of my Lord."

It means, "I cannot see with my own eyes." He has no more sight except through His Lord. That saint is no more: His Lord appears. And when your Lord appears, you can see your Lord. One group of spiritual people call this experience "Complete Emptiness." They reach a station where there is nothing: absolute nothingness, and they say: We have reached perfection. They have reached something, but it is not perfection. They are unable to cross and go beyond that stage, so they think it is the ultimate goal. When you reach nothing, you stand at the door of complete existence—in God's existence.

Return from Annihilation to Real Existence

When some spiritual people reach complete emptiness, they need a means to cross. They do not find that means. With that means, they can cross and find complete existence. Opposite complete non-existence there must be complete existence, just as opposite the creation there must be God the Creator. A bridge is in between. To cross from one to the other, you must take that bridge. God said in a Holy Tradition (*hadith qudsi*):

> *I was a hidden treasure—unseen—and wanted to be known and so I created creation.*

When you don't see Him, you think in terms of nonexistence. No: when you reach complete emptiness—and it is a high station—you must find the bridge that leads to complete existence which lies across it, for there is a higher station, and a higher one yet. Just as God said:

Above every knower there is a greater knower.[14]

We must also know that "*Wa fawqa kulli dhi maqamin muqeem* — Above every one that holds a station there is another one on another station."

The one above can see the one below, but the one below cannot see the one above. How then can we say that the station where we stand is the last one? We cannot see beyond it. That is why God warned that you cannot know all knowledge, as much as you may approach, but only partial knowledge. Complete knowledge belongs to Him. Do not, therefore, say as they say when they reach complete emptiness, that "this is the final station." Never mind, this is a good and a high enough station for you; but there must be someone whom Allah has placed higher. Do not underestimate the power of Allah. God is never limited. There are endless stations. Whatever you reach, there is something more.

Take an example from this life. How can they speak of absolute emptiness? In our limited materialistic knowledge, we speak of empty spaces. This entire galaxy wherein lies our solar system is but a point inside a bigger galaxy. And that bigger galaxy is a point in yet another galaxy. If you take even galaxies millions of light-years away, with all their greatness, they are seen moving at indescribable speeds — in completely empty space. Where are they going? There is no end to this motion in space. According to our wordly knowledge, they are moving into "empty space," and we cannot move to a higher explanatory station. According to spiritual knowledge, however, there is no empty space. Space is always full of creation and knowledge. But

---

[14] Surah Yusuf, 12:76.

you can never understand your Lord, although you may be attaining the highest station in some spiritual order or system of belief. For as high as you reach, there is higher, and higher than that.

The Creator is so powerful that He creates what cannot be understood by the mind. No one can evaluate God's power. That is why saints and prophets declare their weakness. They say, "O our Lord! We are helpless." May Allah send the light of understanding and knowledge to our hearts.

God is never far away. They say "no one can know his Lord," or "no one can see his Lord," but the Prophet ﷺ said, "Whoever knows himself, will know his Lord." If you are not seeing your Lord, it means that you still do not know yourself. If you reach a level where you can know your Lord, it means that you have come to know yourself. But you don't even know the self that is in you; how are you going to know the Creator? It is impossible.

How are you going to know yourself? By surrendering to God's will. Surrendering to God's will mean accepting whatever is going on around you without complaining. If your wife fights with you, you must not complain; if you fight with her, she must not complain. At that time there is surrender. If you find some people complaining about you and cursing you, ignore them. Don't care for what they are saying: that is surrender. Who made them speak? You or your Lord?

You have to know this: nothing can move if God does not want it to move. No one can speak if God does not want him to speak. No one can do anything if God does not make him to. Therefore you have to know that everything is from Him. That is the way saints became saints—they accepted. When they accepted, and effected a complete surrender to God's will, they reached Him. When they reached Him, they reached sweetness and beauty. They were no longer able to come back to this world spiritually. Their spirits are in His presence. If we can reach to that level, God will bless us. What kind of blessing He is going to give no one knows. These blessings are from His generosity. Saints are blessed ones.

There is the Holy Torah and the Psalms, the Holy Gospel, and the Holy Qur'an. Are there any more books? These are the main books of the major religions of the Book. They call these books "holy," which means "sacred." One day our shaykh met a priest and told him, "O Your Holiness!" The priest said, "Don't say 'Your Holiness!' I am not holy!" He said, "How is it that you are not holy? Are you not reading the Holy Bible?" He said, "Yes." Our shaykh said, "If you are reading the Holy Bible and not becoming holy, why then are you reading it? What is the benefit? If the Bible cannot make you holy, or the Qur'an, or the Psalms, or the Torah, or the Gospel, then what are you doing? This means that you are not reading properly! You are reading words!"

"Holy" means "sacred." It means that the reader is present in the Divine Presence! He is right there, in God's Divine Presence, never away from that Divine Presence. This is a holy one: a sacred one, dressed by God with holiness as God dressed His book with the same holiness. If you are not such a one, it means, O Rabbi, O Priest, O Muslim scholar, that you are not benefiting from reading the Bible or the Torah or the Qur'an. If you are not going to become holy people, it means that you are reading as Satan is reading: he too can read the holy books."

Many people follow gurus nowadays. They go to Hindu temples just as they go to mosques, churches and synagogues. People go to all kinds of spiritual gurus. Yet what is the benefit? Are they getting anything? Are they becoming holy? If they are not becoming holy, leave these gurus. It means that they themselves are not finding their way. Try to find your way. The one that does not show you the way is not a holy one. A holy one must have effect on you and on your life. If he cannot affect your life, there is no benefit.

Moses ☪ came and affected some people: these people became holy. Jesus ☪ came and the same thing happened; Muhammad ﷺ came and the same thing happened. That was 1,400 years ago. What about the present time? Were are the hidden saints that still affect people? Search for them, and if you find them, hold on to them and refuse to listen to your ego. One day the ego accepts, the next it rejects. Once your ego says, "Yes, this is a holy man," accept and do not change your mind. If you change your mind, it is a sign that your ego is cheating you. Satan is trying to deceive you. Do not listen. Try to connect your heart with your Creator through that holy person.

Without a means you never reach. There must be a means to guide you and show you the way. Thirty or forty years ago it was still the same as thousands of years ago: saints were ordering their followers to go into seclusion and trained them severely to prepare their spirits to be in the Divine Presence. Nowadays there is no permission for that, because people are running completely after their materialistic life. If one has ten dollars in the bank, he wants to make it twenty. If he has ten thousand or a million, he wants to make it twenty thousand or two million. What for? Everyone is running after the material world, no one is running after spirituality.

Only very few people, like this gathering, and then not 100%. If they run above 50% by one percent, it is enough for them to undergo seclusion. If a person shows his shaykh surrender above 50%, he will train him and send him into seclusion. But no one is yet coming to 50%. We are all under that. When you reach that mark and above, you are going to leave everything and say, "I have finished, I am coming to you, I want to stay in your presence, surrendering myself. Whatever is going to happen, let it happen. I do not care about my family nor anything else: I am caring about my Lord." At that time, he will be happy with you. He will raise you quickly and send you back to your family with more support and more power. But you have to surrender!

May God make us surrender to our master in order that he will support us. Since we came to America, we tried to find some people who are surrendering. It was impossible except for very few, and we say that, "The rare is like the nonexistent."

There are a few surrendering. They are accepting to leave everything and to surrender to God, but they are very rare. That is why what we speak now, we speak through the tongue. When you listen, you are happy sitting there. You feel that light and that power. But when you go, it is over and done. Everything disappears. It does not in fact disappear from the heart but it is veiled: a darkness veils it over, because in that heart darkness outweighs light. From there comes the lack of surrender. When the light outweighs the darkness, there is surrender. All Sufi orders and everything in them is based on surrender. If you don't surrender, you can never reach your aim or your goal.

Surrender of a Corpse is Rejected

A follower once said to his shaykh, "O my shaykh, how am I going to surrender to you? Let me surrender to you as a dead person surrenders!" He said, "No; even a dead person is not surrendering completely. We don't accept in our *tariqah* the surrender of a dead person, for he still has a will. According to all religions, when God takes the soul away, the dead one still sees and hears and feels everything, but he cannot open his eyes or speak: that power is taken away. I want the surrender of tree-leaves in autumn: when they fall down, the wind will carry them. Wherever the wind will carry them, that leaf will never say anything. Go East, go West, go North, go South... It might be that the leaf falls into the fire and is burnt, but it will not say anything.

I want such surrender. If you reach such a level, we accept you in our way."

If there is surrender of the heart, you can taste what our shaykh is saying through us. Everyone can taste and feel at that time. Until there is complete surrender, however, you will feel it only while you are here. When you go away, you will no longer feel it in your heart, only in the mind, even though it is still in the heart. May our Lord give us power to surrender, not to our will but to His will. Our will is unimportant. And if we surrender to His will, He will show us miraculous powers.

SECLUSION

[An address to a gathering of Sahykh Nazim's students at the London Naqshbandi Sufi Center]

Obey God, obey the Prophet, and obey your leaders.[15]

We are meeting in this mosque and we have to ask, as the Prophet ﷺ ordered the Sahabah ؓ and all masters have ordered their followers after him, that one hour sitting here be counted as an hour of seclusion. You are disconnecting yourself from the outer life and coming here for the honor of God, for the honor of the Prophet ﷺ, and for the honor of your shaykh. To be good examples and good followers of the Sufi way, *tariqah*, you are leaving your countries, your homes, and everything, and coming here in order to benefit and learn something. You are not coming here only to spend some time. You are coming to take spiritual advice from your shaykh. That is why you have to listen well and act accordingly. Do not come here and spend fifteen days of vacation, then go back out. In that case, there is no need for coming.

The Prophet ﷺ has ordered all Sahabah ؓ to enter seclusion, to make retreat, to do meditation. This means: to keep the presence of their Lord and the love of the Prophet ﷺ in their hearts. After the Prophet ﷺ, all Sahabah ؓ, and especially Sayyidina Abu Bakr and Sayyidina 'Ali—the two with whom all orders of Sufism originated—taught their followers to enter seclusion.

---

[15] Suratu'n-Nisa, 4:59.

Grandshaykh once said, "One that did not enter seclusion in his life is as one who has wasted his life." If you do not seclusion in your life even one time, it means that you have lived for nothing.

You are not going to take anything with you. You are going to take only what God has planned for you to take. And God has planned for everyone to be a good believer. That is why, when He created the spirits of humanity, He asked them, "Who am I and who are you?"[16] Prophets and saints said, "You are our Lord, and we are Your servants!" The rest said, "You are what You are and we are what we are," which means, "We are not believing in You; if You are God, so are we." Those were the unbelievers. God threw them into darkness for 70,000 years and then called them back and asked them again, "Who am I and who are you?" Some of them said, "You are our Lord, and we are Your servants," and these were also believers.[17] We are those believers. Don't listen to your ego saying, as we said the first time God asked us, "You are what You are, we are what we are!" Only after God threw the ego into darkness did it accept and say, "You are my Lord!" Now, when we come to this earth another time—in a physical body after the first, spiritual creation—we are saying yet again, "You are what You are, we are what we are." No one is accepting.

All masters of the Naqshbandi order have to put their disciples into seclusion, for the same reason that God has put our spirits into darkness for 70,000 years: to polish us and to teach us good manners, and to make us accept later this fact, "You are our Lord"; to break and kill their ego. Only at that time they will say, "You are our Lord; we are Your servants."

---

[16] Suratu 'l-'Araf, 7:172.
[17] Abu 'Abdullah's narration of the threefold division of souls on the Day of Promises and their sojourn in darkness in Hakim's *Nawadir al-usul*, pp. 417-418.

This is what Mawlana is teaching us through all these years: to be good servants to our Lord. To obey our Lord. But the ego does not accept. Grandshaykh therefore said:

> As the Prophet ﷺ has made the Sahabah ؓ enter seclusion, he also had to make his followers enter seclusion. If they do not enter in this life, they have to enter in the grave, for a duration of forty days. This is a must on everyone. Nothing can clean you of your bad manners except seclusion.

If you do not enter that seclusion you will never be cleaned. You will be one of the "colorful" or "multicolored" rank. The Naqshbandi order speaks of our present situation as the "colorful" or "multicolored" position—that is, constantly changing: one day we are good; one day we are bad; one day we are half-and-half. This cannot be taken away and we cannot be constant on one color except by entering seclusion.

Our brothers and sisters, try hard to make your shaykh give you permission to enter seclusion. We are not telling you to go up to him and say, "O my shaykh, give me permission to go to seclusion." This is not the way. The way is to try to accept what he is telling you without using your mind. Keep faith in what he is telling you.

Belief is in the Unseen

Why are some called believers? Because they believed in the unseen. When the Prophet ﷺ came he said, "Believe in God," as did Jesus ؑ and Moses ؑ when they came. Belief, therefore, is in the unseen. When it is seen, at that time it is not a belief but an evidence.

At that time you accept because you saw something, and this is not accepted.

Whatever your shaykh says, do not say *"muhaqqaq"* or "true!" with your tongue. Your heart has to accept. If your heart does not accept, then you are not going to benefit anything. We have to show our shaykh, who knows how we sleep even as we sleep, that we truly believe in him. Do you think that our shaykh is someone like us? *Hasha*! (God forbid), Once, Grandshaykh said, "If an ant is moving on top of a smooth rock in the West and I am in the East, I can hear her footsteps in my ear as I hear the crack of thunder." And he said, "We—the shaykhs of the Naqshbandi order—can hear and feel the movements of our disciples, no matter what they are doing, as loud as if we heard thunder!" And he said, "Keep respect when you are sleeping in bed with your wife, because we are hearing and seeing everything."

We are all under the same shaykh, and that shaykh is presently holding all power in his hands before Mahdi ﷺ. If you do not know this, we know this. All the power that has been given to saints from the Prophet ﷺ has now been pulled out of their hands and placed in Mawlana Shaykh Nazim's hands. Other saints cannot proceed except by way of miraculous power, and the Prophet ﷺ is no longer allowing saints to show any miraculous power in the present day. He wants, as he has foretold in hadith, for corruption and oppression to finally govern this world. If you use miraculous power, you will take away that corruption; but that corruption has to reach its ultimate. That is the reason Mawlana Shaykh Nazim is patient and more patient. When you see him in reality, at that time all of us are going to melt as salt melts in water. Keep then respect to your shaykh in your heart.

Five Heart Levels

You are under your shaykh's supervision for twenty-four hours. You can never move out of his sight. He is looking at you. He is looking at you when you are moving here and there. Yet this is nothing: he can hear the secrets that come into your heart and the secrets that you keep in the recess of your heart as if it were thunder. Leave this also; in every person's heart there are five levels. The first level is *Maqamu 'l-Qalb*, the Station of the Heart. Satan can enter through that level and understand what you are doing: that is why you sometimes have bad thoughts. You are distracted in prayer, you cheat at work or you feel suspicion...

There is a higher level: the Station of Secrets—*Maqam as-Sirr*. They now have the distinction between the conscious and the subconscious. The subconscious is that place in your inner mind where you bury things. It is a scientific expression for the second level in the heart: it knows information, and God has given every human being a secret. We are created and honored by our Lord Who has created us from three lights: His light and the light of the Prophet ﷺ and the light of Adam ൠ.

Human beings are honored beings. They are created on perfection. God said:

Verily We have honored the Children of Adam.[18]

With what kind of honor? Perfection in creation. In many hadiths, the Prophet ﷺ speaks of his Lord in terms of a human being, "I saw my Lord coming to me smiling." It does not mean that He is a human being or similar to a human being, but it means that human beings are created after perfection.

No one can know with what secrets God has endowed the light that He has put into your heart. That is what the teachings of the Naqshbandi order wants to bring out. Divine Law *(Shari'ah)* teaches you the rudiments of how to fight Satan and throw him out of your heart. *Tariqah* affirms *Shari'ah* and then goes to a higher level—to extract the secret which God has given to your heart. This extraction is the duty of the shaykh. This cannot be

---

[18] Suratu 'l-Isra', 17:70.

given to you except through seclusion, and the shaykh can hear and know what is going on at the second level.

The third level is the Secret of the Secret—*Maqam Sirr as-sirr*, then come the fourth level, the Hidden (*Khafa*) and the fifth level, the Most Hidden (*Akhfa*). No one can enter the third level except the masters of the Naqshbandi order. Masters of the forty other Sufi orders can enter the second level only. No one but the Prophet ﷺ can enter the fourth level, and the fifth level is known to God alone, Who alone knows how He has honored that human being.

You can see how human beings are honored beings. There is no discrimination in God's sight at that level: there is no Muslim; there is no Christian; there is no Jew; there is no Buddhist; there is no Hindu. There is only:

We have sent you not except as a mercy for all human beings.[19]

There is no differentiation at that level. Discrimination is from us. It is we who say, "They are Jews"; "They are Christians"; Christians say, "These are Muslims"; "These are Jews." But there are no such things in God's eyes. There are only human beings—period. Allah said:

You are not allowed to speak ill of your brothers and sisters! You would be interfering in God's judgment. But you are not the judge: God is the Judge. Don't interfere, therefore, in God's ways by giving your opinion. God will not ask for your opinion in the Judgment Day.

If God says, I want to put everyone in Paradise, who can say to Him, "What are You doing?" and if He says, I want to punish everyone, who can say to Him, "What are You doing?" No one.

---

[19] Suratu 'l-Anbiya, 21:107.

And do you think that God has created us to punish us? Is He Someone revengeful, Someone who likes revenge or punishment? Someone who created His servants in order to torture them? Do you accept this view? It is impossible. God is merciful, and He is keeping His mercy for His servants.

The Loveliest Title is 'Servant'

The Prophet ﷺ said:

The loveliest time in my life is when God calls me by the name of servant or slave—'abd ....and He tells me, "Come, O My servant."

Mawlana Shaykh Nazim is teaching us how to be good servants. Why are we not accepting and obeying? We come here and sit hours and hours, day and night, in order to get something. Everything we want to get depends on servanthood. He is teaching us to be servants, not to be—as he said yesterday—mighty. The title Mighty belongs to God. We are servants. Moreover we are, as he also said, weak and helpless servants. We cannot do anything. That is why God has given the Prophet ﷺ intercession, and the Prophet ﷺ said:

My intercession is for the great sinners of my nation.[20]

We are weak and cannot be perfect, but we have to teach ourselves to accept what our shaykh says and to polish our hearts.

Shaykhs do not depend on us. They depend on their power which God has given to the Prophet ﷺ and which the Prophet ﷺ has given, to them. That is why God said, "Come to me one step, I will come to you ninety-nine steps." Come to your shaykh one step, you will find him running towards you ninety-nine steps.

---

[20] Ahmad, at-Tirmidhi, Abu Dawud, at-Tabarani, Khatib, al-Bayhaqi, Hakim, as-Suyuti.

When you do not want to come to him one step, how can he come to you? He will not come. You have to show progress on your part.

Grandshaykh's order for everyone to enter seclusion must be understood in this context. Everyone must teach himself how to polish his heart. We cannot enter seclusion now. All of us are sinners and no one is asking really from his heart to enter into seclusion. For that reason, there are other ways. Mawlana Shaykh Nazim is showing us ways in order to pull us towards him fast. Some people ride on donkeys, some people on horses, some people in cars, some people on planes, and some people on rockets. The faster you can go, the faster you can approach.

Powerful Intentions Work Miracles

Grandshaykh said, "I shall teach you a way to approach me very quickly. Whenever you are coming and sitting in an association, or you are praying at night, or by day, or you are making *dhikr*, or reading Qur'an or hadith, or doing anything, when you sit, say:

Nawaytu al-arba'een	I intend the Forty Days
Nawaytu 'l-'itikaaf	I intend retreat
Nawaytu 'l-khalwah	I intend seclusion
Nawaytu 'l-'uzlah	I intend isolation
Nawaytu 'r-riyadah	I intend devotion
Nawaytu 's-suluk	I intend discipline
Nawaytu 's-siyam fi hadha'l-masjid li-Llahi ta'ala	I intend abstinence In this place of worship, for the sake of God the Exalted."

The Prophet ﷺ used to make a similar intention when he would retreat in the cave before revelation came to him. When all Sahabah ؓ and all grandmasters entered seclusion, they made this intention. When you make this intention for this meeting of ours, which lasts one hour, this hour will be deducted from the forty day seclusion which is an obligation on everyone of us. Make that intention before sitting at any meeting: it will take you to your shaykh like a rocket.

How many years have you been sitting with Mawlana Shaykh Nazim? If you added up all these years, having made that intention, you will never leave the room except that it be written for you that you have spent two, or three, or five hours in seclusion. This will be deducted from the forty day seclusion. When you finish the forty days in this way, you will find that the light which God has given to you in your heart will be opened. It is that light which is going to open the eyes of the heart. Without this, you will never find the happiness that is now hidden in your heart. You must bring it out, and this is one "hook" to do that. Use it every time you sit with the shaykh.

Hide Others' Mistakes

> One day, the Prophet ﷺ called Sayyidina Bilal ؓ shortly before midnight and ordered him to give *adhan* for everyone to come to him, "Quickly, for I cannot delay giving this message to my Companions." Sayyidina Bilal ؓ was very frightened and wondered why the Prophet ﷺ was calling everybody at such an hour. Was Judgment Day coming? The Prophet ﷺ was shivering. Sayyidina Bilal ؓ went to the mosque and called *adhan*, and all the Companions ran to the mosque and waited for the Prophet ﷺ.

When the Prophet ﷺ came, they did not receive him in the same manner that we receive Mawlana when he arrives at the mosque. We run to him, unfortunately, like donkeys! We have to give respect. When Mawlana enters, rather than crowding him rudely, you should be disciplined, stand in line at a distance in order to show respect to your shaykh. Instead, we run in chaos like sheep or chicken. You have to kiss his hand, but do not run and make a crowd and block the way. Even when Mawlana Shaykh Nazim wants to go to the car he is unable to enter the car unhindered. Why don't you simply stand and give respect?

One day Sayyidina 'Abdul-Qadir Jilani ق was walking with his followers in an alley of Baghdad and they saw someone coming from the other end of the alley. His Companions were moving with him in accordance with *adab*: all of them behind—no one moving beside him. Here, everyone is trying to move beside the shaykh and pray beside the shaykh! What is your rank to pray beside him? Stand behind in order to keep respect, not beside—except if there is no room in the mosque. Sayyidina 'Abdul Qadir Jilani's disciples did not crowd each other by walking abreast in the same row, as we do today, but they moved behind one another with the shaykh alone in the front. You cannot be in his level! Teach yourself this *adab*, this respect.

A priest came from the other end of the alley, and immediately Sayyidina 'Abdul Qadir Jilani ق gave way, and all the disciples gave way. No one said, "This is a priest." They all give him way. When the priest saw that respect in the shaykh, and he saw that all the disciples were following that *adab*, he bowed to Sayyidina 'Abdul-Qadir Jilani ق from the head. The latter immediately bowed from the waist. When he saw this, the priest said:

"*Ashhadu an la ilaha illa-Allah wa ashhadu anna Muhammadu'r-Rasulullah.*" Priests know the truth and that incident brought it out from this priest. "O our shaykh," said the disciples, "what happened? How did you give so much respect to that priest?" He said, "I gave respect because I am looking at the light which God has given to his heart, and I am giving respect to those two angels that are standing on his right and on his left." It is this respect that made that light jump out and made the priest say *shahadah*. Giving respect is most important.

When the Prophet ﷺ finally came to the mosque, all the Sahabah were in line and were bowing. The Prophet ﷺ passed unhindered until he reached his place. When he reached it, he was shivering as he said, "God has sent the angel Gabriel to me to tell me: 'O Prophet of God!! Call your Companions and give them that message.' It is the most difficult message that the archangel Gabriel gave to me in my life. I am very frightened of this message, and that is why I called you quickly to tell you what must do, and tell you to listen and obey to this message." The Sahabah were anxious in their hearts to know if a big battle lay ahead, or something coming down from heaven.

The Prophet ﷺ said, "God has informed me tonight that He has ordered all his angels in the seven heavens, and swore an oath on Himself, and ordered me and all prophets that have passed away, to curse and send hardships on the one who is not going to obey this message." Everyone was afraid: what could earn such a curse from God, angels and prophets? The Prophet ﷺ continued, "If anyone makes another mention of any bad event or happening that took place two hours earlier in their life, they are going to be cursed."

This means that if something has gone wrong and confusion resulted from it, or someone has spoken harshly to someone else, and you bring back that event into your conversation more than two hours later, you are going to incur that curse from God, the Prophet ﷺ, the angels, and all prophets.

You have to be concealers of your brothers' and sisters 'faults as God is the Concealer of the sins of human beings. You must not show up their mistakes for you yourself are in the midst of mistakes. If you do not show their mistakes, God will never show your mistake. This is the meaning of as-Sattar, the Concealer. Hide their mistakes; don't speak ill of your brothers and sisters, and God will hide your mistakes. For everyone has mistakes they are hiding in their heart. If you take such care to hide your own mistakes, why do you bring out the mistakes of the others? Hide others' mistakes, and God has sworn on His Honor and Greatness that He is going to curse anyone that is not going to hide the mistakes of his brothers and sisters, or hide whatever bad events have passed concerning them.

In our time the Naqshbandi order is based on respect. In the spiritual associations of saints with the Prophet ﷺ, are sitting the saints of the Golden Chain which descends without interruption from the Prophet ﷺ to Mahdi ﷺ, and our shaykh comes just before Mahdi ﷺ. These saints asked our shaykh, "What is the definition of the Naqshbandi order now?" He said one word—and everyone must understand the meaning of that word, "respect." If the Naqshbandi order is based on respect, how can you possibly speak about anyone badly and still claim it as your *tariqah*? Therefore, keep respect for everyone in your heart as you are keeping respect for your shaykh.

Respect Everyone

This is the present foundation of this order. You have to keep respect for the young, you have to keep respect for the adult, you have to keep respect for ladies, and you have to keep respect for men. Sayyidina 'Ubaydullah al-Ahrar was walking in a street with his followers one day. A dog was coming, and he backed up to give way to the dog. You must even give respect to animals, and even stones. As the Prophet ﷺ taught us, if you see something on the path liable to cause harm, you must take it away. A long time ago, one of the followers of Mawlana Shaykh kicked a stone out the way of the shaykh. The latter said, "No! Who is the Creator of that stone, you or God?" The disciple answered, "Of course, God." Mawlana said, "How then do you kick His creation with your foot? Bow down and take it with your hand!" Everything comes into creation from the Ocean of Energy or Power, *Bahru 'l-Qudrah*. Everything comes from the Divine Attribute of The Powerful One. From that ocean, God has created that stone also. How could you remove it with your feet? The order to "Take it with your hand" means that respect has to dominate everything.

We are not even keeping respect with our shaykh. You have to keep respect. If your brothers and sisters run and crowd Mawlana's way, at least you must not run. When you go to the post office or to the bank or in any store to get something, how do you behave at the cashier's counter? Do you rush in front of others, or do you stand in line? Why do you keep more respect in those places than you are willing to keep with your shaykh? As you keep respect when you go to a job interview, entering the room and trembling inside in front of your potential employer; sometimes, you don't even sit but keep standing as he asks you questions; but in front of your shaykh, *masha'-Allah*! All kinds of bad behavior come out... Keep respect with your shaykh and you will reap benefit.

It is *tarku 'l- adab*, against respect, bad manners, to speak in the presence of your shaykh, even to talk with each other, let alone to give lectures. It is against respect even to stand in a careless manner or to turn one's back in his presence—even if he is talking with someone and not looking at us. We are doing too many mistakes in that respect without noticing. Yet you see your shaykh being ever friendly and merciful with you as a matter of course, because he has the behavior of the Prophet ﷺ, and the Prophet ﷺ is dressing him with his power. The spiritual power of the Prophet ﷺ is appearing in this century in the person of Shaykh Nazim ق. By opening only slightly the power of this attraction, many people are coming. If he opened it completely, all of London would not be enough to contain the visitors who would come and see him. Every one of us must therefore keep respect and *adab*, correct manners, when we are in his presence.

If you keep respect properly, God will give you respect. Take your respect from your Lord, not from your ego. Take your title from your Lord, not from your ego. Keeping respect with your shaykh will merit you a title from God, and He will cause everyone to respect you. Open your ears to this advice and let this enter your heart. Do as much as possible. Do not say, "It is another one of these lectures of which we have heard many." Do not say, "We are as we are and we cannot change." It is ego that is telling you not to change yourselves.

A Hindu Shows Miraculous Power

A disciple of Sayyidina Khalid al-Baghdadi—a saint of the Golden Chain who passed away some 200 years ago and is buried in Damascus—was sent to Hajj by his shaykh. His shaykh told him to look for something specific, but he did not find it when he was there. However, he heard about an unbeliever in Bombay who had miraculous powers and could do everything that you asked him to do. The disciple was upset: he had been with his shaykh dozens of years and he could not do any anything miraculous. How did that unbeliever, who was neither in *tariqah* nor even in Islam, possess miraculous powers? "I am going back to my shaykh to tell him, 'O my shaykh, you sent me to look for a saint, and I found an unbeliever who has miraculous powers, while we cannot do anything! What is this teaching?'" This is reality for us: we come and sit with Mawlana Shaykh Nazim for hours and hours, and we are not benefiting for a reason which is coming presently.

The disciple went and told his shaykh about his doubts. Sayyidina Khalid answered, "O my son, don't get the wrong impression. You would be making a mistake. I shall give you the answer tomorrow." That night, Sayyidina Khalid was in India in one second by saying *"Bismillahi 'r-rahmani 'r-rahim."* That is another power which Mawlana Shaykh Nazim is not using. The shaykhs have freed their spiritual powers from the cage of their bodies. Now the spirit can take the body with it, whereas before, the spirit went only where the body took it. They move by putting their body inside their spirit, not vice-versa: thus travel is possible in one second, wherever the spirit goes. As he came to the door of that person in India, he again put back his spirit into his physical body, and thus "appeared" there.

The man from Bombay was waiting at his door. It was a Hindu monk. He said, "O my shaykh, I knew that you were coming through my power, and I ordered a Muslim lady to prepare a meal for you as I know that you do not eat from our food." They sat opposite each other. Before saying anything to him, Sayyidina Khalid al-Baghdadi said to him, "Give *shahadah* now!" The Hindu monk sat in silence concentrating on his heart for half an hour, while Sayyidina Khalid al-Baghdadi did not say anything. After half an hour, the monk said, "*Ashhadu an la ilaha illa-Llah wa ashhadu anna Muhammadan Rasulullah*." He already possessed worldly powers; as soon as he said *shahadah*, he received heavenly powers.

Sayyidina Khalid asked him, "Why did you wait half an hour in unbelief when you knew that belief was Reality?" He said, "O my shaykh, I am very sorry, but for twenty-five years I have not done anything without asking my shaykh, and my shaykh is my ego. I have to ask my ego and see what it will tell me. After I got an answer from my ego, I said *shahadah*. O my shaykh, for 25 years, whatever my ego told me to do when I asked for its advice, I did the opposite. Now, when I asked it what I should do, whether I should take *shahadah* or not, my ego told me, 'Are you crazy? Are you going to go down to the bottom step and climb all the way up again? You are crazy! Be aware of this! Never give *shahadah*!' And I was fighting with my ego whether to say or not. Since my ego insisted not to say it, I decided to say it."

Sayyidina Khalid said, "When you said it, you received heavenly powers. We do not depend on wordly powers. Wordly power is for Satan." When you see non-Muslim people that can perform miraculous feats, you must know that this is worldly power. Satan and devils can do this easily: walking on water, going through fires, walking on nails, penetrating through walls. This is not dependable. We need heavenly powers, and they come from the light of the heart. We need to love everyone as we love ourself. That is what we need truly. We need to respect everyone. We need to be helpful with everyone, humble towards everyone. Be aware of this, and you will find that heavenly powers are open in front of you.

The next day, Sayyidina Khalid went back to his association of hundreds of scholars and disciples in Damascus, and he said to them:

> I have been teaching you for forty or fifty years, and no one is doing something to tame his ego. That unbeliever was able to gain miraculous powers—wordly powers—because he was doing something against his ego. You I have told to fight your ego, to kill your ego, to be good servants, and you are not accepting. For that reason heavenly powers are never going to be opened for you.

Take this story into consideration and be good servants. As you keep respect for your shaykh, keep respect for his followers also. Respect and love each other, be humble with each other, and do not repeat a story that has passed more than two days ago. And if you want to show your shaykh good *adab*, don't rush, just as you do not rush when you are in the supermarket, but act calmly stand in line instead. I will pray in the last row and perhaps my heart will be present at the side of my shaykh to a greater extent than one who is praying thoughtlessly next to him, or to his left or directly behind him in the first rows.

Keep your heart present to this advice or you will never find any benefit from the Naqshbandi order. This order is based on respect. Respect everyone and you are going to win everything. If not, you will gain nothing.

The Smell of the Naqshbandiyyah

In every lecture or association, we place ourselves under that verse:

Obey God, obey the Prophet, and obey those in authority among you.[21]

God also said in Qur'an that:

Whoever obeys the Prophet, obeys God.[22]

Whoever obeys the masters who are showing us the way to the Prophet ﷺ and explain to us how to approach the Prophet ﷺ, is following the teachings of the Prophet ﷺ. We are, therefore, in need for guidance that shows us the best way to do that. There are many ways.

There is a saying in our Way:

The ways to God are as numerous as the breaths of human beings, (i.e. infinite in number).

You can come to your Lord by millions of ways. There are shorter ways and there are longer ways. Each person goes according to the secret that God has deposited into his heart. Each one has a different way. You do not all of you have the same way, because you are not all the same person. Each has a light and a secret in his heart which God has given especially to him. Who can bring that secret out? You cannot do so by yourself. You need

---

[21] Suratu 'n-Nisa, 4:59.
[22] Suratu 'n-Nisa, 4:80.

someone to bring out that secret from your heart and show it to you.

Where to Hide?

The one who will show you your secret must accompany you all your life. If he does not accompany you all your life, how will he know what is in your heart in order to bring it out? One of the masters of his time, Sayyidina 'Abdul-Qadir Jilani, once gave his disciples (*disciples*) the following order, "Slaughter a chicken in a place where no one can see you and bring it to me." Some people took the order literally and thought that they merely had to keep this a secret. Others thought, like some of us sometimes do, that the shaykh was greedy and wanted to stock up on chicken. It is bad manners on our behalf to think in such a way...

After a few hours, the disciples came back, each with his chicken slaughtered. At the time of Maghrib one of them was still missing and did not show up. The shaykh said, "Where is So-and-so?" and no one could tell him. Time for the night-prayer (Salat al-'Isha) came, then the next day came, and still no one knew where the missing disciple was. In the afternoon of the next day that disciple came with the chicken in his hand, but the chicken was still not slaughtered. The shaykh said to him, "Where were you all this time? Everyone brought their chicken slaughtered and brought it to me slaughtered except you. Why is that?" He answered, "O my shaykh, your order to me was to slaughter this chicken in a place where no one can see me. I tried all day yesterday and all night and all morning today to find a place where God is not, and where the Prophet ﷺ is not, and where you are not, and I could not find any such place: how can I slaughter the chicken?" Sayyidina 'Abdul Qadir Jilani said, "This is my successor who will teach you *adab* and give you a good example to follow, for he knows that I am in his heart twenty-four hours, and never leave him."

Shaykhs are not like people who take to the pulpit (*minbar*) and give a lecture. These are not Shaykhs, but lecturers. A Shaykh is not a lecturer. A Shaykh is for *tarbiya*, education, schooling, training. A Shaykh accompanies someone that is a true believer and learns from him his good character and his ways. There are many lecturers that will prepare and deliver a very good lecture for you, but that are not practicing what they are preaching. They give it to you, but what is the benefit? Where will you get knowledge from? Books and lecturers? You have to find someone that is practicing what he is reading and learning. Learning by way of ego is unimportant to the Naqshbandi order. You need to learn to use the ways of the heart. This is the most important point of the Naqshbandi teachings.

Alhamdulillah, you are following someone in whose hands are stored the secrets of the Naqshbandi order. Every twenty-four hours, the Master that you are following is obliged to take away your burden from you and come to the presence of the Prophet ﷺ and say, "O Prophet of God! These are my followers; their burdens are on me, I will accept to carry their burdens, and whatever good I have done that day, and whatever worship, I give to them. Please accept them." Do not, therefore, be a heavy burden on your shaykh. Do not say, "We are doing this or doing that." Keep yourself locked up in your corner doing what you need to do for yourself—not looking at your brothers and sisters and mentioning their mistakes in front of people. Cover them and God will cover you. Veil their mistakes, God will veil your mistakes. Show up their mistakes, and God will show up your mistakes.

In the meeting of the saints, Sayyidina Aba Yazid al-Bistami once said, "If disciples (*mureeds*) knew how saints are going to return the tortures inflicted on them by their followers, they would torture them even more." Saints are under order that whoever tortures and attacks them, they have to give back rewards in return. As for those that say something good to them and show them good manners, they are going to raise their levels.

We are asking our brothers and sisters to be as respectful as possible towards the shaykh. I am insisting on this matter because we need to hear about it. It is easy to open different matters, but this is what we need to know right now: discipline with our shaykh.

You are under the scrutiny of many people, who are looking at the followers of the shaykh to see how they behave. If you behave well, they will say that the shaykh is a very good person. If you behave badly, then a bad reputation will fall on your shaykh and this is unacceptable to everyone. None of you would tolerate this to happen because of our bad character. Therefore correct your behavior both in and out of his presence. It is easy to behave in his presence. Outside it, it is difficult to correct your behavior. Keep him always in your heart: if you keep your shaykh in your heart, you will see that you will behave well.

Who Can be Called 'Naqshbandi'?

Grandshaykh once asked, "Who are the people that will be accepted into the Naqshbandi order?" The people around him answered, "We are Naqshbandis! Can't we consider ourselves Naqshbandis?" At that time Grandshaykh said, to be a Naqshbandi follower and a disciple, the eyes of the heart must be open. You must hear the recitation of the angels. If you go to Ka'bah in Makkah and give *salam*, you must be able to hear Ka'bah give *salam* back to you. This is the first step in the Naqshbandi order. Does one of us have this power? If someone here has this power, let him raise his hand, and I am going to see if he is right or wrong." To enter the Naqshbandi order means that the eyes of the heart are open: you can see everything. Many people among us say that they see angels, they see jinns, they see

Mawlana coming through the wall, or that they see Mawlana everywhere. It is easy to say it by tongue; it is another matter to say this truthfully.

Who is the the person who will claim to stand even at the first level of the Naqshbandi order? Grandshaykh said, "All those that come to me are my lovers (*muhibbeen*), and I love them. I love all of them as I love my children, even more than my own children, because they are sacrificing everything and coming to me. But it does not mean that they have put their feet at the first level of the Naqshbandi order." To smell the perfume of that order, you have to be under the supervision of forty accomplished Naqshbandi Imams who believe both in *Shari'ah* and in Sufism, who must look at you day and night for forty days without your knowledge, and who must see you not deviating from *Shari'ah* nor from *tariqah*. This is to say that you must not commit any sin nor neglect any sunnah of the Prophet ﷺ, even the smallest one—and there are many small sunnahs that everyone has all but forgotten in our day. After forty days of such examination, if you have not deviated, at that time you will get a smell of the Naqshbandi order; but you have not entered it yet.

Our situation is still that of lovers (*muhibb*) of *tariqah*, not disciples (*disciple*). Yet that latter level has been destined for us by Mawlana Shaykh Nazim's promise in the assembly of saints and in the presence of the Prophet ﷺ. His followers will obtain this level, not by dint of their progress, but through Mawlana's progress. Do not, therefore, even give your ego a chance to think, "I am progressing." You are nothing. The only one that is progressing is your shaykh. When you consider yourself to be nothing, at that time you will be everything.

Without this promise, it is impossible for anyone to enter and say, "I am Naqshbandi." We are allowed to say that we are Naqshbandi by tongue, but that light is not yet opened to you, even though it is destined for you: yes, anyone found in this present association is a Naqshbandi. But do you want that light to be opened? Keep what God and the Prophet ﷺ have ordered you to do, and keep the ways that your shaykh has showed you for approaching the Prophet ﷺ, and all correct manners and good behavior.

EAT SIMPLE FOOD AND WELCOME GUESTS

A man prepared a dinner for the Companions of Prophet Muhammad ﷺ one month ahead of time. As soon as the Prophet ﷺ was about to enter his house, the man said, "O Prophet ﷺ, what I have done for you does not amount to your honor." The Prophet ﷺ did not enter. He stepped back and went away. The man was very embarrassed and said, "O Prophet of Allah! What happened?" The Prophet ﷺ answered, "I am accepting this from you. All my Companions will go and eat, but I cannot eat—that word which you said was very hard on my heart, because I saw so many angels at your table, yet you said you did not honor me. What more honor could I want?" And he left without eating.

On his way back, an old woman saw him on the street and ran to him, saying, "O Prophet of God! My husband is blind. He wished to come and visit you many times, but he could not walk. Please enter my house and eat of our dinner." The Prophet ﷺ entered with Sayyidina Abu Bakr as-Siddiq ؓ who had accompanied him. She had nothing in the house but dry bread, salt and water, which she offered to the Prophet ﷺ. He would dip the bread into the water to make it soft, then put it into the salt and eat. And he said to Abu Bakr as-Siddiq ؓ, "Eat until you almost burst from being full! This food is the blessed one."

Honor Your Guests

From the beginning, these were the teachings of Islam. One day, Christian priests came to the Prophet ﷺ. They wanted to see him and verify his way of life, how he ate, spoke, acted in all aspects of his life, and so forth, i.e. in order to observe all aspects of his character. That day, the Prophet ﷺ had grapes in the house. As soon as the priests entered his presence, he took a bunch of grapes and started eating the grapes from the top, near the stem. They said, "They say you are a prophet, but what you are doing now is unprophet-like. Why are you eating at the spot in the bunch where the grapes are most sour?" He answered, "In our way we save the sweet for those we love, and we eat the sour ourselves. I am eating the sour to offer you the sweet. I have been ordered to carry sourness and difficulties in order to keep others feeling easy and happy, and to give them the sweetest things."

Do not take the best to yourself and leave the rest for others, but give them the best first. Even in eating, there is a way. Even if you must give away your food to someone who is coming, give it. Eat olives. If you don't find olives, use salt, bread, and water. If you don't find anything, sleep without eating. But give what you have. Do not be like those who work and work making money and more money to spend a fortune on one night's party while poor people are suffering. When guests come unexpected, don't ever say, "do not come." If someone calls and asks to come, say, "Yes!" Don't say, "I have no time now."

Guests are Allah's gifts. How can you reject them? In the West, if you want to go and visit someone, you have to make arrangements one month ahead of time. What for? It is going to bother you. This is a negative trait of the culture. That is why they are running to Hinduism or Buddhism or Chinese philosophers and away from the strictness of religion. They don't know that the highest spirituality is found in Islam. Muslims themselves are not practicing this excellence and therefore do not understand the point. Search Hindu, Chinese, Buddhist, and world philosophers: you cannot find there what you find in Sufi teachings.

Sufi teachings have integrated all inner teachings. Westerners are not aware of Sufi teachings. They are all running to Far Eastern religions. Where to go? They are running away from themselves to find peace in their heart. Buddhist teachings make your heart feel happy and take depression away. Many will find satisfaction with such teachings but these teachings will not make you stars, only candles. But to become stars you must come to Sufism. If you want to be a moon or a sun, you have to come to the Sufi way. Not all Sufi ways: only that Sufi way which connects you to the spiritual presence of the Prophet ﷺ and to worship, little by little. Don't turn away from worship, saying, "We only make *dhikr* and listen to Rumi poetry." One Sufi master, one Grandshaykh of the Golden Chain surpasses even Rumi ق and all his knowledge! Where is Rumi ق in comparison? But there is no permission to spread this knowledge into the hands of people who will not understand it.

Rumi was Muslim

Jalaluddin ar-Rumi ق was a very, very, very strict Muslim. Never did he do something against *Shari'ah*. And he was a Sufi. Because he wrote something that ignorant people did not understand, they ordered him to be killled, like Muhyiddin Ibn 'Arabi. That is why there is no permission in this time to write these secrets nor to spread the knowledge that is in the hearts of saints. There is need of support, and that support is coming, *Insha'-Allah*, with Mahdi ﷺ, the Awaited Saviour. When the time comes, you are going to see things that will amaze you. You will say, "Is this what we did not understand before?" It is something that you never even dreamt about.

The Second Era of Ignorance and the Coming of Mahdi

Our brothers and sisters, especially newcomers, you are all coming here out of love for the shaykh. You did not come for love of Islam. None of our brothers and sisters have come to London for the love of Islam. All of us, the speaker included, have come for the love of the shaykh, and he showed us the way of reality, and he showed us that the way of reality passes through the faith of Islam.

God has created everyone on the pattern of Islam. The seed of Islam is in everyone. Islam, like *salam*, means "peace" in Arabic, a reference to the peace of the heart. That light of peace God has put into the heart of every human being. Not seeing this, all of us have nevertheless come to our master Mawlana Shaykh Nazim through the door of love, humbleness and respect, and he has brought us to Islam.

Why did the Sahabah, the Companions of Prophet Muhammad, accept him? Why did God choose the best one to be the Prophet? Because good manners always attract people, and bad manners never do. When we saw Mawlana Shaykh Nazim's manners, we were attracted to him. That attraction made us follow his way, which in reality is the way of the Islamic faith.

Many people come to us in America, and after three or four visits they give *shahadah*, the testimony of faith in Islam, and they do not even know why they feel inspired to give *shahadah*— the testification of faith in Islam. After they sit with us and pray with us, when they are asked what their religion is, they answer, "We are Sufis." This is because they do not come primarily for

Islam. After a while, four to six months, they notice that they are Muslims!

Islam is the highest spiritual teaching and it is the religion of God. Moses ﷺ brought Judaism to the Jewish people in their time. When Jesus ﷺ came, Judaism was superseded and everyone was called to believe in Jesus ﷺ. When Muhammad ﷺ came, everything else faded and Islam shone forth. The highest belief, therefore, must be Islam.

Why do we not deny Moses ﷺ, and Jews deny Islam? Why do we not deny Jesus ﷺ, yet Christians, who accept Moses ﷺ, deny Islam? We do not deny anyone. This is the proof of perfection. The imperfect can never be the higher one in level. The Prophet Muhammad ﷺ is the highest one, and that is why the other religions cannot see him. We Muslims, however, who follow the Prophet Muhammad ﷺ and his teachings, accept Christians, because we know that they are right in accepting Jesus ﷺ; and we accept Jews, because we know that they are right in accepting Moses ﷺ. By the same token, those who accept Jesus are higher in level than those who do not, because their belief is more perfect—they can see that Moses ﷺ is a prophet, whereas the others cannot see that Jesus ﷺ is a prophet: they can see neither the higher nor the highest in level.

When Moses ﷺ went to Mount Sinai, God gave him one hundred tablets. When he came back after his forty-day seclusion with his Lord and saw that the people had been steered away from rightful belief, he threw down the tablets and 98 of them disappeared. Only two were handed down to the people. That is one explanation for the relative imperfection of the religion, and a cause for Christianity to supply a continuation and a perfecting process. And the continuation and perfection of Christianity must lie in Islam.

Islam came to take people from darkness into light. That time is called "the era of ignorance." Unfortunately, we are regressing, in our century, to another time of ignorance. Everywhere now you find ignorance. The people on the right path are being opposed, disliked, defamed, and fought. The wrong people are being praised and honored. This was foretold by the Prophet ﷺ who said that in such a time:

> *The trustworthy one will be called dishonest, and the dishonest one will be called trustworthy.*[23]

We are coming to the end of the present world. There is not much time left for this world to continue. Today we heard something very surprising: the Naqshbandi order has been banned in one Far Eastern country. This is due to the influence of the Wahhabi movement. Using their money, they are trying to control and to fight the love of the Prophet ﷺ. They don't like anyone to love the Prophet ﷺ, and for that reason, God shall put them under the feet of the followers of Sufi and the Naqshbandi Order.

Wahhabis are spreading false teachings that go against the person of the Prophet ﷺ and against the teachings of the four *madhhabs* (schools), in order to show Islam as a dry and cruel religion. They are the ones responsible for the present scandal, because of which Islam has received a bad name in the West. They say, it is the unbelievers that are responsible for passing Islam as cruel; this is false and the opposite is true: more harm is coming against Islam from Wahhabis than from unbelievers. The Wahhabis' hatred of the Prophet ﷺ is greater and worse than that of the unbelievers. When Mahdi ﷺ comes, he is going to cut the necks of 70,000 of their scholars who oppose the teachings of love of the Prophet ﷺ and love of human beings, in order to clean this earth from the dirty people who spread Wahhabi teachings East and West with their money. They are buying religious

---

[23] *Kanzu 'l-'Umal*, al-Mutaqqi.

departments and institutions in every country. They are giving as much money as people want in order to induce them to fight the love of the Prophet ﷺ. There are long-standing historical reasons for this.

> *The people of Najd[24] came to the Prophet ﷺ in his time and asked him to pray for them. He said, "O God, bless Sham (Syria) and bless Yemen."*
>
> *They said, "What about Najd, O Prophet of Allah?" He said another time, "O God, bless Sham and Yemen." Again they asked, "What about Najd" and again he did not answer them except by blessing Syria and Yemen. The third time they asked him about Najd, he said, "The two horns of the devil will appear from there, and earthquakes, confusion and corruption will abound there."[25]*

Now is the beginning of the events predicted in that hadith. In another hadith, the Prophet ﷺ said

> *Such a fire will come from the land of Najd that camels in Basra will run away from its heat.[i]*

That happened recently. Prepare yourselves, therefore, not for the best, but for the worst. Dark ages, not progress, are coming ahead. Only after the dark ages will the golden age come, which is the age of Mahdi ﷺ.

In the very near future many events are going to take place around us. Everyone of us must be careful concerning his beliefs, the beliefs of his wife and family, and of his children. Satan is not leaving anyone alone. He is trying to change your beliefs and to remove you from the love of saints, of Sufi people, and of the Prophet ﷺ.

---

[24] Najd is the whole area around present-day Riyadh, Saudi Arabia.
[25] Bukhari, Muslim.

God said:

Were it not for your (O Muhammad), I would never have created a single one of My creation.[ii]

They were fighting the Prophet ﷺ because they thought that he would be coming from their own tribe, from Najd. They did not accept him even in his own time: they are *munafiqun* (hypocrites) now just as they were then, and they are described in the chapter of Qur'an which bears their name. If you read it, you will find their description there. When Mahdi ؏ comes and says "La hawla wa la quwwata illa Billahi 'l-'Aliyyu 'l-'Azhim," ("There is no power nor might except with God the Most High, the Almighty") they will all tremble in fear of what is befalling them.

They are preparing themselves for that event with help from others. They stock up weapons thinking that they will help them to maintain their kingdom. Never! If God wants to do something else, He can send an earthquake and everything will disappear. But God is leaving them because they are *fitna*: they usher in confusion, and God is testing the hearts of His servants and checking who has a good heart and who has a bad heart.

Be happy, for this group of ours, the group of Mawlana Shaykh Nazim, is the best group, and is among the rare ones waiting for Mahdi ؏, *Insha'-Allah*, to appear. Mahdi ؏ sees the current darkness and would love to appear quickly. Mawlana said that if you put that love on all the mountains of this earth, it would burn them down and reduce them to rubble and ashes. Yet, despite such love, he is waiting to appear because permission from God is not given yet. He is waiting for that permission, and that permission will likewise be given to everyone of us *Insha'-Allah*, because his appearance signifies the appearance of our shaykh; and the appearance of our shaykh is the appearance of all of us as his followers.

The Coming Golden Age

The appearance of our shaykh is in the hands of the Prophet ﷺ. Now, we are running after Mawlana to kiss or shake his hand; at that time you will never be able to approach him, for you will see millions of people trying, as we do now, to see him and touch him. That time is the golden age, and *Insha'-Allah*, God will extend our life in order to let us see that event.

As the Prophet ﷺ explained the signs of the Last Days to the Companions and said, "The best nation, the most favored nation, is the last of this nation," Sayyidina 'Umar ؓ raised his hands to heaven and said, "O Prophet of God! I am willing to sacrifice all the rewards you have given me in order to be counted among those of that last nation!" The Prophet ﷺ answered, "No, this is for them only."

Alhamdulillah, we have reached the time which is the time of the last nation. The Prophet ﷺ said:

> *When my Community keeps on the right, it is going to enjoy an age of one day, and when it does not keep on the right, it will have an age of half a day.*[iii]

> **And one day according to Allah's estimation is 1,000 years according to your reckoning.**[26]

According to the Prophet ﷺ, therefore, God has granted us 1,500 years. We are now in the 1,412th year of the Hijri calendar: there is not much time left for this world.[27]

All the signs are present for Jesus ؑ to come and rule over this earth for forty years, and for Mahdi ؑ to come with him and rule for seven years. These events are going to happen no later

---

[26] Suratu 'l-Hajj, 22:47.
[27] This talk was given in 1992.

than in the coming eighty years. We are this near to the end and there is no time left. We must prepare ourselves by preparing our hearts. How to prepare our hearts? By leaving our ego.

We ask, "How can we leave our ego as our master Shaykh Nazim keeps telling us?" Everyone has ego. But if God had not put ego over us, we would all have been sinless angels. Sayyidina Aba Yazid al-Bistami went to Ka'bah one day and held the chain of the door of Ka'bah. "O my Lord," he exclaimed, "give me leave to chain Satan by his foot and imprison him, with the power that You gave me, in such a way that all Your creation can see him, and he cannot see anyone, so that he will leave Your servants alone and they will no longer be sinning!" God had given this saint such great power that he could make such a request. But God called him in his heart and said, "O Aba Yazid, look above you."

This means: Look into the higher stations of your heart. When Aba Yazid looked, he fell unconscious and remained there for one hour. After he woke up, he crawled to the door of Ka'bah whispering: *Ya 'Affuw, Ya 'Affuw*," "O Forgiver of all, O Forgiver of all, forgive me!"

And God said, "O Aba Yazid, to whom am I leaving the Oceans of Mercy that I have created if not to My servants? If I let you chain Satan, then everyone will be sinless, whereas:

I am the Forgiver and the Merciful One![28]

"Whom am I forgiving but sinners? If they become sinless they will be like angels, without levels. Let them sin: I will forgive them and I will raise their levels higher. These Oceans of Mercy are for sinners. Do not, therefore, interfere in My Will. I am the Creator of human beings, and I am the One keeping and

---

[28] Suratu 'l-Hijr, 15:49.

protecting them from Satan, with these Oceans of Mercy; only let them come to Me when they sin."

If a small child is hurt, he will immediately run to his mother or father. When Satan hurts you and causes you to sin, run away to your Lord and say, "O my Lord, I committed a sin, please forgive me." You will get His forgiveness immediately.

Why, O sinners, do you not come to our Lord? Why are we not, with all our ego, still coming to our Lord? We have to come to him. Run quickly and find forgiveness; but if you do not come to Him, how is He going to forgive you?

Keep Account of Yourself

We say, "How are we going to get rid of our ego?" Mawlana Shaykh Nazim has shown a very good way to get rid of your ego. Every day, write down in a notebook as many of the bad manners in your heart as you have done that day. Everyone has in his heart at least seven hundred bad manners. These seven hundred bad manners have to be taken away in order to clean yourself. Some people say, "We have no bad manners." No. Sit, think, and write down what kinds of bad manners remain in you. Everyone knows himself and what his heart hides of bad manners. Write it down, and try every day to eliminate one bad manner. Day after day, you will see that you are leaving these bad manners one after another.

Satan does not let anyone do this. In your heart, when you sit and think, you are going to find that hundreds of bad manners are coming to mind. Everyone of us is a sinner; you know yourself better than anyone. When a saint, however, is looking at your heart, he knows whether you are clean or not. He knows, therefore, when he must put you in seclusion or not. Seclusion means that you are trying to progress and leave bad manners. When the saint sees that you are trying to leave bad manners in your heart, he is going to give you permission to enter seclusion.

When he does not see you trying this, he cannot, of course, give you such a permission.

Fight your ego! Whatever your ego asks you, do the opposite. Do not accept advice from your ego, because he is misleading you:

Do not justify and praise yourselves.[29]

which could be translated as "Don't ever give excuses for your ego."

The (human) soul is certainly prone to evil.[30]

Your ego is always telling you, permitting you and ordering you to do bad things and commit mistakes. Therefore never listen to your ego, as the Prophet ﷺ said, "Do not listen to yourselves, but listen to me." But who is listening to the Prophet ﷺ? No one.

Love is the Key

Alhamdulillah, our group are listening with their love. That love is going to take us out of the darkness of this world and into the light of the hereafter. Mawlana relates:

> A Bedouin came to the Prophet ﷺ as he was at the pulpit delivering the Friday sermon, stood at the door of the mosque, and said, "Ya Sayyidi O Prophet of God! When is Judgment Day?"
> The Prophet ﷺ did not answer him. He repeated, raising his voice, "When is the Hour, O Prophet?"

Hearing and seeing this, the Prophet's ﷺ Companions sitting there were about to kill that person in their hearts for

---

[29] Suratu 'n-Najm, 53:32.
[30] Surah Yusuf, 12:53. Arabic: *Inna an-nafsu la-ammaratun bis-su'i*.

raising his voice, but there was no permission. When the leader is there, the followers are not allowed to do anything.

This is good respect. When Mawlana is sitting in your presence, whatever you see, whoever comes, whoever passes by, don't look at them: your eyes must always be on the shaykh. When he is there, he is the leader and you are responsible for nothing. Even if you see children making noise, or someone doing something bad, do not interfere: he will interfere.

If someone enters as the shaykh is making an association, he must sit wherever he finds a spot. To come up to the shaykh and kiss his hand is *tarku 'l-adab*, against respect; to enter and say *"Salamu 'alaykum"* is against respect, it is considered a bad manner. They have to give greetings in their heart and sit and hide themselves. We also are not allowed to look at newcomers, or give greetings, or answer their greetings. Only the shaykh will give or return greetings. Some people come in, shake hands with the shaykh, then go around shaking hands with everyone, turning their back to the shaykh. This is all disrespect. After you greet the shaykh, you have finished and may sit down.

The Companions were angry but could never say anything in front of the Prophet ﷺ.

> *When he asked loudly for the third time, "When is Judgment Day?" at that time, Archangel Gabriel ﷺ came to the Prophet ﷺ and told him to answer him. Only then did the Prophet ﷺ answer him.*

You can see by this example also how the Prophet ﷺ constantly listens and obeys. Only when the inspiration comes, he obeys and gives the answer. We are neither listening to the shaykh nor obeying him. When his order comes, no one is obeying. We obey only when we can show to everyone the privilege of bringing him his shoes, his cane, or his cloak. When it comes to obeying his order to leave our ego and our bad manners, no one respects him anymore. No one tries to leave their bad manners. Rather, we listen to the ego at that time, rather than to our shaykh. Cease running to bring the shaykh's cloak (*jubbah*) for everyone to see your status. Run in your heart, rather, to his order telling you to leave your ego, and listen to his order, not to your ego.

> The Prophet ﷺ said, "O Bedouin, Judgment Day is a long journey and you need many things for it; what good deeds and acts of worship have you prepared?"
> He answered, "Ala mahabbatuka O Prophet of God! Do I not have your love, O Prophet ﷺ! Your love, O Prophet ﷺ! Your love!"
> And the Prophet ﷺ answered, "Kafi ya 'arabi — It is enough, O Bedouin: you will be with the ones you love!"[31]

The man left and he did not even enter the mosque and pray with the people.

Love of the shaykh is very important. It takes you with him wherever he is going. Never allow that love to become shaky! Whatever happens, do not accept attacks on that love. If Wahhabi people come to you and speak against what you do, saying, "This is *shirk* (associating partners to Allah)," "this is *bid'ah* (innovation)," "this is not good," do not listen to them. Do not try to advise them. They are ignorant people hardened in their ignorance and will never accept you. Do not, therefore, listen to them.

Sufism in not Idolatry or Innovation

Sufism has never been idolatry (*shirk*) or bad innovation (*bid'ah*) in 1,400 years and cannot be declared so just because of the past thirty years. These false accusations come from hatred of the Prophet ﷺ in the heart of these people. Do not listen to them, do not go to their mosques and do not pray with them. If you do not

---

[31] Bukhari.

find a mosque where the imam loves the Prophet ﷺ and praises him, do not pray there—pray at home. Otherwise, darkness will enter your heart.

Be careful! Grandshaykh said:

> One hour spent listening to someone that does not have love for the Prophet ﷺ or love for the shaykhs in their heart, will bring one year of darkness on the heart. It will take one year for that darkness to wash away from the heart!

Take care, therefore, not to listen to such people. Do not be afraid; when they come to you, tell them:

You have your religion and I have mine.[32]

If they deny that you are Muslim, say, "We are Muslim, it is you who is not Muslim."

We are the ones following the right way, the way of the Prophet ﷺ, of the Companions of the Prophet ﷺ, of the Khalifs of the Prophet ﷺ, of the Four Imams of Islam. All four Imams had shaykhs who were Sufis! They used shaykhs in order to gain their knowledge, and their shaykhs were illiterate: Shaykhs such as Bishr al-Hafi and Shayban ar-Ra'i. Whenever Imam Shafi'i was in the presence of Sayyidina Bishr al-Hafi, who used to make seven mistakes in the recitation of Surat al-Fatiha, he always asked him to lead the prayer! Bishr read, not from bookish knowledge, but from the light of the heart. This is what we need.

Insha'-Allah, we pray that that light be given to us out of the love of the shaykh. May the love of the shaykh, therefore, always grow in our hearts. Without it, never can we come to the door of the Prophet ﷺ.

---

[32] Suratu 'l-Kafirun, 109: 6.

This religion is based on love, respect and humbleness. We have to be humble to each other and to everyone else. There is no harm in accepting our brothers and sisters. This religion is based on love. This religion is based on respect. This religion is based on humbleness. If we do not have these good manners, never are we going to find the light of our Lord in our hearts, as God said in a Holy Tradition (*hadith qudsi*):[33]

The heart of a believer is the house of God.[34]

To be a good believer means to be humble, respectful, and loving to people. Without these three good manners, you will never find that light in your heart in this life; as we pass away and give up the seven last breaths—not inhaling, but only exhaling—at that time, our shaykh will be there to take us into his heart. Until that time, we will never find or see that light of the heart unless we first have these three good manners. Try to get them now. Try to induce your ego to accept these traits. Be humble; if someone hurts you, step on your ill feeling and come to him and forgive him; go so far as to kiss his hand or his feet—what is the harm? As far down as you can go before others, go: then God will raise you.

Insha'-Allah, all of us will be one hand for we need unity. Let all of you believe in this and always follow one leader and one shaykh; one initiation, *bay'ah*; one door; one source of light from the Source; one broadcasting station for all hearts. At that time you will be hooked to him truly. The harder you try to go to him, the firmer and tighter this hook will be.

---

[33] *hadith qudsi*: a Divine Saying reported by the Prophet ﷺ.
[34] Ghazali, Suhrawardi.

Accusations of the Ignorant

In every association, I feel shy to talk because the ego is very difficult to control. The ego always tries to be high, proud of itself. That is why speakers, when they want to say something, feel shy to talk. What to say? We are all sinners. We are not perfect. We are trying to say something and people listen, so they are taking us as a good example. If we are not a good example, then our advice will never come to the heart of listeners. So, every time, *masha'-Allah*, they bring a tape recorder and a video camera, I feel shy and I am not inspired anymore, so it stops! But for the sake of our guests we are waiting to see what is coming, *Insha'-Allah*, God-Willing, something good will come.

What subject do we speak about? There are hundreds of subjects. Knowledge never ends. Religion never ends. There are always new things coming, explanations, something new to know. To say something that affects the hearts of listeners, we have to be good listeners. If you are not a good listener, you cannot understand. In a class, there are good students and lazy students. Why? The good students are the good listeners. The bad ones are not listening, so they are not gaining anything. Do you want to gain something? You must be a good listener.

The Perfect Listener

The perfect listener was the Prophet Muhammad ﷺ. He was the best and perfect listener because he was listening to the order of his Lord, Allah Almighty, and announcing it to people for them to take it. We have to imitate our Prophet ﷺ as much as possible—because no one can reach the level of the Prophet ﷺ—in order to be good listeners. This is the first step if we want to understand or benefit. If we are not good listeners, we are not going to benefit anything.

Avoid Suspicion

A good listener is a person that hears what the Prophet ﷺ has shown us, revealed to us, and explained for us. He revealed God's message, God's book, the Holy Qur'an, and God says in His book:

> ***Suspicion in some cases is a sin. Do not spy on each other, and do not speak evil of each other behind their backs. Would any of you like to eat the flesh of his dead brother? No, you would hate doing this.*** [35]

You must not be suspicious. You must always look for the truth. You cannot make accusations here and there without being sure 100%. Even if you are sure 99%, you have no right to accuse anyone except when you are 100% sure. This is Divine Law (*Shari'ah*). *Shari'ah* is very important because it gives you very small details. If you are not sure 100% you cannot accuse anyone.

Islam is peaceful and merciful. Islam tells you that if you accuse that lady or that man of adultery and you do not have proof, God will curse you. Even if a lady and a man stay in a room and close the door, if you accuse them of adultery, you are cursed. Even if they close the door and you know that this is a bedroom, if you accuse them you are cursed. You are not sure that they are making adultery. How do you know unless you see them? This is *Shari'ah*. You cannot accuse anyone. You can accuse them of sitting alone, this is a sin. But you cannot accuse them of committing adultery, even if the door is closed and it is a

---

[35] Suratu 'l-Hujarat, 49:12.

bedroom. *Shari'ah* will never accept. The Prophet ﷺ said, according to what Allah told him, that there must be a witness—someone must see something. If the door is closed, how can someone see? So there is no witness. If there is no witness, you cannot say that there is adultery, regardless of how "certain" you are.

Islam teaches you good manners: how to be peaceful, with love to everyone; not to be proud of yourself but to be humble with all human beings. Sufism is the heart and the essence of *Shari'ah*. It is not against *Shari'ah*. Sufi people who keep everyone's love in their heart have been admired for 1,400 years. Everyone likes them because they are humble.

As Imam Shafi'i said, "If one hundred scholars came to argue with me, I would immediately win against them; but if one ignorant person came against me, I would lose." Because whatever evidence I give as proof, he would say, 'No, it is not true.' So how am I going to convince him? It is impossible."

Let us say, "This is what the Prophet ﷺ, or this Imam, or that Shaykh said. "No!" shout the ignorant, "give me your *sanad* (chain of transmission)!" You give the *sanad*, they say, "This one is a little bit weak, give me a stronger one." Then they find hundreds of excuses. With such ignorant people there is no need for argument. Don't open confrontations with them. Am I going to bring a big library to show that ignorant person each reference one by one? Impossible.

How Did God Sit on the Throne?

Some people have been taught only how to argue. One of them came to Mawlana Shaykh Nazim, saying, "Ya Shaykh!

Kayfa-stawa-Llah 'ala' l-'Arsh?—O Shaykh! How did God sit on the Throne?"[36]

This is a matter that all such people like to argue without end, how exactly did God "sit?" As a body, or as a symbol, or with His Attributes or Names? Now what are you trying to understand? Whatever way God should "sit" on the Throne, what is your business with that? Why are you asking? Mawlana does not answer them because they think they already have the answer, and they ask the question only in order to argue. So he does not answer them except with one question, "What are the conditions of ablution?" This is the first step in *Shari'ah* and everyone knows what the conditions of ablution are. But they cannot answer. And when they cannot answer, he says, "You don't know the conditions of *wudu'* and it is the first step in *Shari'ah*, and you want to know how God is 'sitting' on the Throne? You don't know how to clean yourself before coming out of the restroom, and you are asking how God is 'sitting' on the Throne?"

Don't give them answers. There is no need to argue with them. Say:

You have your religion, and I have my religion.[37]

Or as Imam Ghazali said, "Arguing extinguishes the light of the heart."

Argument is only for politicians. Why debate and argue? If they come to you, say, "Whatever you want to believe, believe. As for us, we are following the majority of Muslims." Ninety-nine percent of Muslims follow the four schools. One percent are Wahhabi, or Habashi, or Allah knows what. If you are going to sit

---

[36] Cf. Surah Ta Ha, 20:5.
[37] Suratu 'l-Kafirun, 109:6.

and argue until morning you will gain nothing except darkness in your heart.

One day someone asked Imam Malik that same question. The only answer he got was a blow on the head and a rebuke.[38] Centuries later, Imam As-Suyuti wrote:

> O ignorant one, you do not even know by what mechanism the food that you eat leaves your body. How dare you ask about the One who sat on the Throne? Don't ask![39]

---

[38] Narrated by Bayhaqi in *al-'Itiqad 'ala madhhab as-salaf ahli 's-sunna wa 'l-jama'a,* 1961 ed., p. 43.
[39] Suyuti, *Hawi al-Fatawi,* 1975 ed. vol. 2 p. 240.

THE POWER OF SHAYKH NAZIM'S ADVICE

A believer keeps his promise...[40]

Mawlana Shaykh Nazim was given permission from his shaykh to give associations or advicee - not lectures, as lectures are for Ph.D.s and advice is for saints - as the Prophet ﷺ said:

Religion is good advice.[41]

He did not say, "*Ad-deenu 'l-muhadara,*"—"religion is lecturing!" Yet nowadays they say, "Doctor so-and-so is going to give a lecture about Islam." Lectures are for newspapers, not for hearts.

When Mawlana Shaykh was given that permission, he said, "I don't want it." How does someone say that to his shaykh? It is big. It cannot be accepted. When the shaykh gives you an order you have to say, "*Amanna wa sadaqna, sam'an wa ta'an*—I am hearing and obeying; believing and accepting." Mawlana Shaykh said, "No." His Grandshaykh ق knew, however, that Mawlana Shaykh was not refusing, but that there was something there. He said, "Why don't you want that permission?" He answered, "O my shaykh, I will accept only when you accept to give me permission from the Prophet ﷺ that anyone sitting in my circle when I give advice, listening to me even for five minutes, must be with me in this life and in the hereafter, wherever God is sending

---

[40] Abu Dawud, Ahmad, Daraqutni, Hakim.
[41] Bukhari, Muslim, Ahmad, Abu Dawud, Nisai, at-Tirmidhi, #7 in Nawawi's *Forty*.

me—that person must be with me. I cannot accept that anyone sitting with me not be raised to my level. Anyone that sits with me even for five minutes, let it be enough for them in order to be hooked to my train—finished: they are with me."

His Grandshaykh said, "What you are asking, none of the previous saints has asked before. I am happy with you because of that, and *Insha'-Allah*, that secret will be given to you." That is why anyone who sits in the talk of our master is immediately raised to his level only by listening. This gift was given to Mawlana Shaykh from his Grandshaykh, coming from the Prophet ﷺ inherited by Mawlana Shaykh Nazim. *Insha'-Allah*, all of us are on the same level in his heart. No one is higher, no one is lower; all are the same.

STATES

The servant of God who is following a Sufi way will pass through different kinds of states. According to the states that he is passing through, he begins to see. Sometimes he passes through states of illusion: he will see illusions. Sometimes he passes through states of reality: he sees reality. Sometimes he passes through states of seeing the shaykh. He might experience all three states in the same day and pass through all of them.

When someone tries to swim and doesn't know how, he struggles with all his body, trying to raise himself above water level. If he concentrates, not only using his body, but his head in the right way, he will float. Also, the disciple or follower, when he is in a state of struggle, will tend to drown and go more into mistakes. That is why they say, in Sufi teachings:

The person of too many states, mountains cannot carry.

The reason for this is that he is not accepting others, he is carrying too heavy a burden on him and thrusting that burden on everyone; people cannot carry him; mountains cannot carry him. The one who would pass that stage with all that love (for such a struggling person is struggling out of love of the shaykh, he doesn't know what to do, every molecule in his body is saying, "My shaykh, my shaykh," or "O Prophet, O Prophet," or "Allah, Allah"), when one who is in such a state of love concentrates on the heart, then he is at peace. No more problems for him: you will find him in a perfect position, not different from the rest anymore.

People are too proud. When they see a *sahib ahwal*, a person of states, they get jealous. They try to fight him and say to him, "No, you are wrong." They are wrong. That person is in that state because he is full of love for his shaykh. He doesn't know what to do, so he is acting every second according to all the inspirations of his body altogether. He is like a crazy person in a mental hospital, acting without knowing what he is doing. That is why they excuse him, even if he were to kill someone in the street. They will never jail him. The person who loves the shaykh is in that state of love, acting differently in body from ordinary people. It doesn't mean that he is not good. It doesn't mean that what he is doing is wrong. No—it is your point of view that is wrong. In the shaykh's point of view or in that person's own point of view he is right.

One must be jealous of that person for one reason only: because jealousy is useful to raise you from one position in worship to another. Jealousy in Sufism is accepted only in emulation of good manners and giving up bad manners. When you see people acting with good manners, therefore, be jealous of them and act like them. Only this type of jealousy is preferable. Anything else is not good.

Now, if I find someone that likes X and considers him to be his shaykh, although X is a follower of Mawlana Shaykh Nazim, you must not come to him and tell him "You are wrong, X is nothing; you must direct your love to the shaykh!" You don't know whether, perhaps, X will be the door to Mawlana for this follower, acting like someone that carries him to the Ocean. You cannot go directly and swim in the Ocean—you would drown. Do not, therefore, come to him and say, "don't follow, why do you follow, they are nothing, etc." That one doesn't know the Grandshaykh; how will he direct all his love to him?

When Mawlana Shaykh Nazim told people to give *bay'ah*, he always said to give it to Shaykh 'Abd Allah. Did you ever hear him say "Give it to me?" Never. When people ask me, I say, "No, don't direct your heart to Grandshaykh, direct it to Shaykh Nazim, because he is your door to go there." Now, if you are taking someone of the group, such as X, as a guide for yourself, X must not see himself as a shaykh. He must see himself as not existing, the only existing one being Mawlana Shaykh Nazim. But that does not prevent the follower who is believing in X, to come through X to Mawlana Shaykh Nazim.

There are many people creating misunderstandings inside our group through many misinterpretations, because they see someone with much love, and try their best to divert him, either by giving him more orders than he can carry, or by pulling him, each to his side. Everyone is fighting in order to show that they are right and the others are wrong. We said many times that all must be one group working for one cause, which is the cause of Allah, of the Prophet ﷺ, and of our master. Don't fight each other by saying, "That one is not trying to be good, or he doesn't know how to approach people, and so on." Everyone has a way to approach people. If his way is not working with some group, you must try your best to approach the other party.

Jealousy and Pride Cause Fighting

The problem is that all of us are jealous of each other; all of us have pride. Everyone is proud of what he knows, so he tries to make himself look like the one who knows everything as opposed to the other. Then there is no cooperation, and that is why you find separation. If everyone comes to each other, helping each other, at that time you will find more power. Two, three, four hands are better than one hand. If each puts in his hand to make one hand, out of eighty people to speak with new people coming, it will be better than having each one say, "I want to try to speak to those new people the way I know." Then we will have fights. This way it is not going to work. Everyone tries to pull the blanket toward his side to cover himself; no one tries to share the blanket so that all will be warmer. Why? You must work for one cause, not many. Everyone must know his position and everyone must know his level.

A Sufi center is a place for everyone, not special people. If anyone tries to come, we must try to encourage him. If he doesn't accept us, he free to leave. No problems must ensue. Everyone must work for Allah, not for his group. There is no discrimination in Sufi ways. All believers are accepted, depending on their righteousness. The best are the most righteous.

Grandshaykh Lowers Himself

Once, Grandshaykh 'Abd Allah was ordered by his shaykh, Mawlana Shaykh Sharafuddin, to enter seclusion for five years. In his seclusion, he was eating, once every twenty-four hours, one small piece of bread and seven olives. We are not going to detail what has happened to him in the seclusion, what he saw, what came to him of all kinds of wisdom and the climbing of the ladder. He was with the Prophet ﷺ; he was sitting with all the saints; he was taking secrets of knowledge that will never be found even in a Sufi book.

At that time there was a crazy person in the village who considered himself to know everything. He was also a disciple of the shaykh, but he was proud of himself. He was mentally ill. He thought himself to be the Qutb, standing on the highest spiritual station in his time, although whatever he said was nonsense and rubbish—like some people now trying to be shaykhs. After five years, when Shaykh 'Abd Allah came out, Sayyidina Shaykh Sharafuddin said, "'Abd Allah Effendi"—God bless his secret—"O Shaykh 'Abd Allah go and sit with that person for forty days, listen and learn from him what he will teach you." With all the love that he had in his heart for his shaykh, with all his desire to sit with his shaykh, yet his shaykh told him not to come to him, but to go listen to someone else, and a crazy person to boot. So he underwent that other test. According to Mawlana Shaykh Nazim, Grandshaykh said, "Even if my shaykh told me, go and listen to that stone, I will go and sit and listen to that stone! I will not say, 'But that stone doesn't speak.' He will make it speak!"

This is faith, *'itiqad*, and you have to have faith. If the shaykh says, "That person is your shaykh," finished—you must take him as your shaykh, even if he doesn't know anything. Obey. This will be a test for you; who knows? Perhaps this is your key to open the door to your secrets. If you don't take it, you lose. Both of you [points to two disciples] are tests to each other. Either you keep each other and come together as one hand, or neither of you is going to find his secret.

Grandshaykh went to that person and sat in his presence for forty days and nights, and the man was happy that he had found a disciple for himself. He was talking nonsense to him for forty days, not letting him sleep, and Grandshaykh was accepting, accepting. When the shaykh appoints someone now, don't ask why he appointed this one; not that one and not the other one. Even if the appointee doesn't know anything and makes mistakes, we must excuse him and say, "No, he is right and we are wrong." That is the meaning of Sufism.

That also is the meaning of Allah's Orders. Why did God not forbid pork for people when Jesus came? When Islam came afterwards, the Prophet said that pork was again forbidden. Why? To check. There may be nothing in eating or not eating but what matters is accepting what God is ordering or not, believing or not believing—not a question of eating or not eating meat. God said that in Paradise He would offer us wine to drink, but that on this earth wine was forbidden in Islam. Why did He forbid it if wine is sometimes good? To see and check if one is accepting or not; not because it is necessarily harmful or harmless.

When the shaykh appoints someone, he is checking your heart and your faith in everything, to see whether you are believing or not believing. If you are believing, you pass; if not, you fail. That is why you have to be very careful in this. Disciples in a far place may be sitting "like kings in their kingdom," then Mawlana sends or appoints someone from outside. It is a test. Those who do not accept Mawlana's appointees are making confusion. However we are not fighting them—we must ignore them as if they were not there. If Mawlana appoints someone finished: all our group must accept. Therefore: ***"do not give excuses for yourselves."***[42]

Keep a Stone in Your Mouth

Sayyidina Abu Bakr as-Siddiq put a stone in his mouth for seven years in order not to talk. You must be blind, deaf and dumb. Your love is with Allah, the Prophet ﷺ, and your shaykh. If people want to come, they can come; if not, let us not create confusion in the group. You have to be very careful in this matter. *Insha'-Allah* it will come to a good end, and by supporting each other, everything will come back to order and the misunderstanding on how to handle a situation will disappear. Keep good faith with Allah, the Prophet ﷺ, and your shaykh, and everything will be all right.

---

[42] Suratu 'n-Najm, 53:32.

FAITH IN THE SHAYKH

In every association, we have to ask support from our Master, Shaykh Muhammad Nazim al-Haqqani, may Allah bless his soul, give him more power, and raise him higher and higher in levels!

Naqshbandi saints say, "*At-tariqatu kulluha adaabun*—the Sufi path, *tariqah*, is all based on good manners." It is based on respect. *Shari'ah* is based on laws; discipline; punctuality. *Tariqah*, which is the heart of *Shari'ah*, is based on respect, *adab*, and love. You cannot find a Sufi way without *adab*, respect, and love. If there is no respect there is no *tariqah*. How can we accept to say about ourselves that we are in *tariqah*, and at the same time, we are not doing what *tariqah* is ordering us? Some people who consider themselves shaykhs, or representatives, or leaders, call us and ask us to speak "about Sufism please, not about *Shari'ah*," because people are not in the mood for accepting religion and therefore will run away otherwise.

Shari'ah teaches us discipline. *Tariqah* teaches us *ihsan*—perfect manners. The Prophet ﷺ said that we have to teach ourselves good manners; to make our hearts become diamonds through good manners. The beloved brothers that consider themselves leaders must feel shy to make such claims. There is no leader: all of us are following Mawlana Shaykh Nazim. We are all, therefore, representatives. A leader is the one you follow. It is not necessary to follow a representative, but it is necessary to learn from him. There is no one in this country to whom Mawlana Shaykh Nazim has given the authority to call himself a leader. Allah knows, and Mawlana knows who is that one who can consider himself a leader for the people to follow.

Attraction comes through love. It never comes through strictness. It is not a philosophy. Those that say it is a philosophy are wrong. We are not philosophers. We are following a real path, not a movement.

Mawlana Speaks from the Heart of the Prophet

It is not an idea. It is a reality. When Mawlana speaks and gives talks, it is from the heart of the Prophet ﷺ. He is looking at the heart of the listeners and giving them what they need. He is taking secrets from all the prophets: from Muhammad ﷺ, from Jesus ؑ; from Moses ؑ; Abraham ؑ, and giving to those that are listening. And they are listening out of love.

Teach people the easy way, the Sufi way, and teach them love. Then you can direct them to *Shari'ah*. We cannot deny *Shari'ah*. We are Sufi people and Sufism is the heart of the Divine Law. It is based on Divine Law. You cannot say, "I am denying Divine Law," as many so-called Sufi groups say. This we don't accept. We keep Divine Law at its highest levels. Why are those who ask us **not** to speak about Divine Law driving the people with a stick? When it comes to you being in authority, you want to drive people with a stick; when it comes to someone else, you want to speak pure spirituality only.

You cannot have two faces. Either you choose this way, or you choose that way. I am repeating for the hundredth time, O our brothers in North America and Canada, in Montreal California and New Mexico, you must lead people through love and good manners. You cannot push them with sticks. And you have to keep good *adab,* conduct, with your shaykh. You cannot throw words around like this and like that. There is always someone in each of these places doing this. They have to correct themselves. They must have faith in their shaykh. If they don't have faith in the shaykh, why are they saying about themselves that they are following the shaykh? Only to get disciples to listen to them? To base their fame on the disciples of the shaykh? Let them find new people then, and teach them their philosophy. If they are saying that this is the philosophy or the ideas of the shaykh, they are wrong, for his philosophy and ideas are different. Why then are you imposing your philosophy on the disciples of the shaykh? Why are you using them? Go and find new ones.

The Worst Sin

You have to have faith in your shaykh, or else you will not progress. When you have the slightest doubt about your shaykh and you declare this doubt, then you are mistaken. If you have doubts in your heart—Satan comes many times to the heart and gives bad thoughts—say, "*Astaghfirullah*," it is enough. Do not believe what Shaytan is throwing into your heart, and don't mention to anyone what is going on in your heart. The leaders of the Naqshbandi order do not look at that. They consider it a usual occurrence, not a sin. But when you believe it, and go outside and begin to spread bad rumors and bad ideas, false ideas about the shaykh... then that is your illness. Because you don't have faith in the shaykh, you are trying to make people lose faith in the shaykh. This is the biggest *haram* (transgression).

The following example will show how much this can be big and small at the same time, in the eyes of the shaykh or the disciple. One of the big Naqshbandi saints said—and this is entirely an example and not a reality: be careful! Suppose a person decides to go on hajj to Makkah and took his mother with him. If you sin in Makkah, it is considered like 100,000 sins. Even a bad thought there is considered a sin. If you pray one prayer there, it is considered as 100,000 prayers, according to hadith of the Prophet ﷺ. Now if that person took his mother inside Ka'bah, committed adultery with her, then destroyed Ka'bah: is there any sin bigger than this?

The above example is to make people understand the greatness of this Sufi way and come back to a Naqshbandi shaykh of the Golden Chain, and repent to Allah. Sayyidina Shah Naqshband said:

> If that person came back to us, he would find our doors open from East to West, and we are accepting his repentance. It is very easy on us to give that person something to recite in order to be forgiven.

He also said that there was no sin bigger than this sin. He continued:

> But if someone says something bad about his shaykh one time only, or breaks the heart of one of his believing brothers, there is no repentance for that person. Our doors are closed. We cannot open any door for him. He has to go back to where he came from.

In your eyes it is a very light thing to speak foolishly. How many times are you breaking the hearts of your brothers every day? Hundreds of times. You wait for them to be a little bit late, for example, to throw them out of *dhikr*. Why? Mawlana Shaykh Nazim assigned duties to other people on specific days. Why are you trying to take everything in your hand? We have to learn our limits. The Prophet ﷺ said:

> *Whoever knows his limit does not trespass it.*

He cannot go further. Archangel Gabriel ﷺ knew his limits and said to the Prophet ﷺ in the Night of Ascension, "I cannot go further with you," and he stopped. But our ego knows no limits. Its freedom will even take us to hell, throwing us in a valley where no one can give us his hand to help us. You have to be very careful.

Are You Mistake-Free?

We must not impose our leadership. Whoever accepts, accepts; if not, let them not accept. We care only for one thing: the love of the shaykh. May Allah keep us in and direct us to, the love of our shaykh, and make us have faith in him more and more, and not to follow our ego. If we follow our ego, it means that our shaykh is our ego, not Shaykh Nazim. You have to decide: will you follow your ego or follow the shaykh? If you decide to follow the shaykh, then follow him. When you make a mistake, as you follow your ego sometimes, repent quickly. But don't, every time, pretend that you are the one that makes no mistakes.

Some people that consider themselves shaykhs never acknowledge that they have made a mistake. They are always right! But in fact they are wrong. You cannot be a perfect shaykh. In every century, there is only one perfect shaykh. There are 124,000 saints: not all of them are perfect, but they are saints; yet they do make mistakes. There is only one perfect one, and he takes directly from the Prophet ﷺ. This is the highest level. The others are saints, they have secrets and miraculous powers, but they make mistakes. Only the prophets are innocent of mistakes. If you think with your mind that a Sufi makes no mistakes you are wrong. A Sufi master makes mistakes, but these are excused mistakes. You must give hundreds of excuses for that mistake. You must not count it in your heart as a mistake.[43]

This is a very important point. Sayyidina Imam Ghazali said, "A Sufi is not always one hundred percent right, but you have to find excuses for him."

---

[43] Prophets are innocent from commiting sins (*ma'soom*) while *awliya*, saints, are protected (*mahfoodh*).

You are doing mistakes in every second. A saint does not makes mistakes every second. Perhaps in a month's time, or in twenty-four hours. We, however, are in mistakes every second! You cannot compare yourself with the shaykhs. The perfect shaykh comes once in every century, and that one makes no mistake. He is always at the highest level. Even prophets made mistakes. Before you object, let me explain.

No Salvation Except Prophet Muhammad

On Judgment Day, every nation is going to come to its prophet and ask for his intercession. And every prophet is going to resply that he made a mistake. All prophets and all nations are going to say at that time, "We have to go to that one who did not commit a sin; go to Prophet Muhammad ﷺ." Prophet Abraham ﷺ will say, "When they asked me, after I cut the necks of the idols, who had done such a deed, I told them to go ask the biggest idol: I told a lie." Prophet Moses ﷺ will say, "I cannot intercede. I slapped one person and killed him, and then I committed a second mistake. I was angry, and threw down the Torah that God had given me." When he threw them down, 98 tablets were broken and taken up, and only two were left to him. Originally it was more than ten commandments. Allah had given him wisdom, as he gave to Prophet Muhammad ﷺ. But when he threw the tablets down, the portion containing wisdom was taken up and only laws remained. The Prophet Jesus ﷺ said, "How can I intercede with my Lord? You called me 'God' and 'Son of God,' how can I speak?" All prophets and their nations will then turn to the Prophet Muhammad ﷺ and they will say, "O Prophet of God! Bring them all through your intercession and let them go to Paradise."[44]

According to the verse in Qur'an:

---

[44] Gloss of the hadith in Bukhari, Tafsir #236.

> **We have not sent you except as a mercy for human beings.**[45]

That is why the Prophet ﷺ said:

I will be the chief of all the people on the Day of Resurrection.[46]

And the Prophet ﷺ will send **everyone** with even an atom's weight of faith to Paradise by means of his intercession, because Allah loves him. For that reason Prophet Muhammad ﷺ said:

My intercession is for the great sinners of my nation.[47]

From that love, Naqshbandi leaders are taking and giving to their followers. O idiotic people! O square-minded people! as Mawlana calls them, O football-headed people! Take from that love, and not from strictness.

---

[45] Suratu 'l-Anbiya, 21:107.
[46] Bukhari, Tafsir #236, Bayhaqi, Ahmad, at-Tirmidhi, Tafsir #3147.
[47] As-Suyuti said this is sound based on the conditions of Bukhari and Muslim.

Cover People's Faults

Do not talk idly. Do not speak nonsense. The Prophet ﷺ said:

It is a duty and an order for human beings to leave alone what does not concern them.[48]

The Holy Stone of Abu Bakr as-Siddiq

If something does not concern you, don't talk too much about it. As soon as Sayyidina Abu Bakr as-Siddiq ؓ heard this, he put a stone in his mouth in order not to talk, and it was a stone as big as one's thumb. Until the Prophet ﷺ received an order from the archangel Gabriel ؑ saying, "O Prophet of God! God is sending you greetings and tells you to tell to Abu Bakr as-Siddiq to remove that stone from his mouth."

The Prophet ﷺ went back to Abu Bakr and said, "O Abu Bakr, what are you putting in your mouth?" When he answered "A stone," the Prophet ﷺ asked "What for?" Abu Bakr answered, "O Prophet of God! O my beloved Prophet, when I heard that hadith from you to leave what does not concern us, immediately I put that stone into my mouth in order not to speak." The Prophet ﷺ asked, "For how long?" Abu Bakr answered, "I have held that stone in my mouth for seven years."

All Naqshbandi saints after Abu Bakr as-Siddiq ؓ have inherited that stone one after another, until it came to Grandshaykh 'Abd Allah ad-Daghestani, who has kept it in his

---

[48] Arabic: *maa laa yaa'nee* — that which is not your concern. Malik, at-Tirmidhi, Ibn Majah, al-Bayhaqi, #12 in Nawawi's *Forty*.

mouth for forty years. Then it was inherited by Mawlana Shaykh Nazim, who put it in his mouth for a number of years, and he was ordered to take it away and to keep it as a trust for someone— Mahdi ﷺ.

There is a famous saying in Arabic: "If talk is silver, silence is golden."

Look Under Your Own Turban

Silence will never make you fall into problems, but talking will make you fall into sins, make you yell at people and curse. So it is an order for us according to teachings inherited from the Prophet ﷺ and Sufi teachings, that a person has no right to look at the bad manners of others. Everyone must look at what is "under his turban," that is, look at himself or herself. You have no right to tell another, "O So-and-so! You have to do this; you have to do that; you are wrong; you are right." It is not your business. It becomes your business when you are perfect.

When you clean yourself, you can correct others. When I will be perfect, when I will be a good example. At that time I will get permission from my master to give corrections or advice to people. When I am in sin and dirt, I have to clean myself before going to clean people. It is a big mistake people are committing nowadays, thinking themselves perfect and entitled to look at the mistakes of others so that they tell this or that person, "You are a *kafir*, unbeliever, or you are making *bid'a*, innovation," while forgetting everything about themselves. This is an illness spread now everywhere, East, West, North and South. There is no cure for it except when Mahdi ﷺ comes.

Everyone must be aware that they must clean themselves first. Mawlana Shaykh Nazim once said that we are like houseflies. Houseflies go around and around and look where the dirt is to go there. Wherever there is filth, dirt and smell, you will find houseflies. And we are houseflies, because we are after the dirt of our brothers and sisters. We are not going after our own dirt. We think ourselves to be clean, and never see our own filthiness. After getting the dirt, the housefly will then go and look for a clean place in order to put the dirt there.

This comes from the fact that we are not minding our own business. When we mind our own business and our own concerns, at that time we will cease to be houseflies. That is why Sayyidina Abu Bakr as-Siddiq ؓ put that stone in his mouth for seven years; in order to teach himself not to run after the dirt of other people.

Don't Stir up Waste

Unfortunately, as I am saying, everyone nowadays is running after the dirt of his society. He is not looking for clean things, but always for filthy things to dig up and bring out. When you bring it out, it gives a bad smell.

I will now give a bad example, but never mind, because it will help people understand. Some animals, or even some people, leave their waste in the streets or behind trees or in the desert and sometimes you will pass and find this on your way. If you turn it upside down, what will happen? You will smell a very bad smell. On the top side there was no longer any smell, because it was dry. So if you leave your brother's dirt and let it "dry" by hiding it, the bad smell will go away and no one will know about it. This is the meaning of veiling and hiding the faults of others. But if you turn it upside down or dig it up, everyone is going to smell it. It is as if you are making your brother seem lower than the rest. We have to leave that bad habit. It is the one bad habit that the Prophet ﷺ has most ordered the Sahabah ؓ to leave.

One day, the Prophet ﷺ was coming out of his house around midnight shaking and trembling. He told Bilal to give *adhan* (call to prayer). It was midnight, not the time for prayer. Bilal gave a very loud *adhan*, and all the Companions of the

Prophet ﷺ were very afraid. They were wondering if another order for battle was coming to defend their young community from aggressors, for they had just recently returned from battle and were very tired. They all ran to the mosque to see what the Prophet ﷺ wanted from them. He said to them, "Tonight was the hardest revelation that came to me, and it left me shaking." They said, "O Prophet of Allah! May our fathers and mothers be sacrificed for you, as ourselves and our children! Are we being warned of some great punishment?" He said, "We are carrying a very great burden on our shoulders." They were all afraid to hear about that burden. He continued, "Gabriel ؑ came to me tonight and said that God swore by Himself to Himself, and said, 'O my beloved Muhammad ﷺ, if anyone is going to mention a bad event that took place two hours before, or a problem out of which came confusion, a story that causes hearts to feel depressed or confused; if anyone is going to repeat or relate that event from one person to another person within two hours time, I am going to throw him out of My Presence and place him in the most severe punishment.'"

This means that if you are going to bring up what causes confusion between brothers and sisters instead of veiling it, God is going to punish you. "Because," God said, "it is very difficult for Me to accept anyone that breaks the heart of another by bringing out his fault. If you commit a sin—any kind of sin—and repent, it is easy for Me to forgive you. But when you bring out someone's fault, hurting, cracking, breaking a heart that I have created with My hands and My love, it is a very great thing to Me, and I don't accept it from anyone. I will throw you into severe punishment."

All the heartbreak and confusion many people now commit by saying to others, "Unbelievers, innovation," and all kinds of nonsense, is interference in God's Power. We are human beings, not creators. The judgment of whether someone is clean or dirty belongs to Allah. And who can be clean, except the Prophet ﷺ and his inheritors, the saints? No one. All the rest are dirty with their ego! No one is clean, as much as he may rise in bookish knowledge. You know that you are clean when you hear the *dhikr* of angels. If you do not hear the reciting and chanting of angels, then you are not clean. When you begin to hear, you know that you are on the way to cleanliness. It is the first step in real faith. Who is hearing this among those people who are calling others names, bringing out people's faults and causing confusion?

Thus the Prophet ﷺ said this to his Companions in order to warn them. If we examine ourselves now, can we say whether we repeat a story that happened two hours ago or not? I will tell you that not only do we repeat a story that happened two hours ago, but we are repeating even one that happened fifty years ago—even if we could reach to a dirty story that happened in Noah's ﷺ time we would repeat it. That is why it is very important to keep our tongues, as Sayyidina Abu Bakr as-Siddiq ؓ did—by putting a stone in his mouth. When you put something big in your mouth, you cannot talk. Otherwise you cannot control yourself. In this way he was able to protect himself.

We must learn to first clean ourselves. We have no permission to clean others until we clean ourselves. When we clean ourselves and hear the chanting of angels, at that time the Prophet ﷺ will give you an order to clean others. It is not difficult for the Prophet ﷺ to come to you through any kind of means, such as a dream, and say, "O servant of God, you are clean, go and teach." Until that time that an order and permission comes to you, try to clean yourself, make ready and prepare yourself first. You have no right to do otherwise. Then your shaykh, who has more experience than you, will give you permission. As God said:

> ***O believers, be righteous and accompany true people.***[49]

---

[49] Suratu 't-Tawbah, 9:119.

Sadiqeen, that is "good people." When you accompany a true person, he will tell you, "O my son," or "O my daughter, now you are clean from your mistakes, go and teach others." Until you find such a person to give you that permission, try to clean yourself. Prepare yourself for that day that is coming before all of us.

ON SURAT AL-KAHF, 28-31

Restrain thyself along with those who cry unto their Lord at morn and evening, seeking His countenance, and let not your eyes overlook them, desiring the pomp of the life of the world; and obey not whose heart We have made heedless of mentioning and calling Us, who follows his own lust and whose case has been abandoned.
Say: it is the truth from the Lord of you all. Then whosoever will, let him believe, and whosoever will, let him disbelieve. Lo! we have prepared for disbelievers fire. Its tent encloses them. If they ask for showers, they will be showered with water like molten lead which burns the faces. Calamitous the drink and ill the resting-place!
Lo! as for those who believe and do good works, lo! We suffer not the reward of one whose work is goodly to be lost. As for such, theirs will be Gardens of Eden, wherein rivers flow beneath them; therein, they will be given amulets of gold and will wear green robes of finest silk, and gold embroidery, reclining upon thrones therein. Blest the reward and fair the resting-place![50]

"Don't ever follow that one whose heart we have made heedless from Our remembrance," refers to someone who always

---

[50] Suratu'l-Kahf, 28:31.

denies the remembrance of the Lord. There are many good people in society and in the community who do not remember their Lord. They don't believe in Allah. Even though they are good, do not follow them, because their teachings will deviate you from the path of your Lord. Their teachings are only for this life, but not for the hereafter. Their teachings will not take you through the hereafter. For the hereafter, you must belive in your Lord.

The Atheists and Sayyidina 'Ali

Atheist people do not believe in God and say, "This is the only life." So they act according to this life's needs. But when they are going to find that there is another life, they are going to find themselves in misery and sadness. Some atheists came to Sayyidina 'Ali ﷺ, saying, "O 'Ali! You are worshipping day and night, teaching your followers not to take pleasures from this life, losing the short time that you have on this earth in worship, disconnecting yourself from the pleasures of this life. We, however, are taking pleasure from everything. We are happy and must take pleasure from everything around us for sixty or seventy years. We cannot leave anything—if we can womanize day and night, we are going to do it, and we drink as much alcohol as we wish. We are going to take our pleasure from this life." This is what people do today everywhere.

Sayyidina 'Ali ﷺ said, "Is not a day coming when you and me are going to be in the same spot?" He meant, and these wise men immediately understood that "spot" is the grave. He continued, "The pleasures you are enjoying in this life are going to end with death; what difficulties I have endured are going to end. So we are the same: your pleasures and my sufferings are ending and we are going to be equal. If I am going to find that what God has said is true, that there is an eternal life, I am not going to suffer, but you are. I suffer sixty or seventy years in this life, but compared to eternal life, that time is nothing. And I am going to be in happiness for eternal life, and you are going to be in sadness and misery for eternal life. Which is better?"

God is saying, **"Don't follow someone that doesn't have remembrance of his Lord in his heart."**[51] Many people teach fine things but do not keep their Lord in their hearts. A good guide is someone who keeps his Lord always present in his heart. When you do that, you are going to find wisdom and knowledge coming on your tongue. When you do not do that, you are disconnected and will receive no inspirations.

All of us have to try our best—when we gather for such associations, leaving everything for three or four days to come together—in order to progress. Ask yourself how much you have progressed since the last meeting. If you find yourself to have progressed, you must be happy. If you find yourself not to have progressed, then you must not be happy.

You are a disciple who has been put in charge of a region. You have just spent three months with Mawlana. What have you gained there? What new wisdom or inspiration have you brought into your heart? I want an answer and I am going to check that answer. Don't tell me with your tongue. Tell me what you have gained and put into practice. By tongue we can say many things, but what are we keeping? That is what you have to know.

Sayyidina 'Ali:

Take care of them as long as you are in their houses,
And salute them as long as you are in their district,

---

[51] C.f. Suratu 'l-Kahf, 18:28.

And make them happy as long as you are in their land.[52]

You have to take care of everything as long as God is taking care of you. Take care of everything as long as you are living in this world, God's world. It belongs to Him. How can you come against His Will when you are living in His Belonging? Our brother invited us today in his house. Can you come against his will in his house? You cannot. He has a right to say to you what you must do. The deeper meaning is that the owner of the house—which means your heart—is God. You cannot and must not come against Him.

We are in the House of Allah. So we have to take care of ourselves and our behavior. We cannot overcome the Will of God. Yet we are trying to overcome everything without limit. But God said, "This belongs to Me." Americans are polite and do not write "Stop!" outside their lands, rather they post, "Private Property, No Trespassing." Yet even this is not polite because it shows pride. They are proud of their belongings, as if it were private for themselves. But everything belongs to Allah. If people are putting their own laws and limits, what about the Owner of this world? Doesn't He have a right to put down laws for His Property? Why are we not believing? Who is asking himself this question? It is not necessary to do it with the tongue—do it in your heart.

Association to Combat the Ego's Tricks

Associations, spiritual gatherings, are not only for *dhikr*—reciting the remembrance of God. *Dhikr* is good, it makes the

---

[52] Arabic: *daarihim ma dumta fee daarihim, wa hayyihim ma dumta fee hayyihim, wa ardihim maa dumta fee ardihim*. Al-Jarrahi, al-Asbahani, Al-Bayhaqi.

heart happy. But we need teachings in order to know our limits. Ego knows no limits. It will take you to the ocean and throw you there to sink. It doesn't care. If you let go of the bridle of your ego without controlling it, it will destroy you. We are letting go of the bridle of ego. The ego is clever. It is tricking you. To destroy you, it uses tricks. It doesn't come directly to you to tell you, "Follow this!" You would know that you might fall. Instead, it takes you only slightly in the false direction, then again some more, by telling you, "This is a very small sin, never mind, no problem." Once you make one step, you are ready for the next step. Then you find yourself in the middle, you cannot go back. Finished.

Let us give respect to the House of Allah, His creation. If we don't give respect, we are going to lose everything. We have to be careful. Grandshaykh said, "Since in our time not everyone knows what is right and what is wrong, there is *rukhsa* now, permission or excuse for everyone, that if he wants to do something, he can think about it in his mind. If he finds that there is no harm in doing it, then he can do it. If there is harm, leave it." That is why he said, responding to many people who come to him saying, "Muslims discriminate against ladies and do not listen to their wives' advice" that whenever your wife gives you advice, you must take it and evaluate it. If it coincides with Sufism and Divine Law, take it, for it will be valuable advice. But if you see that it clashes with Sufism, good manners and Islam, then leave it. There is no need for it.

A Lady Corrects the Caliph

Sayyidina 'Umar went to the pulpit and was saying to the people, "Don't ask for too great a dowry; it is not allowed." (In Islam, you must give a dowry to your bride before marriage, and if you divorce her you cannot take back what you gave.) One lady ot up in front of everyone and said, "God has given permission for women to take dowry, as Qur'an said, even more than a ton of gold, which you cannot take back!" Then she recited:

> *If you decide to take one wife in place of another, even if you had given the latter a whole treasure for dower, take not the least bit of it back; would you take it by slander and a manifest wrong?*[53]

Sayyidina 'Umar was the *khalifa*, Successor of the Prophet, but he did not say anything. In fact he said, "'Umar was wrong and the lady was correct." He accepted what the lady was saying. How, then, is there discrimination in Islam? Islam gave ladies the right to say what they like. As they gave it to men, they gave it to ladies, without discrimination. Crazy people in our day are claiming that Islam did not give equal rights to ladies in order to lessen its value. But God never lets His religion to appear lesser in value. *Insha'-Allah* we will keep our hearts clean from such thoughts.

---

[53] Suratu 'n-Nisa, 4:20. This hadith is narrated by Abu Ya'la and is strong.

BE MERCIFUL

Everything is based on love. Because God loved the Prophet ﷺ, he created this world.

> *God said to Adam ؑ, "If he [Muhammad ﷺ] were not created, I would not have created you or the skies and the Earth."*[54]

Why did He say "If not for Muhammad ﷺ"? He meant the love that He has for him, and that in turn means that everything is based on love, and that without love there is nothing. Nowadays you don't find love between people. Now, love is taken away — true love, that is. We are not speaking about what they consider love nowadays, but the love of Allah, the love of the Prophet ﷺ, of secrets, of masters and of each other. Pure, honest love is now erased from the earth and you find nothing but tyranny. You can find some special people that still have that love, but they are very few. It is not for everyone.

Adam was Forgiven for the Sake of Muhammad

> *When Adam ؑ committed a sin by eating from the tree, he raised his hands to his Lord and said, "O my Lord, for the sake of Muhammad, I am asking you to forgive me." God said to Adam ؑ, "How do you know about Muhammad?" Adam ؑ said, "I saw his name on the Throne, beside Your name, and I knew that You loved him above all creation." Allah answered, "O Adam! I*

---

[54] Ibn Asakir from Salman al-Farsi ؓ.

have forgiven you! If it were not for Muhammad, I would not have created you."⁵⁵

From the beginning, God has that love for the Prophet ﷺ. If it is true for the Prophet ﷺ, then from the beginning God has that love for everyone. Everything, therefore, is based on love: if there is no love, there is nothing.

If we love each other, we don't want each other to be harmed. What do you think about your Lord who loves everyone? Isn't He going to protect us? Do you think that He is going to harm us? Should everyone fear Allah and nothing else, when Allah has said:

My Mercy encompasses all things?⁵⁶

And again, in a Holy Tradition (*hadith qudsi*) the Prophet ﷺ relates:

*When Allah decreed the Creation, He pledged Himself by writing in His Book which is laid down with Him: My Mercy prevails over My Wrath.*⁵⁷

This means, "Come to Me: I have decreed this for you; I bless you; I grant you Mercy." Why are you afraid? He is not One to be feared for He is the Merciful Lord, the loving God that has created us with His love.

God Tests Abraham Severely

One day, Prophet Abraham ﷺ was sleeping. God had given him a child after his hundredth year. Abraham ﷺ saw a

---

⁵⁵ al-Hakim in his *Mustadrak*, Bayhaqi in *Dala'il an-Nubuwah*, Tabarani in his *Kabir*, Abu Na'im in his *Hilya* and ibn Asakir in *Tarikh Dimashq*.
⁵⁶ Suratu 'l-'Araf, 7:156
⁵⁷ Bukhari, Muslim, Nisai, Ibn Majah.

dream. We say this for us to understand. In reality he was not dreaming but receiving inspiration. God is talking to him in this vision, "O Abraham, for My sake, go and slaughter your son Ishmael."[58]   Religion at that time entailed going out into the countryside, making an oath to God—*nadhr*—and approaching God by leaving fruit from the crops or a lamb on the altar for fire to descend from heavens and consume. When the fire came to take up the offerings, it meant it had been accepted. If it was left, it was a sign that it was not accepted.

Abraham ﷺ woke up and thought, "I might be wrong. Is it possible that I have to slaughter my only child?" Who can slaughter his child, created by God from His love? "How can I slaughter my child? It must be Satan trying to play with me. I am going to sleep another time." He slept another time and saw the same dream, "O Abraham, go and slaughter your son." He woke up rubbing his eyes and said to himself again, "Is this true or false?" He knew that it was true, but he was trying to find an excuse so that the order might be taken back. But it was finished: when God orders something, you cannot take it back.

It was a test for Prophet Abraham ﷺ, to teach him a lesson not to be rude with his people. God had sent him to his people saying, "O Abraham ﷺ, these are My servants, I created them, but they are ignorant: go and teach them, and preach to them that I am there. Teach them to leave idols and come to Me."   And Abraham ﷺ was teaching and preaching for many years; but they rejected him and tortured him. What did they do in the end? They put him in a fire and tried to burn him. At that time he said, "O my Lord, they are burning me." The archangel Gabriel ﷺ came to him and said, "Do you need any help?" Abraham ﷺ said, "From you? You are a creature like me. The One who sent you knows more than you whether I need help or not."

---

[58] cf. Suratu 's-Saffat, 37:102.

That is why God said:

We said, O Fire! Be cool and safe for Abraham. ⁵⁹

After that, Abraham ﷺ raised his head and said, "O my Lord, these people did not believe in me: destroy them." The prayers of prophet are always accepted, so God immediately destroyed all those people with an earthquake. So now, years later, He was testing Abraham ﷺ by telling him to go and slaughter his son.

After the third time that he heard the order, Abraham ﷺ said to himself, "This time it is finished: I am accepting the truth. God is ordering me and I cannot find excuses anymore." The next day, he took his seven-year old son and went to the mountain in order to slaughter him for God's sake. Let everyone take a good lesson from this for this is what we need. How to pray, how to make ablution—this is easy. You can read it in any book and understand it—it is not difficult. But such teachings as God is giving us through wise men, true men, good men, you cannot find anywhere.

Abraham ﷺ went to the place of sacrifice, where there was a big stone for that purpose, and tried to cover the child's eyes. He could not bear to tell his son that he was going to kill him. The love in Abraham's ﷺ heart, was like a fire burning.

What would happen to you if someone told you to slaughter your son? You would die over him. Even if you run over a cat on the street, you feel bad for it. And a son is something very big. So Abraham ﷺ was burning and crying, inside and out. This is how angry God is when someone kills another. There are many people that are killers, having no mercy in their hearts, and

---

⁵⁹ Suratu'l-Anbiya, 21: 69.

God is going to punish them. People that kill each other are abhorrent to God and it is an enormity in God's eyes to kill someone that He has created. As your heart would burn for your son, so does God feel pity for His servant that has been killed. And what if you were breaking the heart of a believer? It is just as if you had killed someone, and God does not accept it. We will come to that later.

Abraham ﷺ was trying to cover his son's eyes. Ishmael ﷺ said, "O my father, why are you trying to close my eyes?" Abraham ﷺ wanted to find an excuse, but Ishmael ﷺ said, "O my father, there is no need to find an excuse. Since God has ordered you to slaughter me, continue and fulfill His order. I am ready and am putting down my head for you. Come and slaughter me." That child of seven years knew that the order had come, because he was a prophet also. Immediately he put his head down, without being tied.

The Fire of Love

Abraham ﷺ took a very sharp knife. Anyone who has slaughtered a sheep knows that according to Divine Law the knife must be very sharp and that the head of the sheep must be thrown back in order for the neck to be stretched. This way, as soon as one says *"Bismillah, Allahu akbar"* and cuts across, the animal will die quickly; otherwise, it will suffer. Prophet Abraham ﷺ took the head of his son and raised it up—immediately God ordered the knife not to cut. That was to bring more pain down upon Abraham ﷺ. When the knife is not sharp and you are trying to slaughter an animal, it is as if you are sawing his neck and it is excruciating. Abraham ﷺ was sawing his own son's neck; and his heart was burning. His son told him, "O father, what is that smell of burning flesh?" Abraham ﷺ answered, "O my son, don't ask. This is my heart burning for you."

At that time God sent a very big lamb, as the Qur'an says:

***We ransomed him with a great sacrificial offering.*[60]**

No one knows the significance of that greatness referred to in the word *'adheem*: it is a secret also.

After Abraham ﷺ slaughtered the lamb and God saved the child, God said, "O Abraham ﷺ! Now is your court date, the time for your judgment. For one son, your heart was burning—what about My slaves that you ordered to be burnt and destroyed by Me? Did you not know that I was also burning for them? Why did you accept Me to destroy all My servants, and you did not accept for your son to be destroyed? Are they not also My servants as your son is My servant? Why do you invoke harm on others and good on yourself? O Abraham ﷺ, I am swearing by Myself, if you repeat this another time, I shall take prophecy away from you."

God then sent Abraham ﷺ a nation worse than the first. Abraham ﷺ tried very hard to teach them; they accepted nothing and tortured him more instead. In the end he said, "O my Lord, these are Your servants; whatever You want to do with them, do. It is Your judgment, not mine."

Two Wings Are Needed to Fly

This is what we have to learn lessons from. This is what we are being taught through the Prophet's ﷺ teachings. We have to purify ourselves from bad manners. This is what Sufi masters are trying to teach us: good manners. It is easy to teach you how to pray. Everyone knows it. But there are many people in our countries who may pray behind the imam in the mosque, even for the dawn prayer (Salatu 'l-Fajr), five times a day; but during their business day they are cheating, deceiving, trading with all kinds of unacceptable business according to Islam. When they go to Europe the first thing they do is go to the Playboy, and when they

---

[60] Arabic: *wa fadaynahu bi dhibhin 'adheem.* Suratu 's-Saffat, 37:107.

come to America they go to Las Vegas. But they don't miss their five daily prayers behind the imam. Is this Divine Law? When we speak a little bit about cleaning the heart or being a good person in society, they say all this is *bid'a*—innovation. It is they who are *bid'a* and innovation! As for us we are the heart of Divine Law. According to Imam Malik:

> Anyone who accepts Sufism without obedience to Islamic law (*Shari'ah*) is a hypocrite and anyone that accepts and studies Divine Law (*Shari'ah*) without accepting Sufism, will be corrupted.

This is because he will have bad manners—just like these people who go and lose millions of pounds in London in one night. The third thing Imam Malik said is:

> And anyone who accepts Divine Law and Sufism together, has certainty and truth within his reach. Then he will have attained both external knowledge and internal knowledge of his religion.[iv]

This is what is needed for everyone of us, to be of two wings. An airplane or a bird will not fly with only one wing. According to Sufi people, one wing must be the external knowledge and the other wing must be the internal knowledge. That is why all Sufi masters were rising up. Otherwise you will not fly, but you can walk. You clip a pigeon's wings in order to make it stay in one place. That is what happens if you have only one wing.

Jalaluddin Rumi was a very great saint and his books are still being studied, particularly here in America. One day a Rumi group in San Fransisco invited me to make *dhikr* with them. They are nice people but they don't practice Divine Law. They said they wanted a lecture, so I spoke a little bit. I said that by whirling during *dhikr*, we were doing what Jalaluddin Rumi was doing, with only one difference; he was rising up as he was whirling around. What they now call *"sema* dancing" was a whirling—we may not call it dancing—that Rumi practiced with his followers by rising up to the ceiling, because they were carried up by their knowledge. Now, we are imitating, but we are not rising, because there are no wings. And they said, "What are the wings?" The wings are external knowledge and internal knowledge. If you can take these two knowledges, at that time you will find yourself rising. This is needed from everyone of us.

Internal knowledge is the polishing of the heart from the dirt of this life. You have to always keep your heart present in the love of your Lord—always, without disconnection, as the Prophet ﷺ was always keeping his heart present to the order of God, listening and obeying. As for us, God wants us to be good servants, to love one another, and to be humble with each other. *Insha'-Allah*, we hope that all of us will be on that path, the path of reality and the path of certainty, not swerving left or right, but always moving straight towards God, towards the Prophet ﷺ and towards true people. This is what God has ordered us in His Holy Book when He said:

O ye who believe! Fear God, and be with true people.[61]

Therefore find a true person and follow him. God did not tell you "Be a true person," for it is very difficult. He said, "Be with true people." We have to accompany true people. They are very rare, like diamonds. *Insha'-Allah* we shall be accompanying them in this life.

---

[61] Suratu 't-Tawbah, 9:119.

MIGRATING TO GOOD MANNERS

Friday is a holy and blessed day, especially when it coincides, as it does today, with the third day of the new Islamic year, which commemorates the migration of the Prophet ﷺ from his hometown to a new place, from Makkah to Madinah.[62] That is the migration from evil to goodness, from a place where people tortured him to a place where people loved him and respected him.

There has been torture and killing on this earth from the time of our parents Adam ﷺ and Eve. Of Adam's two sons, the brothers Qabil and Habil, the first killed the second—Cain and Abel in the Bible. Thus killing began from the first days of man on this earth. The spirit of evil starts on the first day, like the spirit of good.

Evil spirits are always after good spirits, because evil tries to bring us down towards it; but since we are created of light, we always try to run back to our origin. We are created from the Ocean of Power, and one of God's Attributes is "The Powerful One," al-Qadir. That is why we are always running towards our origin in God's Presence, and evil is trying to pull us back, and has caused all prophets to suffer from the beginning of history until our time: from Adam ﷺ to the Seal of Prophets ﷺ.

---

[62] Muharram 1, the new year in the Islamic Hijrah calendar which is based on the phases of the moon.

All Prophets Suffered

All prophets suffered. They did not say, "Life is pleasure." They did not say, "Life is to earn money." They did not say, "Life is for going to picnics, to be always happy and at ease." No—they were suffering a lot, all of them, from the beginning. Not one prophet lived his life in peace—although each in his heart lived in peace. Do not, therefore, expect no suffering from this life.

If you are on the way to Allah, you are going to suffer. If you are going to be on the way of Satan, you are not going to suffer, but you are going to lose eternal life. Ways to Allah entail much difficulty in this life. The prophets' lives were not easy, so don't say to yourself, "I am a good person, so why are all these troubles coming to me?" They come to you because God loves you and He wants to reward you in the hereafter with eternal life. When you face a difficulty, therefore, surrender and submit to God's Will. At that time, you will find that your difficulty is easy. When you do not surrender and submit to God's Will, you are going to be in trouble.

All prophets, when they suffered, said, "You are our Lord, we are not going to ask for anything; whatever You like to do with us, do." Then everything was opened before them. When the Prophet Muhammad ﷺ, the Seal of prophets, saw his followers and Companions tortured by ignorant people, he decided to migrate from Makkah to Madinah, leaving the ignorant people and going to people who were believers. It is a duty for us, and an example to follow, that we have to migrate from bad characters to good characters. You have to leave your bad manners. Anyone that does not try hard to find good manners, is never going to find happiness and satisfaction in his heart. This is God's order. This is the order found in all traditions. This is the order found in Sufism.

***O believers! Be righteous and good people in your society.*[63]**

---

[63] Suratu 't-Tawbah, 9:119.

It means that you have to know there is a merciful God, a loving God waiting for you to come to Him and ask Him—and He is generous with you—to give you more and more. Don't think that God is far away from you, or that He is someone from whom you have to be afraid. Don't be afraid of your Lord. Come to Him, for He loves you: He created you with love, with passion, with His Hands. He put in you a secret, as He did for every person—a Divine secret in the heart. He tells you, "Come to Me, and I shall give you the key to that secret. But if you do not come to Me, how can I give you that key?" Any door one wishes to enter demands a key. If you do not ask the key from the owner of a house, that house will never be opened to you. Who is the Owner of our hearts?

The Prophet ﷺ said:

The heart of a believer is the House of God.[64]

This means that in every person there is a house of God. When you are a believer, He will give you the key. The key to your house is to be a true believer.

You must not be believing one day and angry, cursing the next. You must always be happy with your Lord, saying, "O my Lord, if Your will is that I be in trouble, never mind, I will be patient." If you are patient, God will give you more.

Be Patient with Difficulty

We have to be patient with difficulties. We have to be patient with each other. We have to be one hand and one heart. The Companions of the Prophet ﷺ were one hand. That is why the teachings of the Prophet ﷺ were spread from East to West and from North to South. There were no media at that time, but

---

[64] Imam Ghazali mentioned it in his *Ihya' 'Ulum ad-deen*.

through that light which is in the hearts of the Companions, these teachings were spread, and now everyone knows about Islam. The essence of Islam is purity of the heart, and that is Sufism. Everyone knows these teachings, and they are spread everywhere, because they were speaking something which was coming from the heart. They were not cheating. They were true believers. This is what is demanded from us.

The Prophet's Favorite Name

God asked the Prophet ﷺ, "By which name would you like Me to call you?" The Prophet ﷺ said, "I like to be called *'abd*, Your servant." That is why he said that the happiest time for him is when he reads that verse in Qur'an:

> **Glory to Him Who took His servant for a journey by night from the Sacred Mosque to the Farthest Mosque, whose precincts We blessed, in order that We might show him some of Our signs; He is the One Who hears and sees all.**[65]

The Prophet ﷺ said, "I am very happy because God has mentioned me in the Holy Qur'an by the name 'servant.'"

Nowadays if you call someone "servant," they get angry. "Me, a servant? I am better than you." He would think himself to be inferior if he were a servant. Never. A servant to God, a slave to God is the highest honor. We are trying to be accepted by God as servants and slaves! A slave to God means that one is accepting all of God's orders, not disobeying a single one. This is the meaning of being a slave. A slave cannot disobey, or he would be in trouble. The Prophet's ﷺ happiness for being called a slave meant, "I am obeying my Lord, not disobeying." When you are obeying, God is going to be happy and satisfied with you.

---

[65] Suratu 'l-Isra, 17:1.

This is the first step for us on the way to God: to be decent servants to our Lord Allah Almighty, to go according to His will, not according to ours. And if you are going according to His Will, then why are you angry with what is going on around you? Know that it is His Will, and we are inside that will, waiting for Him to call us to come to Him. This is the key for your heart and your house. Come to your Lord, and you will find Him there. Do not move towards your Lord and you will find Satan waiting for you. Choose which way you want—the way of Satan or the way of our Lord? Some of us are one day here, one day there. They are mentioned in the Holy Qur'an:

One day believing, one day disbelieving... [66]

That is why they are not progressing. If you want to progress, choose your way. If you prefer the Satanic way, chose that way; you are going to progress and you will be a big devil in this world. If you go to Allah's Way, you are going to be a purified human being, clear, honest, transparent. Secrets will come to your heart; you will give people the knowledge of an inspired person. Choose your way, for life is passing quickly:

No one knows in what land he is going to die. [67]

Perhaps you are going to die in Woodstock, perhaps in Chicago, perhaps in China. No one knows when; perhaps this very second, perhaps after two seconds. Perhaps tomorrow. What have you done for your Lord? Are you remembering? Are you thinking or not? If you are thinking, then you have to be careful.

This is not to make you fear from your Lord, only to prevent you from being ashamed when you are going to see Him

---

[66] Suratu 'n-Nisa, 4:137.
[67] Surah Luqman, 31:34.

giving you blessings and mercy! If someone steals something from a car, and the owner sees him, and they both happen to be from this group, how ashamed is the thief going to be? We don't want to be ashamed in the presence of our Lord. We come to Him with sins—never mind, but we are coming to Him. Don't try to run away. He sees where you are going. Are you going to His enemy, Satan, who caused your father and mother to be sent out of Paradise? Don't run away from your Lord, in order not to feel ashamed. He is merciful and is running after you even as you run away, to tell you, "Come to Me, come to Me, come to Me." So don't run away; come to your Lord in order not to feel ashamed later. He is a Merciful Lord and a Forgiving Lord.

Insha'-Allah all of us will be going to our Lord as one group and one hand, and to our Prophet Muhammad ﷺ, and to Jesus ﷺ, and to Moses ﷺ, and to Abraham ﷺ, and to Noah ﷺ, and to Elijah ﷺ, and to all prophets because we believe in all of them. They are our guidance, our teachers and our spiritual guides. We are accepting all of them. If you accept all of them, it means you are accepting your Lord. If you deny a single one, you are not going to be considered a believer. This is what we have been taught and this is reality. We are seeing this through our hearts, through our God-given lights, through our teachers and masters. This is the real way, the real order and the real path. There is no other path except this path, the path of believing in all of them. And this is believing in God.

DO NOT USE MIND IN *TARIQAH* BUT LOVE

In every meeting and association we have to ask support from our Lord Almighty Allah, and from all His Messengers. We are so weak that whenever we want to say something, it is our ego that speaks. Our ego always says "I, I" and never "We, We." The ego never accepts anyone else save itself.

You can go all over this world trying to find someone that says, "O my Lord, I am sacrificing myself for the benefit of Your servants and Your creation." Such people exist, but they are very rare. These people are the saints that Allah has sent to us in this century. Praise be to God that he showed us one of his saints, our master Shaykh Muhammad Nazim al-Haqqani, may Allah bless his soul and raise him higher and higher, and make his life longer and longer! Without him, we would be like orphans. We are asking for his support, for without his support we are nothing.

Everything Depends on Love

Support means love. Without love, there is no familiarity. Without love between two people, how can they come together? It would be impossible. Therefore everything depends on love. That is why the first level after *iman* (belief) is love. We have to believe in God and His Messenger, the Seal of Prophets, Muhammad ﷺ. After this, the basis of faith is love. Without love, you cannot reach your goals or your aim. In this country, when a couple love each other, they marry. This means that love makes people form a union and put a contract of marriage. Marriage means that each is giving his word to the other that he or she will not leave him or her.

Love is the foundation of the building of your heart. If you want to build the heart of a believer, love must be there. All this world is depending on that love. There is nothing else. Because God loved His servants, He created them. If He did not love them, why create them? He not only created them but said,

> **He has put in your service all that is in the heavens and all that is on earth,**[68]

He is saying, "All this is for you." If someone has a son or a daughter, he gives them everything because he loves them. If he doesn't love them, he gives everything to a charitable organization, punishing them by not writing them into his will. Allah has given you everything and said, "This is for you; use it!" He put into your service heavens and earth. This means that He loves you greatly.

This is a sign and a teaching: we have to learn and understand that love is the foundation and basis of everything in this life. Without love, peace will never be on this earth. Jews are fighting Christians and Muslims; Muslims are fighting Christians and Jews; Christians are fighting Jews and Muslims... All of them believe in one and the same God; why are they fighting each other? Because there is no love. Love makes peace. Hatred makes enmity. You must choose your way. If you want peace, you must have love; if you want enmity, put hatred into your heart.

Religions—Judaism, Christianity, Islam—were not sent by God to put hatred among human beings, but love. Why then do we have this hatred for each other? This is the ego. Ego does not accept anyone save himself. "Don't accept except from yourself. Who are they to accept anything from them? No need. I am the only intellectual, the only genius, the only this and the only

---

[68] Suratu 'l-Jathiya, 45:13.

that..." This is what the Prophet ﷺ called *ash-shirku 'l-khafiyy*, the hidden *shirk*—idolatry—when he ﷺ said:

What I fear most for my Nation is the hidden idolatry.[69]

This means that you are blanking out your God and putting up your ego as your god.

We have presented the heavens, the earth, and the mountains Our Trust to carry, but they refused to carry it and shrank from it; and man accepted it. Indeed he was unjust and foolish.[70]

Trust also comes here in the sense of the thinking mind. This trust the heavens, earth, and mountains were afraid to carry. Mind is a great responsibility. The mind that God gave you either will destroy you or will raise you. That is why mind is very dangerous, and why heavens, earth, and mountains were afraid to carry that responsibility. "Never mind... We are happy, satisfied with Your Will, O our Lord," were their words. "It is an honor for us that You have created us, and made us Your creation. It is enough for us and we don't want anything else. We are swimming in the Ocean of Peace and Satisfaction. We don't want that trust of Mind." Allah continues, **"And human beings accepted it."** Human beings accepted mind: they were ignorant transgressors for carrying that heavy, difficult responsibility. It is so dangerous to use your mind.

Leave Behind Your Mind

Why is a saint a saint? Because he does not use his mind. Never! A saint never uses his mind. If he uses his mind it is finished: he cannot be a saint. A saint uses only his heart. A

---

[69] Ibn Majah, al-Hakim, Ahmad.
[70] Suratu 'l-Ahzab, 33:72.

mind is only a physical material object. Ego has control over the mind, but ego cannot control the heart. The heart is spiritually connected to God. The mind is connected to the ego. Thus a saint knows everything through his heart and does not use his mind. This is in order not to make anyone upset and not to make any mistake. A saint is accepting the Will of God and accepting what God has created him for. He is looking at the Preserved Tablets and doing what he is seeing there. He does not change the Will of God or interfere with it. All of us, however, are using our mind. In the Naqshbandiyyah Order, therefore, we are not allowed to use our minds. This is the first step.

The foundation is love. The first step is not to use your mind. If you use your mind, you cannot progress: you are going to see everyone has mistakes. You will think of yourself as the only one not making mistakes. All the others are crazy, sinners. Hatred and jealousy entered that way, and people began to fight each other. They are using their minds. A Muslim says, "I am better than that Christian." Christians say, "Who are those Jews? We are better than them," and so forth.

Anyone who uses their mind and tries to make others to follow him by force, by discipline or punctuality, he and all his teaching and knowledge are rubbish. *Tariqah* is never built on strictness. Sufi orders are built on love and leniency. You cannot be a dry person. You have to give your heart to followers. You cannot keep your heart for yourself. This way, we are all followers to our shaykh, for he shows us his love; if he were not, why follow him? It is that love which is catching us. Without it, we are weak servants of this earth.

We must teach ourselves. We are sitting here for one or two hours, each of us thinking, "Yes, he is right." After we go out of that door we are forgetting everything and nothing is left. But that light is going to be with you until the end of your life for this is the power of our shaykh. The light of this association, even though you are going to forget, is going to remain with you all your life. If I give you a page to memorize now, you need time. The heart, however, is not like the mind. As soon as you read with it, it takes that page immediately and keeps it forever, like a computer. As soon as you put the information into a computer, even hundreds of pages, you press one button and it will give it back to you. What about the heart? The heart is more powerful. But there are veils of darkness on our hearts. When we need this information to come back, that "virus"—as in the computer—interrupts the flow of this information: these are the veils of darkness on our heart.

For a saint, there is no veil of darkness. Whatever information he wants, he can bring it forth immediately. That is why the past, the present and the future are the same for a saint: all information. When God created this world, He created everything with it, even then. He put down what that servant is going to do in his life. For a saint, therefore, it is already there and he knows it! He knows your past, he knows your present, he knows your future. But why tell us? You do not throw diamonds between the feet of the ignorant; and we are ignorant people. As long as we are using our minds we are ignorant. As long as we are using our heart, we are intellectual. No one is using his heart. All of us are using our minds and that is why we are falling into mistakes. If you use your heart, Allah is going to open the eyes of your heart, and then you can see the unseen and know the unknown and hear the unheard and speak the unspoken.

That is one key: don't use your mind. If your shaykh calls you and says, "Go to the Atlantic Ocean with a bucket, and empty the ocean with that bucket in order to find a hidden treasure buried there for you," immediately you have to take your bucket and go. Once you reach the shore, say, "*Bismillahi 'r-rahmani 'r-rahim!*" and begin to empty the ocean. After two or three hundred bucketfuls, the water is going to go back to the ocean. You must not use your mind and say, "It is impossible. Even though I believe there are diamonds down there that are my trust, yet how am I going to empty the ocean with that bucket? Even with all the buckets of this world one cannot empty that ocean." If you say this, it is finished—you cannot take your trust: you used your mind.

How Imam Ghazali Became a Saint

With your power you cannot do anything. How did Imam Ghazali, a big Sufi saint, reach sainthood? All his life he had doubts about God and even about himself; even questioning whether he was living or not. He asked himself, "What is the proof that I am living? Perhaps it is an image, an illusion." *"La tusaghghir ma'rufan*—never consider any good deed small." However small it may be, do it. "And do not consider a sin small, either—*wa la tusaghghir dhanban*." Always consider it very great. One of Imam Ghazali's relatives was going to be hanged, and he had to write to the prince at that time that his relative was innocent. If that letter reached the prince, he was going to forgive the accused. The day was Monday the 12th of Rabi'u 'l-Awwal, coinciding with the birthday of the Prophet ﷺ.

Grandshaykh says that this day does not always fall on a Monday. When the date and the day coincide in certain years, there is a *tajalli*—manifestation—of mercy, coming down, and this is not every year. That is the reason why you must ask the shaykh, when you want to go to Hajj, if you may go that year or not. If there is no blessing, he will tell you not to go, because if you go, you are not going to get any benefit.

As Imam Ghazali was writing that important letter, a black fly came on his pen and began to drink the ink. Although he was in a hurry, he stopped writing. If it were us, we would have killed that fly; but saints are full of mercy. He stopped and said, "Allah has created that fly for the sake of the Prophet ﷺ, and He has created me for the sake of the Prophet ﷺ, and he has created that person who is being prosecuted for the sake of the Prophet ﷺ. All of us are the same: creatures, servants of Allah, even though it is a fly and I am a human. I am leaving her to drink until she is sated. When she leaves, I will continue." For doing this, Allah immediately dressed him with His blessings, and raised him to one of the same stations that the Prophet ﷺ reached in the night Journey and Ascension, carried by the same creature, Buraq, that the Prophet ﷺ rode to go the heavens.

That was all because of a small fly. "Do not devaluate a good deed," therefore, for you don't know how God is going to reward you. When the shaykh tells you to empty the ocean with a bucket, don't say, "How?" The *adab* of *tariqah*, the good manners of Sufism, demand that you obey the order of the shaykh and nothing else. If we keep this in our hearts, at that time we will find that we are progressing, we will find happiness, we will find peace, we will find satisfaction in our hearts. But if we are going to say, "No; how can I empty the ocean?" it means that you are rejecting the shaykh's knowledge. Such are the ignorant people who say that the shaykh doesn't know anything. They are not aware of the fact of his wisdom. He knows everything but he is testing you; are you going to accept what he says or not? Are you going to empty that ocean or not? If he gives you a broken pick and tells you to dig to the seventh earth because your trust is there, don't say, "How am I going to dig with that broken pick?" Say, "I can dig with that broken mind!" It is your mind that is broken, not the pick. Say, "This is my shaykh's order! O my ego, don't interfere; O my mind, don't interfere; I am going to dig day and night." Allah's Mercy will reach you. But if you are going to use your mind, you are going to fail.

You cannot use your mind in *tariqah*. You must have *taslimiyya mutlaqa*—absolute submission, without even one millionth of a percent of reservation. It must be a complete surrender to the will of the shaykh. If you can reach that, at that time you will find your treasures. Yet if you stay hundreds of years in the company of the shaykh—all your life—and you are not surrendering, you are not going to find even one treasure.

In the time of Sayyidina 'Abdul Khaliq al-Ghujduwani, one of his disciples at a very high level of surrender and belief in the shaykh was tested by his shaykh as the time had come to check him. The shaykh called him and said, "O my son, there is no need for you to stay with the disciples in my association, because your spiritual illness is so great that it is spreading through the hearts and poisoning the other disciples. So it is better for the others not to see you. I am therefore sending you today to that cemetery. Go and take a lesson from there." If Mawlana Shaykh Nazim tells that to anyone, what will happen? Not only will he run away, but he will curse the shaykh also! That disciple's heart never changed. He said, "*Sam'an wa ta'atan*, I hear, I obey." The shaykh was looking at his heart to see if his love was changing or not, and he did not find any change in his love. It was as before and he did not care what the shaykh said. His love is for the shaykh, even if the shaykh is going to cut him into pieces.

Visit to a Cemetery

He went to the cemetery. As soon as he reached it he saw that the gate was locked. Someone was sitting on top of the cemetery wall, dressed all in green: that was Khidr ﷺ. He told him, "O my son, come to me, I am Khidr and I will give you your trust. I have been carrying it and waiting for you for a long time. Take it." The disciple looked at him and did not care for him. Anyone of us would have run, "Give me my trust! I have been waiting for that moment." But how will that disciple care about Khidr ﷺ when his shaykh did not tell him that he was going to see Khidr ﷺ? And Khidr ﷺ was not his shaykh: why listen to him? This is how high he kept his shaykh in his heart, and such was his belief in his shaykh. Never mind Khidr ﷺ: if one of us finds another person, immediately he will run after him and change

Shaykhs. That disciple said, "*Basaree 'ala shaykhee*, my sight is on my shaykh!" As soon as he said it, the lock on the gate opened by itself and he entered.

Khidr ﷺ was by his side again, this time in front of the first grave. Khidr ﷺ said, "*Subhanallah*, that person died with an age of three years." The disciple looked at him and said, "How can that be? His age was eighty years. He had been with my shaykh a long time. Are you Khidr or Satan, coming here to make me busy with nonsense? Go away! My shaykh sent me here to take wisdom." He left him and went to another grave. Khidr ﷺ followed him and said, "Praise be to Allah; that person died when five years of age." At another grave, "This one six years." "That one seven." None of the people Khidr ﷺ mentioned had reached maturity—meaning fifteen years—even though they were all very old people, fifty, sixty, seventy, and eighty years of age. All of them were still *tahta' t-takleef*—"under age" or "not responsible." We know that, according to religion, no sin will be written against you until maturity. Allah is Merciful and will not write a sin until after maturity. Until then, you are not considered as having a responsible mind. Those people, therefore, were not considered responsible for what they were doing!

Who is Considered Responsible in Tariqah?

There is a secret here. Allah's Mercy is so great that even elderly people, if they are not responsible and not yet mature, how is God going to judge them? How then is God going to punish human beings? Not one of them is mature. This is one secret of the Naqshbandi order.

God burdens no one with more than they can carry.[71]

---

[71] Suratu 'l-Baqara, 2:286.

You are not responsible before God except according to what you can carry. If you are a boy under age, therefore, how are you going to be responsible? Even if a boy under fifteen kills someone, they put him in a juvenile prison for correction to reform him and then forgive him. Now if all people are not yet mature, how is God going to judge them and not forgive them? So great is the Mercy of Allah Almighty.

The disciple answered Khidr ﷺ, "What are you saying? All of these are old people. How can they all still be immature boys?" Then he left and went back to his shaykh. Before he arrived, Khidr ﷺ was already in the presence of the shaykh, telling him, "O my master—for that Naqshbandi shaykh was of very high standing—I am ready to sacrifice everything that God gave me to carry to be a follower like that follower, with that love in his heart for you." As soon as he said this, the disciple entered and saw Khidr ﷺ there, sitting beside the shaykh. Khidr ﷺ began to swear at him and curse him, saying, "this is a bad person, a very inferior person, with a great illness..." He was trying to put him down as much as possible. The shaykh was doing the same also, cursing the disciple. Both Khidr ﷺ and the shaykh were looking at the heart of the disciple to see if he was changing or not and they cursed as much as they could. Immediately the Prophet ﷺ appeared and said, "Enough; what are you doing? You can see that his heart is not changing. Why are you cursing more?" He did not care what they were saying. Out of love for his shaykh he only waited for the next order. He was not listening to what they were saying. When the Prophet ﷺ said those words, the shaykh opened the eyes of the disciple's heart.

This is how we must have faith in our shaykh. That disciple had many excuses, with all this cursing, to say, "My shaykh is wrong, Khidr ﷺ is wrong." Yet his heart and his love never changed. How then do you accept someone to say that your shaykh doesn't know anything? How am I going to accept that person? Never will I accept such a person! It is a very great thing to say such a thing: it is grave backbiting and a very big sin. Mawlana Shaykh Nazim said, "Whatever we are doing of sins, there is an excuse for, and the shaykh will find that excuse for you in order for God to forgive you. There is only one thing for which there is no excuse to be found: to have a bad thought about your shaykh. This is the only sin that the shaykh cannot clean you from. Finished: you are thrown away. We must therefore be very careful in our belief and our love for the shaykh."

The summary of this association is that the basis and foundation of our hearts is love. To climb and build the buildings is done by not using our minds but by using our hearts. Our minds cannot help us. If you stop using your mind in the ways of *tariqah*, you are going to find yourself rising up.

USE THE MISWAK

Do not leave the Sunnah of the Prophet ﷺ. Keep the Sunnah of the Prophet ﷺ. Many times we say, "Use the *miswak, miswak* (wooden toothbrush)." No one understands. In the time of the Prophet ﷺ, they were dying for the reward of a *shaheed* (martyr). People died in their country in order to get the reward of a *shaheed*, and the Prophet ﷺ said:

> *Whoever revives my Sunnah when there is much corruption (in the last days of this world), will get the reward of a hundred martyrs.*[72]

When you use the *miswak*, therefore, you get the reward of a hundred martyrs. Why aren't you using it?

---

[72] *Mishkat* 1, 6, al-Hakim. Arabic: *Man ahya sunnatan min sunanee 'inda fasadi ummatee falahu ajru mi'ata shaheed.*

The Meaning of Religion

We are children of Adam ﷺ. When Adam ﷺ came, there were no Christians, no Jews, no Muslims. They were all children of Adam ﷺ. Adam ﷺ showed his children his Lord, by saying, "Our Lord in heaven." Then, the Prophet Noah ﷺ came, calling people to one God. Abraham ﷺ came, calling to one God. Moses ﷺ came and said, "This is my Lord." Anyone who believed him was called "believer," while anyone who rejected him was called "disbeliever." After Moses ﷺ by many years, Jesus ﷺ came and said, "This is our Lord in heaven, and I believe in Moses ﷺ." If Jesus ﷺ had denied Moses ﷺ, he would not have been a Holy Spirit from God. God, Who has created everyone, had sent Moses ﷺ. How could Jesus ﷺ deny Moses ﷺ? If he had denied him, he would have denied God. Again, those who believed Jesus ﷺ were called "believers", and those who rejected him were called "disbelievers." Moses ﷺ and Jesus ﷺ showed they were believing in one God.

The God of Moses ﷺ is not different from the God of Jesus ﷺ. God is God; He never changes. It is we who change, but there is no change for God. How then does one group say "Our God" and the other group says, "Our God"? Are there two gods? As God sent Moses ﷺ who preached his Lord, so He sent his Holy Spirit, through the Virgin Mary, and he preached his Lord. 572 years after Jesus ﷺ showed his people the way to worship God, the Prophet Muhammad ﷺ came. As Jesus ﷺ did not deny Moses ﷺ, the Prophet Muhammad ﷺ did not deny Moses ﷺ, but believed in Jesus ﷺ at the same time. The Prophet Muhammad ﷺ did not deny Moses ﷺ and did not deny Jesus ﷺ. On the contrary, he said, "Anyone that denies Jesus ﷺ, or Moses ﷺ, he is denying me." And he said, "Our Lord in heaven." So where is the difference? The

God of Adam ﷺ, of Noah ﷺ, of Abraham ﷺ, of Moses ﷺ, of David ﷺ, of Jesus ﷺ, of Muhammad ﷺ and of us never changes. It is we who are changing our Lord because of hatred in our hearts—Jews hate Christians and Muslims; Christians hate Jews and Muslims; Muslims hate Jews and Christians. But Moses ﷺ doesn't hate Jesus ﷺ, and Jesus ﷺ doesn't hate Moses ﷺ, and Muhammad ﷺ doesn't hate Jesus ﷺ and Moses ﷺ.

We have invented that hatred in our hearts in order to make enmity and fight each other. Real Islam, real Christianity and real Judaism believe in the same Lord. That is why you cannot deny anyone. If you deny anyone, you are denying your Lord.

Accept All of God's Messengers

We believe that Jesus ﷺ is coming another time. We are waiting for him. This is our mission, and what we preach to our people. Muslims believe in Jesus ﷺ and are waiting for him. On what can hatred be founded? Islam is peace. It is not what they show today as representatives of Islam. Islam is one thing and the Muslims in our day are another; they do not represent Islam. There are good Muslims and there are also bad examples. You see them praying and speaking on pulpits, then they go out and do all kinds of wrong things.

Look at the mercy of real Islam. The Prophet ﷺ said in hadith:

> *In spite of Abu Dharr (who was surprised at this), whoever says "There is no god but Allah" has entered Paradise.*[73]

He did not even go on to say, "and Muhammad ﷺ is His Messenger." He only said, "Whoever accepts God is saved."

---

[73] Bukhari and Muslim from Abu Dharr ﷺ and when he (Abu Dharr) used to relate this hadith he would say, "In spite of Abu Dharr."

Islam has all kinds of mercy for human beings, trying to save them.

The problem is that every person is proud of himself. He doesn't accept advice from anyone, and thinks that his knowledge is the highest knowledge—that there is no knowledge above him. But God says:

> **Over every knowledgeable one there is another one more knowledgeable.**[74]

There is no difference between real Christianity and Islam; it is the same. There is no difference between real Judaism and Islam.

We have already related how one day a follower of Mawlana Khalid al-Baghdadi, a great saint, discovered another saint in Bombay that had miraculous powers, but the other saint was neither Muslim nor Christian nor Jewish. The follower went to his shaykh and said, "O my master, if that man were Muslim, we would say, 'Fine, he has miraculous powers.' If he were Christian, I might still say, 'Yes,' because God said in Qur'an:

> **And there are, certainly, among the People of the Book, those who believe in Allah, in the revelation to you, and in the revelation to them, bowing in humility to Allah.**[75]

And:

> **The nearest to you are the Christians.**[76]

---

[74] Surah Yusuf, 12:76.
[75] Surah Ali 'Imran, 3:199. People of the Book refers to those communities who received heavenly revelations prior to the advent of Prophet Muhammad ﷺ.
[76] Suratu 'l-Maidah, 5:82.

But he is not Muslim, nor Christian, nor Jewish. How can he have those miraculous powers?" Mawlana Khalid answered, "O my son, I will give you the answer tomorrow."

At night, by saying "Bismillahi 'r-rahmani 'r-rahim" he was, in one step, at the door of the other person 6,000 miles away, in Bombay. He found that that person knew that he was coming and was waiting for him at his door. He said, "O my Master—for he knew that Mawlana Khalid was higher—I had food prepared for you by a woman of the Book." He knew that Muslims, Christians and Jews do not eat the food of Hindus. Sayyidina Khalid entered, sat in front of him across the table, looked into his heart and said, before saying anything else, "Say: *Ashhadu an la ilaha illa-Lllah wa ashhadu anna Muhammadan Rasulullah.*" The other man sat and thought for half an hour. After half an hour he said, "*Ashhadu an la ilaha illa-Lllah wa ashhadu anna Muhammadan Rasulullah.*"

Anyone sitting here right now and hearing me say this has entered into the blessing of this affirmation with me. It is enough to be sitting here for five minutes to be mentioned under the name of Muslim and he or she will be with us under the same umbrella of the Prophet ﷺ in the Judgment Day. The light of the acceptance of God and all prophets is in all human beings. Why are all people called to Islam? Because the Prophet ﷺ came at the end. First Moses ൺ, then Jesus ൺ, then Muhammad ﷺ. If there were other prophets after the Seal of Prophets, people would be called to another thing, and we cannot, as Muslims, deny another one who would be coming. But since Muhammad ﷺ was the last one to come, it means that Islam is the last religion. Everyone in God's creation has the light of that religion in his heart, and one day it is going to come out. It cannot remain inside. The Prophet ﷺ said:

*Every child is created in purity and innocence, then his parents make him Jewish, or Christian, Zoroastrian or idol-worshipper.*⁷⁷

That light, therefore, is there from birth.

If one has an inflammation in his hand, he feels that he must scratch, and the more one scratches, the more it spreads. The light in the hearts will spread like an itch when the time comes, except that scratching will be as polishing to remove the dirt from under which that light will come out and shine.

We Sufis do not call non-Muslim people "Christians," "Jews."" Since they believe in Allah, we leave them to Allah's judgment. It is not in our hands and we cannot use terms such as *kafir* (unbeliever) and *mushrik* (idolater)—it is not our duty, but the Lord's. There are many Muslims that are Muslim only by name, and many Christians and Jews better in manners than Muslims. That is why the judgment of human beings belongs to Allah alone. And all human beings are slaves before one God. This is what the Prophet ﷺ has taught us.

That Hindu guru could do miracles within the realm of the world. As soon as he said *shahadah*, he penetrated as if on a rocket into the realm of the miraculous powers of heaven. For God said:

> **O human beings and jinn! If you were able to penetrate through the regions of heaven and earth, go! But you cannot except through use of a means.**⁷⁸

That means is, *La ilaha illa-Allah, Muhammadun Rasulullah.* All heavenly miraculous powers opened to him.

---

⁷⁷ Bukhari, Muslim, Tirmidhi, Abu Ya'la, Imam Ghazali, Zubaydi, al-Baghawi, Barudi, at-Tabarani, Bayhaqi, Ahmad and al-Hakim.
⁷⁸ Suratu 'r-Rahman, 55:33.

Sayyidina Khalid al-Baghdadi ق asked him, "Why did you wait half an hour before saying this?" He answered, "O my master, forgive me. For 25 years I was fighting my ego."

Judaism, Christianity, Islam teach you to bring down your ego and bring out your spirituality, which is the light in the heat; to make it come out. That is the meaning of all religion; not hatred and fighting! As God is God, there is, therefore, no difference in religions, "Ways to God are according to the number of breaths of human beings." If you want to take real Judaism, take it; or real Christianity, take it; or real Islam, take it; who is telling you not to? But if you are lucky, you find the shortest way. If you find a rocket, you don't ride on a car or a plane: the rocket is better for you, so you will be more advanced, quickly, and it is not going to harm you. Yet the plane will get you there, and the car, eventually; but the rocket will get you there in one second.

He continued, "For 25 years, I consulted my ego about everything I set out to do; if my ego said to me, 'Do it,' I didn't do it; if my ego said to me, 'Don't do it,' I did it. I always did the opposite, to teach myself not to give my ego anything it liked. In this way I gained these miraculous powers."

God is merciful:

***My Mercy encompasses all things.*[79]**

And:

***He is the Compassionate, the All-Merciful.*[80]**

God is providing every human being with His mercy. He doesn't discriminate. He doesn't say, "This is inferior, this is superior." No. To God it is the same, for He is giving everyone,

---

[79] Suratu 'l-'Araf, 7:156.
[80] Suratu 'l-Baqarah, 2:163.

Muslim, Christian, Jewish, Hindu, Buddhist. When God sees you—no matter what you are—trying hard to oppose the negative self, your bad side, trying to improve your manners, fighting your ego, not committing sins, He will be merciful with you. But He will never give you heavenly power; He will give you worldly powers, which are to Him like the wing of a mosquito, next to nothing compared to Divine powers, for the Prophet ﷺ said:

> *This world does not amount to the wing of a gnat in the eyes of God.*[81]

He said, "When you ordered me to say, *La ilaha illa-Allah*, I consulted my ego. I said, 'O my ego, my master. The shaykh is telling me to enter into into Islam; what do you say, O my ego, do you accept or not?' My ego answered, 'Are you crazy? For 25 years you have been progressing in your way until you are now famous among your people for having miraculous powers, giving talks while everyone is listening to you; you are at the top of the stairs. Now, you want to enter Islam and go back to the first stair? Don't do it! Never!' As soon as my ego said never do it, I did the opposite—because it is cheating me—and I said, *Ashshadu an La ilaha illa-Allah wa ashhadu anna Muhammadan Rasulullah.* You were right, O my shaykh; I am accepting you, I am accepting the Prophet Muhammad ﷺ, and I am making prostration for Allah, my Lord in heaven."

God is merciful. His doors are open. If you want to enter, you are welcome. If you don't want to enter, He is still waiting for you. He is not like human beings who might kick you out. Anytime that you come, He is accepting you. Therefore, don't make it long. What is it going to cost you to say, "I accept God, and all the prophets, and Moses ؑ, and Jesus ؑ, and Muhammad ﷺ?" Is this the problem, the fact that you must say, "Muhammad

---

[81] Gloss of a hadith narrated by Tirmidhi.

ﷺ?" Don't let your ego hold sway over you. Accept all of them, and you are going to win. If you believe in Muhammad ﷺ, it does not mean that you stop believing in Jesus ؑ; and Jesus ؑ came with the Gospel, and Moses ؑ came with the Torah, all of which we cannot deny. If one denies this, he is not Muslim, for he is denying Allah.

It costs non-Muslims one word, *"Muhammadun Rasulullah*—Muhammad ﷺ is the Messenger of Allah," to overcome their block and to enter into Islam. As for Muslims, it costs them nothing and they have no credit for accepting Judaism and Christianity—none of the three religions can reject us, for we naturally believe in Moses ؑ and Jesus ؑ.

TARIQAH IN THE QUR'AN

This is the first day of the new year according to the solar calendar. May Allah make our heart begin from now to seek the better and the best for our brothers and sisters, and then for ourselves. We have to put our brothers and sisters ahead of ourselves. We come second. The Prophet ﷺ never said, "Myself, myself," but always said, "*Ummatee, Ummatee* — My Community, my Community!"

When Allah brought the Prophet ﷺ out of his mother's womb, the Prophet ﷺ immediately went down from the hands of the midwife and into prostration. His mother and all present heard him saying, "Ya Rabbee! O my Lord! My Community, my Community!" This is not difficult for the one whose name Allah ordered the Pen to place beside His Own Name on the Divine Throne before He created creation:

La ilaha ill-Allah Muhammadun Rasulullah.[82]

No one knows at what time Allah made the name of Muhammad ﷺ accompany His Name.

The name symbolizes the person named. This means that the creation of the Prophet ﷺ was at that time. Allah created the Prophet Muhammad ﷺ before He created anyone else. That is why He said to our father Adam ؑ, "*If Muhammad ﷺ appears in your time, you must follow him. You cannot be his father, but he will be your father.*"

---

[82] Bayhaqi, Abu Nu'aym al-Isfahani, al-Hakim, Ibn Asakir.

When Adam ﷺ ate from the tree and committed a sin, he went into prostration and said, "O my Lord, forgive me for the sake of Muhammad ﷺ!" and Allah asked him, "How do you know about Muhammad?" Adam ﷺ replied, "O my Lord, when I raised my head, I found his name written beside Your Name on the Throne. I knew that he is your beloved one. Forgive me for his sake." Allah forgave Adam ﷺ and said to him, "Were it not for Muhammad, I would not have created you."[83]

Today Friday is a holy day for Muslims and especially Sufi people. Take a decision today, therefore, and say, "O my Lord, I am going to be going Your Way, and not Satan's way. For Your sake, I am coming towards You. O my Lord, give me that power. Support me, because I am weak. Help me to follow that Way."

They say *tariqah* is not mentioned in the Qur'an it is mentioned:

If they kept steadfast on the Path, Allah would shower them with blessings and mercy.[84]

That Path is the path of prophets, the path of spirituality, the core of Islam and the heart of Islamic teachings. Allah did not say, "If they keep straight on the path of Islam," rather He said, "on the Path," using a definite article for the word "path." Allah here is emphasizing *tariqah*.

Degrees in Religion

It is understood that everyone has to follow Islam:

The religion with Allah is Islam.[85]

---

[83] Al-Hakim, at-Tabarani.
[84] Suratu 'l-Jinn, 72:16
[85] Surat Ali 'Imran, 3:19.

In the time of Moses ﷺ came the Torah; the Gospel came in the time of Jesus ﷺ. What did Allah send at the end? There must always be an end. When you graduate from high school you take a diploma. After that you take a BA or BS degree, then you may go on for a Ph.D. At that stage, you no longer mention your high school, even your Bachelor's. You say, "I am a Professor or a Doctor," not "I am a High School graduate!" That is finished. Similarly, when Islam came, all previous religions entered into Islam, and Islam surpassed what came before. It replaced everything. Moses ﷺ came with laws, obligations and rule; Jesus ﷺ came with spirituality; Islam added both sides together. You find rules **and** spirituality in Islam.

Allah said here, "***If they kept steadfast on tariqah.***" That word, in Arabic, means path, way. And it is the "Ways to God," as the Prophet ﷺ said, not the "Islam to God," that are according to the number of the breaths of human beings. There is a secret that must be sought out, therefore, in that verse of Qur'an. Shallow scholars do not understand. Scientists that find something through technology say they "made a discovery." This discovery shows very clearly that such-and-such a compound has such-and-such powers and properties. To everything there is a process of discovery. Allah never gives everything out in the open. Yes, He gave you Islam; but there are things inside that you are called upon to discover.

Discover Qur'an's Secrets

Discover the secrets inside Islam. Do not take Qur'an as literature! Qur'an is not literature! Is Allah's Word limited to your understanding of letters? Qur'an is not Shakespeare! There is no limit to Allah's Word. For that reason you must understand that there are discoveries to be made. If you do not run after these discoveries they will never come to you, just as discoveries never come to scientists sitting idle. They run after scientific discoveries, and you must run after Qur'anic discoveries through your heart.

You are then going to find secrets that have never been opened to human beings before.

In every century there are saints filling this world. This world is full of the saints. Search for them through your heart. You will find at least one whom you can choose. Hold tight to him. He will take you to the presence of saints and to the presence of the Prophet ﷺ. Say: "From this day we want to begin a new chapter." And may Allah give us the power for that new chapter. We have to stick more and more to our goal in our heart, and be steadfast with our brothers and sisters because we can learn through each other; by ourselves we cannot learn. Allah has created this world with cause and effect. We are causes for each other to progress. Sit together; make more associations; grow. When you increase your number, *"inayatullahi tudrikukum—* Allah's Divine Care will reach you." If you think someone is trustworthy, trust him, and you will not lose but gain many blessings through this trust. May Allah support all of us and give us His blessings.

God's Messengers Free One from Depression

Everyone must have support from his Lord Almighty Allah before he begins to say anything. We also have to ask support from all the prophets that God has sent to teach us and show us the way.

What does Allah want for his servant? To be happy. All His messengers came to show us the way to happiness. God wants you to be happy, to live in peace with a serene heart, and to feel satisfaction in your heart! You have to ask support from your Lord, therefore, in order for Him to make you happy and satisfied. For God said:

> *I am happy with My servant when My servant is happy with Me.*[86]

When you are satisfied with the position that God has given you in this life and when you are satisfied with the level God has raised you to in this life, He is going to be happy with you and satisfied with you. If you are going to complain about the situation He has put you in, He is not going to be happy with you.

He sent His messengers to show us the way to happiness in all our lives. Why are we not following them and asking for their guidance? None of us is trying to say, "O my Lord, what is the purpose of my creation? What are my obligations?" Everyone dislikes to carry obligations. Everyone wants to be free. You are

---

[86] Gloss of hadith in Bukhari and Muslim.

free, for God gave you freedom. But to be free, you must be happy, or else you are going to feel miserable. Every day, I am receiving calls from people who are depressed. Why are you depressed? You are in a free country, living a free life. Yet there is no happiness with all this freedom. It means that this freedom, provided by the government for the people, is not a perfect freedom. If it were, you would never find depression in your heart.

Psychiatrist, Cure Yourself!

Only God gives you freedom. He says: "If you want perfect freedom, listen to My messengers." This government gives you freedom, but your ego catches you in its snares. You are in the prison of the ego. That is why Americans are depressed, as well as Europeans, or anyone living in the world nowadays? There is no happiness, because we are running away from our Lord. We are not trying to find the way of happiness—we think we already know our way. If you know your way, why then are you in need of psychologists and psychiatrists, the best-paid people in this country? Why go to them? Are you mentally ill? Or do you think that this psychiatrist or psychologist will take away the pressure from you? Don't you know he is depressed also? They call us too. How are they going to treat you, being ill themselves?

There is no possibility for finding your way except in repenting and coming to your Lord, by listening to His messengers who show you the way to happiness. Allah does not want you to be tortured and punished. He did not send you messengers for that purpose. He sent them to make you see the way, and every person has a way to reach his or her Lord.

Yes, every person has a way to reach their Lord, and all of them come to a circle with the same center. We are living on a circle, the circumference of which has an infinite number of points, all taking from the center. The source is the same. God is the same for Muslims, for Jews, for Christians, for Buddhists, for Hindus, for Arabs, Americans, Europeans, Malaysians, Indonesians, Chinese... Allah is One and the same. All of them have to take from the same source. No one can take from a different source. If we listen, we find our way. If we don't listen, then we are going to live all our lives in depression, and anyone who says to you "I am happy" is a liar: when they sit together they say they are happy, but when they go back home they are fighting with their families, their children, their neighbors, their businesses, and themselves. They are in depression.

Anyone that comes to the way of messengers will find himself no longer fighting. Gof will dress him with a beautiful robe. One of the saints asked: "Why are people attracted to saints? What makes them different from others? Why do people come to saints for *tabarruk*—to take blessings from them?"

He answered his own question: "Because God has dressed them with some of His Attributes. According to that attribute with which God has dressed you, people will be attracted to you and coming to take blessings from you. In fact, they are taking blessings from God and not from that person, but that person is dressed with God's Attributes. Anyone that found his way to his Lord is dressed with these attributes, and if you are so dressed, you are going to be living in God's Existence. You are going to feel happiness in your heart and never experience depression. Depression comes from the ego, happiness comes from God."

May God grant us that happiness. May God dress our hearts with His attributes in order to take depression out. There is no house I enter except such problems are there, because they are not finding their way to their Lord. Saints never complain because they found their way. Why complain after that? When they look at themselves they only see their Lord, as the hadith of the Prophet ﷺ says:

Whoever knows himself, knows his Lord.[87]

You don't know your Lord because you don't know yourself. That psychiatrist can never cure you because he does not know himself either. As for scholars, rabbis, and priests, they may talk for hours—and what they say is good—but the results are rubbish, because they are not doing what they say. The reason is, they don't know themselves. If they knew themselves, their talk would hit the target immediately. But a scholar proud of his knowledge—as they are found to be wherever you go—is ineffective in curing people. Know your limits. Even a computer program, however powerful, has its limits. The workings of the computer itself are unknown to those who made it! Allah is causing it to work.

Why are there billions of Christians in this world? It means there is support through the heart of these great messengers and saints, sent by God to this world. They must come to know themselves, and when they do, God dresses them with His power. We therefore say about the Prophet Muhammad ﷺ that he is carrying Divine Power, and about Jesus ﷻ that he is carrying the power of the Holy Spirit within himself. It is with that kind of power that they were able to spread religion. They knew themselves, and God dressed them with His power. After the Prophet Muhammad ﷺ we know, according to tradition, that there are no more prophets—he is the Seal of prophets—but there are saints. In every century there must be 124,000 saints on this earth, each one of them representing one of the 124,000 prophets that Allah has sent since the beginning of creation. These saints are spread East and West, North and South, teaching people the ways of self-knowledge.

---

[87] Ibn 'Arabi, *Fusus* I, p. 81, 122, 145, *Futuhat* 1, 328, 331, 347, 353; II, 298-299, III, 536; IV, 245, as-Suyuti, Mawardi, Al-Jarrahi; also attributed to Yahya b. Mu'adh ar-Razi.

At any time, even if you are in a discotheque, God may send someone to you that will attract you to Him. You might be in a mosque and the shaykh is speaking up, but there is someone next to you that you find yourself attracted to, more than to the speaker. Do not belittle anyone. A saint might be passing you in the street: no one knows. Many saints come to you on the street as poor beggars or in any other shape they like, in order to show you the way: do not underestimate them.

Give Whoever Asks

I was walking with my shaykh on the street in Damascus one day. He always kept change in his pocket. He said, "Never reject a poor man who asks. Always keep change in your pocket. You don't know when a saint comes in the guise of a poor person to test you: are you generous or not?" That day we met many beggars on the way. He kept taking from his pocket and giving, taking out and giving. On our way back, someone came and my shaykh had no more change in his pocket. That beggar asked for something. Mawlana Shaykh Nazim took his watch—it was very important for him because it came from his shaykh—and gave it away. What to do? He only had the watch to give. After he gave it, we walked away and he said to me, "Look behind you." I looked and that person had disappeared. He said, "He is one of them. If I had not given the watch, I would have failed the test."

You don't know when Allah comes to you through His saints, reaching out for you and showing you the way to His knowledge. Allah loves everyone. If He did not love you He would not have created you. He created us with His love. Because of that love, God will never allow you to suffer. God will always support you through your life until you meet Him. All of us are going to meet Him. No one is running away from that meeting. We may be running away in this life—or thinking that we are running away. He said:

We are nearer to him (man) than his jugular vein.[88]

If He is so near to us, why are you running? You cannot run. If you do, immediately He sends you a difficulty to bring you back and tell you: "Come here! Yet you are not learning." What can we do?

People sit and spend time on television, on their food, gossiping, working, sleeping. Never mind: you are free, and God gave you all this. But spend some time for Him also, such as this meeting. We are spending a little time for Him and it does no harm. On the contrary, it will bring blessings for you. At that time, you will never find depression. What did the Prophet ﷺ say?

Contemplation for one hour is better than worshipping for seventy years.[89] *v*

To worship for seventy years is impossible. No one can do that. Many people wait until they are forty to worship God. Until then, they worship only themselves. When they come to forty, they feel near the grave and they start remembering their Lord. So they worship for the next twenty or thirty years. No one worships for seventy years. Supposing one did, yet rememberance of Allah, the Prophet ﷺ said, is better even than that. "Remembrance" means sitting by yourself, thinking of nothing else, and asking forgiveness of your Lord, "O my Lord, I am a weak servant; forgive me." This is better than seventy years' worship.

---

[88] Surah Qaf, 50:16.
[89] *Nuzhat al-Majalis.* Similar ahadith with variant wording are narrated in ad-Daylami and Abu ash-Shaykh related in *al-'Adhama*h from Abu Hurayrah ؓ.

This is a true narration of the Prophet ﷺ, and it is to be heeded especially by those who promise Hell to non-worshippers. Remembering carries a heavier reward than worship. For you must remember Allah with humility, with a broken heart; but in prayer, you often worship Him with your ego. Those who say, "We are going to the mosque, or "to the church," or "to the synagogue," are proud of themselves. That pride will veil them from the light of God. But when you remember God with humility, that veil of darkness will never be on your heart. It will be thrown away. That is why one hour of remembering Allah with humility is better than worshipping Him for seventy years with pride.

May Allah give us the power of understanding and of remembering Him as He wants us to remember Him. May He give us the power to be as He wants us to be: decent people, people who are looking for the right path, *as-Siratu 'l-mustaqeem*, the path that Allah wants for everyone. And this is the way of truth. Allah has said to you, "I gave everyone his own way to take:

Each one is swimming in his orbit."[90]

Stars are swimming in their orbits, the moon is swimming in her orbit, the sun is swimming in its orbit; every star and galaxy is swimming in its orbit, and so is every human being. Every one has a way.

Find your way. You cannot find it except if a guide shows you a way. Without guidance, it is very difficult.

Whoso knows himself knows his Lord.[vi]

---

[90] Surah Ya Sin, 36:40.

The first step, therefore, is to know yourself, and you begin this by sitting by yourself and thinking. No one is doing even that. Meditate through your heart. Remember what you have done all day long. Ask yourself if you are a good person or not, or if you have broken someone's heart. Evaluate yourself. If you do this for forty days, God will throw into your heart a light that will help you understand yourself quickly, and understand what is around you. When you understand what is around you, you will be able to understand your Lord. Without that light, you can never understand your Lord. The period of forty days is a period of seclusion, without interference of anyone, neither wife, nor husband, nor children, sitting for one or two hours in your room by yourself every day, remembering.

Give God some rights! He created you! No one gives Him a single right. We are giving more attention to dogs and cats and horses and fish in aquariums, than to Allah, the Almighty and Exalted. Is this justice? That is why God sends depression over you. As much as you listen to rabbis, priests, Muslim scholars, or Buddhist monks after that, no one can take you out and raise you up unless you come back to yourself, correct yourself, and give time to your Lord.

THE WORTHLESS CENTURY

The title of every lecture is:

> ***Obey God, obey the Prophet, and obey those in authority among you.***[91]

Alhamdulillah, praise be to Allah Who has gathered us tonight for a holy night. Every night of this month is a holy night, for it is the month of Rajab. The Prophet ﷺ said

> *Rajab is the month of God, and Sha'ban is my month, and Ramadan is the month of my nation.*[vii]

Allah looks at His servants throughout the year. In Rajab, He looks at His servants in order to prepare their hearts for the month of Ramadan, which comes after Sha'ban. The Prophet ﷺ therefore used to fast in the month of Rajab, mostly Mondays, Thursdays, in its beginning, and in its middle. In Sha'ban, Sayyidatina 'Ayesha said that she hardly saw the Prophet ﷺ break his fast.[92]. He fasted because, as he said, "*Sha'ban is my month,*" and it was a special fast for him. We are mere imitators and we cannot be like the Prophet ﷺ, but he showed us his way.

> *I have left the Qur'an and my way of life (Sunnah) for you to follow.*[93]

Everyone, therefore, must follow the Holy Book of Allah, the Qur'an, and everyone must follow the Sunnah of the Prophet

---

[91] Suratu 'n-Nisa, 4:59.
[92] Bukhari and Muslim, cf. *Mishkat* VII, 7, 1.
[93] Malik and al-Hakim.

ﷺ. That means that one has to follow Divine Law—as it should be, not half the way. It is an order from the Prophet ﷺ, "*I have left it for you.*"

May Allah give us power to keep the Divine Law of the Prophet ﷺ and the Divine Law of Islam high, in order to be good examples in this society at large, the society of human beings. As we said, Sha'ban is the month of the Prophet ﷺ, at which time he used to fast days and worship nights, until his feet were swollen. People are now accustomed only to fast in Ramadan during the day, and worship in Ramadan at night by praying Tarawih.[94] But there are eleven other months besides this month. Why are we leaving them? Everyone must remember in his heart that the Prophet ﷺ never left a night without worship—not only Ramadan. And that was true all year round, especially in Rajab and Sha'ban:

> *Rajab is the month of God, Sha'ban is my month and Ramadan is the month of the Nation.*

What Allah will give His servant no one knows, not even the Prophet ﷺ, for God has no partners: Allah is in not need of anyone, and everyone is in need of Him. May Allah give our hearts the power to renounce *shirk*, association. As the Prophet ﷺ said:

> *What I fear most for my Nation is the hidden idolatry (shirk).*[95]

We all fall under that address: we are all, therefore, associating partners with God in our heart. That means that when we are stubborn, or angry, we refuse to listen to Allah and instead listen to our ego. Everyone must listen to Qur'an and to the Sunnah of the Prophet ﷺ. You cannot listen to your ego when you

---

[94] *Tarawih*: Additional congregational prayers performed every night in Ramadan.
[95] Abu Sa'eed and a similar hadith was transmitted by at-Tabarani.

like, and leave Qur'an and Sunnah, then listen to Qur'an and Sunnah when you like and turn from your ego. We have to teach ourselves never to listen to our ego and always to follow Divine Law.

Unfortunately, we are living in the 20th century, a time that is said and assumed to be the most civilized century. To us, it is the most ignorant century. It is the worthless century, with tyranny and oppression everywhere, with the increase of evil people everywhere, and no one is found who tries to remember Allah and the Prophet ﷺ, the way of Companions and Successors, the way of the great scholars who have paved the way of 1,400 years of Islamic religion. No one is trying to remember the culture founded by the Prophet ﷺ and kept by the great imams and scholars. No one is trying to understand and to learn. We live in a century where everyone believes that what he thinks is right. This is not true. We might be mistaken. The Prophet ﷺ said:

> *You have to follow the majority of Muslims.*[96]

World Filled with Tyrants

The majority are always right, they are not wrong. Thus we are finding that, in this time, we are wrongly following a minority of Muslims; Muslims that are not thinking about others, only about themselves, tyrants! These are the leaders of our Muslim countries, and Allah is never going to leave tyrants in peace. The Prophet ﷺ said:

> *After me there will be khalifs, after them princes, after them kings and after them tyrannical kings.*[97]

---

[96] Ibn Abi 'Asim, al-Qurtubi and al-Hakim.
[97] At-Tabarani, Abu Nu'aym, Ibn 'Asakir, Suyuti.

The Sahabah asked the Prophet, "O Prophet of God, is Judgment Day coming after you?" He said, "No, after me khalifs will come." These are the Four Rightly-Guided Successors, may God be pleased with them. *They said, "Will Judgment Day come after the khalifs?" He said, "No, after khalifs, princes are coming."* [These are the Umayyad and Abbasid princes.] *They said, "O Prophet of God! Will it come after the princes?" He said, "No, after the princes, kings are coming."* [These are the sultans of the Ottoman Empire, until 1920. Now there are kinglets left here and there.] *They said, "Is Judgment Day coming after the kings?" He said, "No, tyrants are coming."*

Now, all the world is filled with tyrants. There is not one Arab country except its president or king is a tyrant—and not one of them is thinking except about his chair and how to maintain it high. They are leaving Muslims to their sufferings everywhere. And yet we ask how Muslims are going to be successful? What happened to the order, **"Obey God and obey the Prophet"**? The Prophet said

According to how you are, God will send someone to govern you.[98]

We are in mistakes and sins, and that is why there are tyrants over us. Tyrants do not care for anything except eating, drinking, and womanizing. No one is caring for Islam and Muslim societies. Muslims are suffering everywhere and are being slaughtered. When they see peace in a Muslim country, they try to penetrate and make wars and sufferings. This is coming from tyranny, from "slaughter and killing."

---

[98] Ad-Daylami, al-Bayhaqi, al-Hakim, at-Tabarani, at-Tabrizi's *Mishkat* XVII, 1, 3.

The Prophet ﷺ said that, in the Last Days, one of the indications of the Hour is:

There will be much slaughter and killing.[99]

Look everywhere. East and West, North and South, you will find killings, especially Muslims killing each other also. Who is caring? No one. What are they going to do? You can organize thousands of demonstrations: if leaders themselves do not demonstrate good will, what will change?

Rulers of Muslim countries must come to their conscience. We are Arabs, and we cannot even go from one Arab country to another without a visa. Why? How do Americans and Europeans not need visas for Arab countries? In Egypt, Westerners are rarely bothered: Come and feel welcome, you are a civilized one. But Muslims? They are feared and considered backward. If I say *La ilaha illa-Allah Muhammadun Rasulullah* ﷺ, they will say: this is finished! Either you have a visa or you don't enter. They deny what is written even on the gates of Egypt, at the airport in Cairo:

Enter in peace and security.[100]

How then is Islam going to revive? If we Muslims are not good to each other and if we fight each other, how come we want America and Europe to help Bosnia, Afghanistan, Pakistan and Kashmir, Somalia and Ethiopia and Sudan? This is where we have arrived, and this is what the Prophet ﷺ announced as indications of the Last Days. Jesus ﷺ and Mahdi ﷺ are coming. Do not say it is too far. The Prophet ﷺ said:

I have been sent as near to Judgment Day as these two fingers are near to each other.[101]

---

[99] Arabic: *al-harj wa 'l-marj*. Bukhari, Muslim.
[100] Suratu 'l-Furqan, 25:46.

There is nothing left to do except prepare our hearts to receive that big event. How to prepare our heart? Let us not sleep happily with our families and children, not caring about others. God will never accept this. We have to care for Muslims. We have to pray day and night that Allah take the burdens away from the people who are in pain, especially Muslims and non-Muslims who are suffering under the scourge of a war which they have contributed to cause.

"*La hawla wa la quwwata illa bil-Lahi 'l-'Aliyyi 'l-'Adhim* — There is no power nor might except in God Exalted and Mighty." Allah knows, and we don't know. That is why we do not interfere. "Whoever knows his limit does not trespass it." What can we do in the world?

One time Allah sent an unprecedented earthquake to Egypt, but still they did not learn anything. The money Saudi Arabia sent for relief was shared by the people at the top. How dare they say after that: We are Arabs and love Arabs? Allah said in Qur'an,

> ***The desert Arabs are the worst in unbelief and hypocrisy.***[102]

> ***Do not say: We are believers; say: We are Muslims.***[103]

Believers (*mu'minun*) are one thing and Muslims are another thing. Islam (submission) is something, Iman (belief) is something else. Islam is the first step; the second step is Iman.

Continued from previous page ...
[101] Bukhari, Muslim, Ibn Majah, at-Tirmidhi, ad-Darimi, Ahmad and at-Tayalisi.
[102] Suratu 't-Tawbah, 9:97.
[103] Suratu 'l-Hujurat, 49:14.

That is why there are five pillars to Islam, and six pillars to Iman. It is inside Islam, but it is a higher level. Not every Muslim can say of himself he is a *mu'min*. For he can be in Islam, but a heretic, a hypocrite, a corrupt one and not a believer. And if he is teaching, such a teacher would be dispensing corrupt teachings to innocent and ignorant people who think this is Islam.

Sincere Ones Treated as Criminals

In Arab countries, they are catching and throwing into jail scores of people only for saying: *La ilaha illa l-Lah Muhammadun Rasulullah* ﷺ. If you grow your beard a little bit, you are accused and thrown into jail for being a fanatic or a member of extremist organizations. This is for keeping the Sunnah of the Prophet ﷺ. People are thrown into jail and forgotten, tortured with electric shocks applied to their private parts, hung by the legs and doused with water. When they die, their bodies are disposed of by means of acid and not even buried properly.

See the prisons everywhere in Arab countries, countries calling themselves Muslim. The conflict in Bosnia was clear, against Muslims and Islam, but what about the deprivation of human rights that starts at the airports of Arab countries against anyone who looks Muslim?

One day on our way to one Muslim Arab country and a group of us were stopped at the customs and my brother was taken away from us. They told us, "You cannot speak to him because he has been incarcerated for something he did against state security." This is one of the big charges our countries level against their people. They took him and we could not do or say anything: they kick you out, beat you and it could get worse. We knew some people in the government, but we had to trace my brother and find out where they took him. We went and met with the Minister of Defense whom we knew through family connections. Immediately he called immigration service at the border, about 100 miles from the city. They said, "We transferred him to another place." He called that place, and again it was the wrong place. We stayed there until 1 A.M. and we were very embarrassed in front of that minister. He said, "I will ask about him tomorrow." They found him after two days 400 miles away. Why did they send him there? After investigation—it is a long story—they said, "Oh, we are sorry, it is a mistake between identical names..." They did all this because of suspicion, and because they are afraid for their president's chair.

This is tyranny. This is what the Prophet ﷺ warned about. I am sorry to say this, but it must be said: tyranny is everywhere. Let us correct ourselves. If we correct ourselves, Allah will correct our leaders.

For *"As you behave, Allah will send people to control you."* Let us control ourselves. Let us come back to our faith, and not fight each other. Let us be as Allah said in Qur'an:

Hold fast to the rope of God as one hand, and do not separate.[104]

and Allah will make us successful. Then He will take tyranny away from tyrants by sending Mahdi ﷺ.

Don't think there is deliverance except by the coming of Mahdi ﷺ. Tyranny is everywhere, and all that the Prophet ﷺ said about the Last Days has happened. Bedouins are erecting big buildings[105] and turning deserts into paradises. Women are imitating men in dress and vice-versa. Oppression and *riba*[106] (interest) is everywhere. *Halal* has disappeared. How can you say

---

[104] Surat Ali 'Imran, 3:103
[105] "...you will see the barefoot, naked, destitute bedouin shepherds competing in constructing tall buildings." *Sahih Muslim*.
[106] *Halal*: What is lawful, especially in relation to food and money.

"halal" for meat? Because of the method of slaughter? Ask yourself, "From where the money is coming?" It is coming from banks. How can you say it is *halal*? Everything is *haram* now. That is why the Prophet ﷺ said:

> In the Last Days, there will come a time that who is keeping his religion, it is as if he is holding fire in his hand.[107]

Who is doing this now? No one is carrying money in his pocket anymore. All of you are carrying cards. It is all interest money. Even if you don't take interest with your money in the bank, nevertheless it is being used for interest, and then used to buy food. There is *shubhah* there, doubt, and that is enough to consider that food corrupt.

There is nowhere to run. It is finished. We are in the Last Days, and we are coming to the darkest times. The meat may be *halal*, but where did the purchaser and the slaughterer of the sheep get his money? He is slaughtering hundreds of sheep every day, and chances are he is using a check for his transactions. Where is that check from? It is *riba* (interest) money even if he is not taking interest, for he must ask himself, "Where is this money coming from and where is it going?" In the time of the Prophet ﷺ, they used to exchange: "I give you wheat, you give me barley; I give you dates, you give me meat; I give you golden coins, you give me golden coins." They exchanged similar products. This is *halal*. They have everything with them. Now you cannot carry anything with you: the next day thieves will carry everything away. Even if you want to buy a mosque, you go to the bank! Even if you don't use the bank's money (avoiding loans), ask yourself: "What place are you taking the money from?" Where then is *halal*?

---

[107] At-Tirmidhi and Ahmad Ibn Hanbal.

Awaiting Mahdi

We are in the Last Days and there is no salvation except through Mahdi ﷺ. He is the one that can come and whom all Muslims will accept as a khalifa. If there is no khalifa, where is there going to be peace? The Prophet ﷺ said:

> One of my descendants will come and fill the earth with justice and peace as it was filled before with ignorance, hypocrisy and corruption.[108]

No one can deny the Prophet narrations (ahadith) concerning Mahdi ﷺ. Muslims must know that these narrations are certain, authentic and numerous. It is sure that Mahdi ﷺ is coming: but Allah alone knows when. We do not say about ourselves that we know. Even the Prophet ﷺ said:

> **Nor do I know what will be done with me or with you. I follow but that which is revealed to me by inspiration.**[109]

It means, "I only know what Allah tells me, and what He does not tell me, I don't know—I am a human being."

No one can reach the level of the Prophet ﷺ, and if Allah does not tell the Prophet ﷺ, he will not know. Unseen things, al-ghayb, is in Allah's secret—but we have knowledge about it from the numerous indications and Prophetic Traditions uttered by the Prophet ﷺ. You may not ignore them. Prepare yourself, therefore, for that day.

May Allah give us long life for that day. It is a Golden Age. If Mahdi ﷺ comes in our own time, we will be lucky. May

---

[108] Ahmad, Abu Dawud, at-Tirmidhi, Ibn Majah, at-Tabarani, Abu Nu'aym, ad-Daraqutni, al-Hakim
[109] Suratu 'l-Ahqaf, 46:9.

Allah give us such luck. Whatever the Prophet ﷺ has said concerning the signs of the Last Days has appeared already. What else do you want? It is finished. Open any book of hadith concerning ʿAlamat as-Saʿat (Signs of the Hour). Look at Ibn al-Qayyim's book *Madarij as-salikin*. You will find all these Prophetic Traditions there; then look at the society and the world around you: you will find that everything that the Prophet ﷺ has announced has appeared.[110] What else do you want?

We want only one thing: to come to each other with love and respect; to be one hand. The Prophet ﷺ said:

God's Hand is over the community of people.[111]

May Allah join us together as a community of good people for our intentions are good. We don't know whether what we are doing is right or wrong, but our intentions are good, and as the Prophet ﷺ said:

Actions are judged according to intentions... [112].

Every deed is according to your intention. If your intention is good, Allah will reward you even if you mistakenly do wrong! And if your intention is bad, Allah is going to give you what you are asking for.

We are trying to bring each other and the people at large to the love of Islam. May Allah accept this intention from us, and accept the same from everyone that is trying their best to raise high the name of Muslims and their religion. Let them know that, when they speak in the name of Muslims, they must not think

---

[110] Many of these Prophetic narrations are cited in the author's work: *Approach of Armageddon? An Islamic Perspective*, Islamic Supreme Council o f America, 2003.
[111] *Mishkat* I, 6, 2, at-Tirmidhi, al-Hakim.
[112] Bukhari and Muslim.

about themselves. They must think about the people. If you think first about yourself, then about Muslims, you are not a true believer.

> *No one will be accepted as a believer unless he will like for his brother what he likes for himself.*[113]

This is the first level. The second level is:

> *No one will be considered a believer until he loves me more than he loves his father and mother, more than he loves his wife and children, more (and this is the third level) than he loves even himself.*[114]

Until people love the Prophet ﷺ more than they love their own selves, they will not have *Iman* (Faith).

Praise the Prophet for He Hears You

Islam is based on the love of the Prophet ﷺ. Without the Prophet ﷺ there is no Islam. Allah has sent Islam through the Prophet ﷺ to all people, and the love of the Prophet ﷺ is a must upon every human being, "Praise," God said, "my beloved one."

> **Allah and His angels are praying on the Prophet;**
> **O believers! pray on him.**[115]

That is why it is our duty to send prayers, blessings, greetings, praise and salutations on the Prophet ﷺ. There never was, never is, and never will be any wrong in it.

> *A Muslim does not send prayers on me except that Allah revives my soul to return the salutations.*[116]

---

[113] Bukhari and Muslim.
[114] Bukhari and Muslim.
[115] Suratu 'l-Ahzab, 33:56.

The Prophet ﷺ is alive and hears our salutation. Before he left this world he said, "I am fresh and alive in my grave: whoever prays on me one time, Allah prays on him ten times."

In another narration he ﷺ said:

I am fresh and alive in my grave: whoever gives me greetings, Allah has sent my soul back to my body to return his greetings.[117]

In another narration he ﷺ said:

Allah has forbidden the earth to eat the bodies of prophets.[118]

And finally:

The prophets are alive and pray in their graves.[119]

Islam is based on love for the Prophet ﷺ, and on his obedience. Allah said:

Obey God and obey the Prophet...[120]

and He also said:

Whoever obeys the Prophet obeys God.[121]

Continued from previous page ...

[116] Ahmad, Abu Dawud, Al-Bayhaqi, as-Suyuti.

[117] Abu Dawud.

[118] Ibn Majah, Ahmad, Ibn Abi Shayba, Abu Dawud, al-Nasa'i, Ibn Majah, al-Darimi, Ibn Khuzayma, Ibn Hibban, al-Hakim (*sahih*), Tabarani in his *Kabir*, and Bayhaqi.

[119] Al-Bayhaqi, Ibn 'Adiy, Ibn Abi Hatim, al-Khatib, al-Bazzar, Ibn Hajar, as-Subki.

[120] Suratu 'n-Nisa, 4:59.

[121] Suratu 'n-Nisa, 4:80.

How then can you obey someone if you don't love him? "Lovers always obey the ones they love."[122] I cannot obey anyone unless I love him, or unless he imposes tyranny over me, and the Prophet ﷺ is not a tyrant. Allah said to him in the Qur'an

If you had a hard and cruel heart, they would run away from you.[123]

The Prophet ﷺ is not a tyrant and since he is not a tyrant, he is coming to us with love. Our obedience to him comes from love. Our love for the Prophet ﷺ is therefore part of our faith and not against it.

May Allah put the love of the Prophet ﷺ deep in our hearts, and the love of Islam, and the love of each other, without discrimination of color, races, or anything else. We are all brothers and sisters. May Allah accept our good intentions from all of us.

---

[122] Rabiʿa al-ʿAdawiya, quoted in Bayhaqi's *Shuʿb*.
[123] Surah Aali-ʿImran, 3:159.

KHIDR AND MOSES

We are all students of the same teacher who is inspiring us through his station in the Divine Presence. We are all in need of that one. We cannot be self-sufficient. We cannot say, "I know everything." What do you know? You know nothing.

There are close to six billion human beings on this earth. Out of these six billion do you think that you are the most clever one? Where are the rest? Do they know nothing while you know everything? You need advice from everyone. There may be hundreds, thousands upon thousands more knowledgeable than you. You know something, yes—Allah gives everyone something to know. But you must know also that above you there is another one more knowledgeable. And Allah said in Qur'an:

Above every knower there is a higher knower. [124]

That means you are nothing. Your knowledge is yet nothing. "You are rubbish, garbage!" This is what we have to teach our ego.

Moses was a highly powerful prophet, one of the five greatest Allah sent to this world: Noah, Abraham, Moses, Jesus, and Muhammad, God's peace and blessings be upon them all. Moses was higher than Noah because he brought with him a great religion. It is contained in the Torah which God gave him. This means he is a highly knowledgeable person to whom Allah

---

[124] Surah Yusuf, 12:76.

gave a special trust, for Allah does not give revelation to just anyone.

Moses ﷺ was a Divinely-supported person. Prophets cannot be ordinary people. Ordinary people derive their knowledge from others. They cannot bring their own knowledge. You can find some saints, in Sufi teachings, bringing that knowledge from the secret that Allah gave to the prophets. But Allah gave it to very few saints. The majority of people are taking from each other.

Yet with the high knowledge of Moses ﷺ, Allah caused him to be in need for Khidr ﷺ, the Green Man, even though Khidr ﷺ was not a prophet:

> ***They [Moses ﷺ and his servant Joshua] found one of Our servants on whom We had bestowed mercy from Ourselves and whom We had taught knowledge from Our own presence.***[125]

Moses ﷺ said to him, "I would like to accompany you." He answered him, "You cannot be patient enough to accompany me." Moses ﷺ was surprised and insisted that he could. Khidr ﷺ said, "You cannot, but if you do, do not ask about what I am doing no matter what you see me do. On that condition alone you may follow; but if you want to ask questions, don't follow me."

This means that Khidr ﷺ was going to do something that Moses ﷺ does not understand, although he was the messenger of this great religion. He was in need of Khidr ﷺ to learn something.

They took a boat and crossed Tabaraya River in Palestine. When they were in the middle of the river, Khidr ﷺ made a hole in the boat in order for it to sink. Moses ﷺ was unable to keep quiet, "Why are you doing this childish act? Those people gave you the

---

[125] Suratu 'l-Kahf, 18:65.

boat, are you now scuttling it?" Khidr ؑ replied, "Did I not tell you you were unable to keep patience with me?"

Moses ؑ had not yet understood, even though he was a prophet and could read hearts, that there was something he did not know. They continued and found a young boy. As soon as they saw him, Khidr ؑ killed him. Moses ؑ said, "What are you doing? You broke a boat, and now you kill a child? This is against all laws!" Again Khidr ؑ said, "Did I not tell you you could not keep patience with me? The third time you ask me, we will part ways."

Then they reached a city where they asked for food. No one gave them any food, rather they threw them out. On their way out, they found a wall which was about to fall down. Khidr ؑ rebuilt that wall and made it straight. Moses ؑ said, "Why are you doing this? They refused to accept us as their guests in this city, and yet you are building their wall for them?"

Khidr ؑ said, "This is the point where we separate, for you did not understand the wisdom of what I was doing. What we do is what Allah tells us to do. First I caused this boat to sink because there is a tyrant who is taking every boat from the poor people on this side of the city. In order for these people not to lose their boat, I am causing it to sink. That tyrant is going to die tomorrow, and tomorrow, they can retrieve their boat and use it safely. I killed the child because Allah did not want that child to cause his parents, who believe in you, to leave and run away from your religion. Allah will give them better children than him. Finally, I built the wall which belonged to a man who was in life very generous to poor people. When he passed away, he left a treasure buried under the wall for his two orphans. Were that wall to come down, people would discover the treasure and take it. I built it back in order for the two children to receive their treasure later. You did not understand God's wisdom."[126]

How can we consider ourselves knowledgeable if the Prophet Moses ﷺ, with all his personality and knowledge in the Divine Presence, was himself unable to understand certain things? With all the honor bestowed on him by God, Moses ﷺ found himself ignorant before Khidr ﷺ. We human beings in our day, are so proud of what we know! And what each one knows is nothing! Your knowledge is not worth mentioning. There are others more and highly more knowledgeable than you. As high or deep as you travel into knowledge, there is deeper depth and higher height than where you stand.

Listen Humbly to Advice

That is why, when someone sits to give advice, he must sit with complete humbleness and complete respect for the listener, and he cannot consider himself higher than them, otherwise that light will never come to their hearts. Scholars of our day—churchmen, clergymen, rabbis, shaykhs, imams—are proud of what they know; and what they know is like a matchbox where you may find one, or two, or three matches; when you shake the box it makes a sound. They make a sound. Or they are like a big balloon full of air; prick it with a needle and nothing is left.

A wise man, a spiritual man is not proud of his knowledge. He is like a matchbox which is full and makes no noise no matter how much you shake it. He is not trying to show that he knows anything. There is a wise saying:

> Do not throw diamonds under the feet of foolish people.

---

[126] Cf. Suratu 'l-Kahf, 18:65-82.

When that wise man sees that he is among ignorant people, why throw them diamonds? They are not going to accept anything. That is why he keeps quiet until he finds suitable listeners.

In our time, very few people understand spiritual teachings. The rest are stubborn in their beliefs. They are not accepting advice, they are not willing to believe that Allah did not create human beings in order to punish them, but in order to love them and keep them respected and honored. Every religious group is trying to send the other party to Hell and save themselves. They are not trying to extend a helping hand to their brothers and sisters in other groups. Why? Paradise is so vast that it can contain everyone.

Paradise is in your hearts. They say, "Paradise is in heaven." But where is heaven? Heaven is in your heart. Your heart can be Heaven and Paradise to you; and it can at the same time be Hell to you. If you can correct your heart, then you will find happiness. If you do not or cannot correct your heart, you are going to find Hell in your heart. Everything depends on the heart.

Allah said to the Prophet ﷺ:

If you had been harsh and cruel-hearted, they would have run away from you.[127]

This shows that Allah based everything on the heart. Because the heart signifies love, it follows that Islam is based on love. Unfortunately, the people who consider themselves the scholars of our century are presenting Islam as an rigid, fundamentalist religion. This causes people to run away from it.

From the seventh century until the nineteenth century and the beginning of the twentieth, Islam was full of Sufi teachings.

---

[127] Surat Ali-'Imran, 3:159.

Most of the Sufi teachers are originally Muslim, although they say that Sufism started very long ago. Knowledge of God cannot be for one group of people at one time! Allah has been sending that knowledge to the heart of people from the beginning of creation. Sufism, in reality if not yet in name, was therefore present from the beginning of creation. The way of the heart cannot be confined to a historical period. But after Islam was spread everywhere in the world, Sufism as we understand it spread quickly.

Scholars Must Open Their Minds

It is advisable for our scholars to open their minds more and more towards the many people asking for spirituality. These scholars are closing their mind to this and are trying, with their strict ways, to stop people from accepting spirituality. This is true for Judaism, for Christianity, and for Islamic teachings. Allah's Mercy is always available for everyone, not for a special group of people.

> *Say (O Muhammad)!, "O my servants who have transgressed against themselves, do not despair of the mercy of God."*[128]

God is the Creator of everyone. You cannot limit him to your group. How can you limit your Lord? Your mind is the one that is limited! But your heart is not limited. Crazy scholars are limiting the heart. They are saying that nothing concerns the heart, and everything goes by the mind. They use technology, which is a product of the mind, as a standard for religion. Ignorants! Have they not heard of God's saying in a Holy Tradition (*hadith qudsi*):

---

[128] Suratu 'z-Zumar, 39:53.

My earth and My heaven contain Me not, but the heart of My faithful servant contains Me.[viii]

This means that your heart is unlimited. The mind, however, is limited. Do not take everything through the mind. The mind cannot handle everything. Hearts can take everything; and everything can enter inside them. Now, they are saying the opposite: they are saying hearts are nothing, and everything depends on the mind. What is this? What can you understand then?

God is the Creator. You and I are not the Creator. We are created. He is the Engraver, we are the engraved. All of us, therefore, are His engravings—without discrimination. Allah has engraved us, each one according to this shape and those features. A famous artist like Picasso exhibits paintings, and the paintings do not care about your criticism: only the artist does. Who is our artist? Who made us? God has made us, everyone in a different way. If you are going to put one person to shame, or speak to them in an ugly way, you are not addressing them, but Allah directly—and Allah will never accept this.

One saint said:

> If a person comes to us after having committed all kinds of sins, he will find a way of purification in our methods. Come to us with all manners of dark deeds, and you will find a means to shed that burden of sins. But, don't ever come to us after having broken the heart of a human being: for this heart cannot be glued back together after that.

To break the heart of a human being is a very big mistake. Nowadays people do nothing except speak ill of each other—*kafir, mushrik, bid'a; kafir, mushrik, bid'a*—"unbeliever, idolator, innovator, atheist, Buddhist, Hindu, Jew, Christian…" This is all they know. No one looks with a wide angle.

God is God. Do you understand? He is the Creator. We, all of us, are His creation. How many has He created like us? Billions and billions and billions. Allah is Great! Now, when your clothes become dirty, what do you do with them? Do you throw them into the fire to burn them? Have you no mind? Do you not wash them, or send them to the cleaners or launderer to clean them for you? And if this is what we do with our clothes, what do you think God will do with us to clean us from our sins?

Do Not be the Judge

Allah, with His light, can turn a stone into a diamond. He can turn a non-believer into a believer. Do not, therefore, be a judge of human beings. Leave them to their Lord. Leave everyone connected to His God. And God is one—the same for Jews, Christians, Hindus, Buddhists, atheists—even for those not believing in Him, He does not care! He is taking back what He entrusted to you.

> *We have offered the heavens, the earth, and the mountains Our Trust to carry, but they were unable to carry it and recoiled from it; and man accepted it. Indeed he was unjust and ignorant.*[129]

Heavens, earth and mountains recoiled from fear. They are creations like us, and all of creation is alive. Allah said:

> *Everything in creation is praising Him.*[130]

Even mountains are praising Him, nature is praising Him, tree leaves are praising Him, birds, animals, water, skies, stars, paradises... Creation has life and everything that appears appears only through the existence of Allah.

---

[129] Suratu 'l-Ahzab, 73:72.
[130] Suratu 'l-Isra, 17:44.

Allah gives you appearance in this life through the same secret of life that is behind the appearance of elements such as inanimate solids. If this were not the case, you would not appear and the solids would not appear. That is the secret of creation, and everything that has that secret is praising God. This we know from all religions and all Sufi teachings and all philosophies. Call it "superpower" or "natural power," there is a Power and that Power is the Creator.

The Ignorant Trust-Bearer

When Allah gave that trust to the mountains and heavens, they recoiled and were afraid, but human beings accepted immediately because they are ignorant oppressors. It is a trust and as such it must be returned. On that day Allah will ask, "Did you keep it or did you lose it?" You must keep it well. That means you have to keep His servants well! This is what makes Allah happy with you.

If you work for a king, you cannot make his children angry with you or he will get angry with you. By pleasing his children you will make him happy. Look at President Bush's dogs: everyone is trying to make them happy in order to make Bush happy. The White House may be spending untold amounts to keep these dogs! What about human beings? Will you not please God by spending on them and pleasing them? Keep them under your protection and don't try to hurt them. Then you can return what was entrusted to you.

Allah is not in need of your worship. Your worship is for you. You can either be good to yourself or not, it concerns you. But you have to know that you must be good to people. This is what is needed. Sometimes you sin, and all of us are weak: but do not cause your sin to harm others. You must always ensure that people are not harmed because of you. If you break one heart, Allah is not going to accept it from you. But if you break your own heart, never mind! You can bring it back together again. That cannot be done with others' hearts.

Let us prepare ourselves, therefore, to be more open in understanding and visualizing the nature of things. We must accept everyone that comes to us. We must not say, "We accept this one, but not that one." The prophets, when they came, accepted everyone. Allah did not say to Moses ﷺ, "I am sending you to Jews." He did not say to Jesus ﷺ, "I am sending you to Christians." He did not say to Muhammad ﷺ, "I am sending you to Muslims." There were no Muslims, Christians or Jews in their respective times. How dare we say now, "No, we won't accept this or that one?" On what grounds? Allah said, "I sent My Prophet ﷺ as a mercy to everyone. Every one of My servants who likes to come to Me is invited, I am not going to reject them." You and the next person are meant by that "Every one" which refers to **all** human beings!

The Limits of God's Mercy

One day Satan came to a spiritual scholar, a saint, and asked him this question:

"Allah said:

My Mercy encompasses every thing.[131]

Am I included in that 'every thing' or out of it?"

That saint did not know what to answer. If he said, "Yes, you are included," that would mean Satan is under God's mercy, but because Allah has cursed Satan he was afraid to tell him "yes." And he was afraid to tell him "no" because Allah had nevertheless said "everything" unconditionnally. He was afraid to give either answer. If he said "yes," Allah might get angry with

---

[131] Suratu 'l-A'araf, 7:156.

him, and if he said "no," Allah might also get angry with him, "How do you say 'no?' Satan also might be under My mercy!" So that saint did not give an answer. He stopped there and, tradition tells us, so did his knowledge.

Five hundred years later another saint came and gave the answer. That answer boggles the mind but can never shake the heart. He said to him, "You fall within 'every thing!' You are under the mercy of Allah!" And we shall not explain more but leave you to meditate on whether Satan is under the mercy of God. God is just. His justice rules everything and everyone. If Satan is under that mercy and God is just, where is Satan going to go? And if Satan benefits from this, what then of people and human beings? Where will they go, Paradise or Hell? Think about this.

This is knowledge of the spirituality that accompanies Divine Law. May Allah make our minds as open as our hearts. May He make us understand what He wants us to understand, and not make us ignorant of this high knowledge. You cannot find such knowledge everywhere; only through people that have devoted their love and their heart to their Lord, and to human beings. Such is our master and shaykh, our wise and holy man, Mawlana Shaykh Nazim, who sends us inspiration through our heart, may Allah bless him and raise him higher and higher! He is teaching us these things and they come from his knowledge. This knowledge is not to be found in books but is the privilege of hearts. There are hidden troves of this kind of knowledge in the hearts of saints. And may Allah make saints of all of you.

The Prayer of Salvation

Why do tape recorders remember everything they record? Allah inspired human beings to invent these machines to show us His perfection. "This small machine made by you can remember every word; I gave you a heart which can remember everything even better, and you are not using it! Use it!" Now, listen, and remember every word.

The more your say that God is merciful and that He is going to send everyone to Paradise, the better. Never say God is going to punish anyone and send them to Hell. Never. You might be that very one. If you like people to go to Hell, then you might be the first. Why say such a thing? Let us say, instead, that Allah is going to close His Hell. One saint is enough, if he puts his finger inside Hell, to bring it down. Not even a finger but one person's tear coming out for the love of Allah, of the Prophet ﷺ, and of saints, is enough to bring down all seven hells and finish them.

If Allah is the Punisher, why did He create us? Does He not know we are weak servants? "O our Lord, we are weak! Since You created us, protect us. If You don't protect us, it is not our problem! We can do nothing." We are happy now, speaking about Allah, then we go out of that door and fall into sins. Why did He put ego in us? Since He put ego over us, let Him protect us, as He protected His prophets who never sinned, because they were perfect. There is no influence of the ego on them. Yet even if there were influence of the ego Allah never punished them. Moses ؑ killed two people. Allah said nothing. Why say nothing for him and say everything for us?

Allah said, "I created you, and I am putting ego over you. You are therefore going to fall into sin." For that reason, Grandshaykh (Mawlana Shaykh 'Abd Allah al-Fa'iz ad-Daghestani) and Mawlana Shaykh Nazim taught us a prayer. After we pray Salat an-Najat (the Prayer of salvation), we make a long prostration: at that time we make a invocation (*du'a*) and it is never rejected. If you make that invocation before Fajr (dawn), Allah will accept it and never reject it at that time. They taught us to say, at that time:

> O my Lord! You have created angels sinless and without ego, You have created prophets and made them perfect and sinless also, and You have protected them. You have created us and You put ego in us. If You are not going to save us as You saved Your prophets and Your saints, what is the difference? As You saved them, You have to save us. If You had created us prophets or saints or angels, we would be like prophets or saints or angels. But You created us with ego. Then it is Your business, not our business. You have to deal with that. We are weak, we are sinners; therefore expect from us sins, do not expect perfection—unless You protect us. And we are coming to You, asking for Your protection.

Grandshaykh and Mawlana said, "That way of approaching is very acceptable. God loves those who bargain with Him! Say something and keep something, as in business." It is God's business to protect us. We cannot protect ourselves, because we are so weak.

Don't Arrogate Yourself

One day I was bringing Mawlana Shaykh Nazim from Damascus to Beirut. It is a three to four-hour drive. I was seventeen or eighteen years of age at the time. We reached downtown Beirut and were approaching my father's house. We have a feast in Lebanon called Eid as-Salib, the Celebration of the Cross, a tradition of our country which takes place on the first of September. They put huge crosses everywhere in the streets, hoisting and hanging them overhead.

Hear now how Allah protects everyone through the saints. The mercy in the hearts of saints is so great that they don't differentiate between people. As soon as we passed under one of these crosses, I said one word that caused Mawlana to get out of the car. He said, "Stop right now, I want to go out." What did I say that was so offensive? I said *"Alhamdulillah"* (Praise or Thanks to God), and Mawlana said, "Stop the car." I stopped and he go out and said, "You go alone." I said, "O my shaykh, what did we do?" But he was adamant and said, "Finished; I will not ride with you." So I parked the car and said, "Let the police tow the car away, but if you walk, I will walk together with you, unless you come back in." So he relented and came back. I will now tell you another story before I finish this one.

Ibrahim ibn al-Adham was a saint *"yahimu bi hubbi-llah—* enraptured with the love of God," who had left everything and was running after Allah, not minding hot or cold weather, hunger or thirst. How did he become like that? Every night, he used to sleep with seven to ten women. He was a great king. He slept with them and drank, enjoying. One day, they built a special, sky-lit room on top of his palace, and his palace was built high up in the sky. At that time his building was the only high building. So they built for him a big dome for him to look at the sky when he was womanizing. One day, he heard someone walking on top of that dome, making noise.

Look at Allah's good care coming to people. Allah never leaves anyone without taking good care of him. But when help comes, catch it quickly and don't let it get away. Ibrahim said to the noisemaker, "What are you doing on my roof'? Don't you know that I am the sultan? (At that time, he was surrounded by

God knows how many women and men.) What are you doing up there?" The answer came, "I am looking for my camel!" Half-conscious, Ibrahim bin al-Adham nevertheless caught that word, "camel," and dimly felt that it was absurd for someone to look for his camel on top of the king's domed palace late at night. "What did you say? Your camel? You are looking for your camel on my dome?" "Yes," answered the voice. "Is it so hard to understand? I am looking for my camel."

"Are you crazy, O ignorant one! Or are you Satan, and have you come to confuse me more? Can your camel be on top of my dome? Is it possible?"

The voice said, "Yes! It is very possible. There is at least some probability that I might find the camel here. But it will never be possible for you, in your present situation, to find your Lord."

Those words entered like arrows into Ibrahim's heart. The voice came from Archangel Gabriel ﷺ, the Holy Spirit. Some people say, "The Holy Spirit stopped coming." This can never be true, for God keeps sending him and he comes to the saints. Ibrahim understood the message and thought, "Who sent that person there? He is right." He got up and took a shower and ran—to his kitchen. He called his servants and maids, the chief chef and whoever comes under the chief chef and aides. He went to the lowest one and said, "O my son, remove your clothes." The sultan took his own clothes off and they exchanged them. Then he called his treasurer and ordered everything that he had distributed, which was done in a few hours. Then he gave the minister full powers until his son reached maturity. He removed a special ring which bore the picture of Archangel Gabriel ﷺ, and gave it to his son. His wife ran after him but it was finished. He told her, "Look after our son; I am going after my Lord and will no longer stay here."

Holy Diamonds

Allah has placed diamonds at the bottom of the ocean engraved with the image of the angel Gabriel ﷺ and they have their purpose in the ordering of the world. Rare are the people who have seen such diamonds. One of them was in the hands of the Prophet ﷺ, and he passed it down until it came to the hands of our Grandshaykh. This is the sign of the secret of the Golden Chain. This is how you know that the shaykh is what he claims to be: he must have that diamond. If he does not have it, it means that he is not carrying the secret. It is a large diamond with the picture of Archangel Gabriel ﷺ on it, shining with light. It is now in the possession of Mawlana Shaykh Nazim. And if the shaykhs of this *tariqah* do not give you power to do and speak, you are nothing.

Ibraham ibn al-Adham left his palace and went out alone never to be seen as a king again. One day he was in a forest. It was snowing heavily and he found no shelter other than a hut built on top of some stairs. Under the stairs there was some space half covered by the snow, so he huddled there to take his rest and wait for Fajr (dawn) to enter. While he slept, three people came and climbed the stairs leading to that secluded room, bringing with them bottles of alcohol to drink. He wanted to sleep, but these people kept clanging the glasses together, toasting each other and making noise. What did he say? He said one word, "*Alhamdulillah.*"

As soon as Ibrahim said this, he heard a voice speaking to him and saying, "I shall throw you out of My Presence if you say it in this way another time!" Allah punished him immediately and caused someone to come out at that moment and to pass water on him. A drunk urinated over Ibrahim ibn al-Adham, the Sultan. Consider the levels through which one goes to kill the ego. It is very difficult.

With what intention exactly had he said "Praise to my Lord?" He said it with the sense, "Thank God that my Lord did not make me like them, a drunkard. He has shown me His light and made me a good person." He praised God in that sense and it was wrong. That is why Allah was not pleased and punished him. It is good to say, "*Alhamdulillah*," but not to say it to mean, "I am better than them."

Let us go back to the first story. We were passing under a cross that day, and I said, "*Alhamdulillah*." Mawlana said, "Stop the car." I was barely eighteen at the time, and I exclaimed, "What did I say? '*Alhamdulillah*' is good!" He said, "No, it is not good in this way." He had read in my heart that I was saying, "Thank God that we are believers, and they are unbelievers, and we don't do things as they do." That is why Mawlana got out of the car. When he came back to the car, he said, "Allah created you this way, and Allah created them that way. If Allah changed your positions, you would be their way and they would be your way. At that time they would be saying '*Alhamdulillah*,' and you would be left in a corner. Therefore, never say '*Alhamdulillah*' with the intention of belittling others and aggrandizing yourself, thinking that you are better than them. It is within Allah's Justice that He made this people like this and that people like that. It was done in order for this world to move.

"Never say that you are better than anyone. Always tell yourself that you are the lowest one of Allah's creation, and lower yet. If Allah had made you Christian, you would be putting up crosses just the same as Christians. Allah made you Muslim and gave your heart the light of spirituality to be a Sufi follower. Once you enter our Path, it is finished: everyone is your brother and sister, there are no more differences to be seen. Allah created them Christian, and He created you Muslim. He created others Jews, and others Buddhists. When Allah wants them to become Muslim or enter a Sufi way, the time will come and they will change. Therefore don't ever repeat that word in that way! Always consider yourself lower, and lower, and lower."

Be happy if someone curses you, for you are being taught not to be angry. This way, you will learn to calm down. But if you are going to get mad and upset when someone curses you, it will be no good. Sufism will give you teachings, but will not yet open up to you and your heart will not obtain its secrets. When cursing and praising are all the same to you, at that time you will reach your goal. When your heart reaches the degree that whatever your shaykh tells you, you will not be upset, at that time, your shaykh will give you your secret. This reality is known in the heart of the disciples who hear this, but they have to practice it.

The Cursing of the Shaykh

"The loveliest and the best time that the shaykh is happy with his disciple," said Mawlana many a time, "is that when he curses and curses him in front of people, yet his love never changes. But if I praise you, run away! Say: 'my shaykh is giving me candies.'" That is, he is treating you like the child that you are, because your ego will not take more. The shaykh wants others to hear something. He wants to tell them that they are sick with such and such an illness, but indirectly. How to tell them? He will look at the heart of the highest disciple that can carry the weight. If the shaykh curses him, mentioning his name in a derogatory way—but for others to hear—yet his love will never change. You cannot tell just anyone that he is wrong; you will hurt their feelings. Some, however, do not care whether you hurt their feelings or not. Their love for the shaykh will never change. This is the best manner and the one for which the shaykh is happiest to see in the disciple. This is the highest disciple because the shaykh can pass the message without hurting the other (the actual destinator of the message) nor the disciple he is addressing (the apparent destinator).

Whenever the shaykh says something derogatory about you in your face, do not run. Keep that love intact. You will progress. The shaykh likes for his disciple to accept everything. If he kicks him out of the house, throws him out the door, the disciple must not be upset. If he tells you, "I don't want to see your face another time," come back from the window. He will never get angry.

One time, when we were in our twenties, we were coming to Grandshaykh's house to visit. It was 'Asr time (the midafternoon) in the summer. To reach his room, you had to pass through his mosque and then go up. We were coming, and we heard Grandshaykh shouting, shouting, **shouting** as we had never heard him do before, and he sounded extremely angry. We froze like cement and no one dared approach. He was shouting at Mawlana Shaykh Nazim, "Get out of my face! I never want to see you again! Get out of here!" And he was cursing and not leaving anything out. After half an hour—God alone knows when this had started—we were still standing under the window, hiding, afraid to make our presence known lest we catch some of the anger ourselves. When we saw Mawlana Shaykh coming down after that half hour of cursing, he was laughing and said to us, "Go up, go up!" We went up and heard Grandshaykh's voice. He shouted at anyone in the house that approached him and all the disciples were keeping away. But Shaykh Nazim had told us to go so we had to go.

We came to the door. He was shouting, but we knocked on the door and entered. He said, "Close the door!" We closed the door and instantly he laughed. He saw our puzzled expressions and said, "He (meaning Shaykh Nazim) surprises me. Whatever test I put him through, he is not failing. Today I was ordered by the Prophet ﷺ to give him a hard test. I had to throw him out of here and test his heart." At that time there were more than one hundred disciples there, and they were ignorant, thinking that he was shouting at Shaykh Nazim. They had sickness in their heart.

But Shaykh Nazim did not care, and Grandshaykh did not care! They want to test the heart and do not care but for one in a hundred. Shaykhs want one star, and not everyone is a star. Yet everyone is a smaller star; but there is only one large star.

Grandshaykh said, "Sit down. I have to continue shouting." He wanted to keep the test for Shaykh Nazim until the end, and also to check the hearts of the other disciples. What are they thinking in their hearts? Are their beliefs changing toward Shaykh Nazim? If they did, they also failed. Every action of the shaykh is your pitfall in many ways! After one or two hours, the test was over, and Shaykh Nazim entered again, laughing, as if nothing had happened. This is what the shaykh loves on the part of his disciple.

Shaykhs test you in many ways. They make you see things not to your liking. In reality, it is by the order of the Prophet ﷺ. Sayyidina Muhyiddin Ibn 'Arabi was being accused by scholars who did not understand what he wrote in his books and who kept telling the Sultan, "You have to put him in jail." The Sultan, knowing that this was a big saint, but under pressure from people, called Ibn 'Arabi to the palace to interrogate him. He came and the two sat in the garden, under a fig-tree which happened to be dry and no longer gave fruit. As soon as the saint sat under the tree it became green again. The sultan interrogated him and then said, "We cannot excuse you, you have to go to prison," and he sent him to prison.

The Sultan had his own daughter serve him food in the prison, day after day. Allah's order came to the heart of Ibn 'Arabi, "That sultan loves you. He is sending you his daughter to serve you. Return him the favor and marry her." According to Islamic law, you have to have two witnesses, and one person to conduct the marriage. But Sayyidina Muhyiddin, apparently disregarding this, married the daughter inside the prison. He slept with the daughter of the sultan after two angels had appeared to witness, and the Prophet ﷺ himself conducted the marriage. That was yet another big test for the scholars outside. When they asked him, and the sultan came and asked him how he could so transgress *Shari'ah*, he said, "It is Allah's Will for me to marry your daughter as it is Allah's Grant for me to restore your fig-tree. I cannot disobey even if you came against me with all your people."

Don't Let Your Love Shake

Saints impose tests that some people will not accept in order to try them. They do not care, except for Allah and the Prophet ﷺ. When it comes to high levels, they are not under the laws that rule; they are above that, because they see what you cannot see. Therefore do not judge the behavior of saints according to your mind. It never works. What saints do is always beyond your limits. Keep that in your mind. Keep your love to your shaykh unwavering, never changing, whatever happens. That will keep you safe, and don't evaluate the shaykh's manner sand behavior, whatever he does! It might be wrong in your eyes and right in his. This is my advice for everyone in the United States, in Europe, in the Far East, and everywhere: Don't evaluate your shaykh's behavior. Don't look at what he is doing when your mind is stranded and cannot accept. It is your mind that is standing still; as for the saints themselves they are reading what Allah has written.

Do not try to understand your shaykh. One shaykh prepared his disciple until that disciple became became very powerful, to the point that he could see the inscription on the Preserved Tablets.[132] Very rare disciples get to that level. Every

---

[132] Preserved Tablet, Arabic: *al-Lawh al-Mahfudh*. A heavenly record in which God has written the destinies of all created beings, prior to their creation in this world.

twenty-four hours, he read what he had to do that day. The first day, he read that his shaykh, according to Allah's Will, was going to be sent to hell for punishment! He began to think, "What kind of a fake shaykh is that?" O foolish one! If he is a fake shaykh, how did you reach the point of reading the Preserved Tablets! And he said, "I cannot leave my shaykh to such punishment, even if he were a fake shaykh. I am going to pray and ask Allah to change his name and let him go to Paradise."

Have mercy, therefore, for all people. Do not go saying "Unbelievers, Jews, Christians, Buddhists etc." Pray rather for Allah to change their path and direct them to the quickest way to reach their Lord. They chose a path that might be long—but they will reach. Allah is always just. However, it will take a long time. If there is a shorter and quicker path, may Allah bring all of them to that path. Is not this way of ours a good prayer?

The disciple prayed and prayed day and night for one year. Then he found that his shaykh's name had been removed from Hell and placed in Paradise. And he made a prayer of *shukr*, giving thanks that Allah had allowed his shaykh to go to Paradise. That night the shaykh called him. He said to him, "What is this? I shall break you as I break this tooth-stick[133] in two and throw you out of my presence, the next time that you interfere with my private business! Go back and pray to God to change my name to its original place, and do not come back to my presence until it happens!"

The disciple was very afraid, for this meant that his shaykh knew everything. He was doubly afraid, for not only had he changed the destiny of his shaykh, but he had also considered him to be a fake. Day and night, again, he prayed. It took him another year in seclusion to change that name back to those destined for

---

[133] *Miswak*: the root of a tree used to clean the teeth. It is a practice from the Tradition of the Prophet ﷺ to use this before every prayer.

Hell! You see how disciples love their shaykhs! What can we do? They indulge their childish ways!

That night he came back to his shaykh who was very happy and said, "Now I can accept you in my presence. For thirty-five years I have seen my name on the Preserved Tablets as one going to Hell. I did not interfere because this was God's Will. I am not worshipping God to go to Hell or to Paradise. He will throw me in Hell; He will throw me in Paradise; I don't care, as long as my love is with Him. Are you crazy, interfering with God's Destiny? Who do you think you are? Do you want every benefit for yourself? I myself may burn, but my heart will never burn. The love that is in my heart can itself burn the fire of Hell! O my son, next time, do not interfere with your shaykh's business."

Never evaluate shaykhs with your mind. They are higher, and higher, and higher, and higher. As much as you may think of shaykhs, they are above that. As high as you may think they are, they are above still. You cannot see where they stand. When you want to know your shaykh, you have to look at him. How will you do that? He is not below you but always above you, much higher. How then are you going to know him? What you know is only what you are seeing of his good manners. This is how you are judging your shaykh. You cannot judge how the Prophet ﷺ sees him. You cannot judge how God is seeing him. You cannot judge how he is seeing himself. You cannot reach.

You look at stars at night and you say, "This one is five million light-years away; that one ten." What are you seeing except little dots of light? Such are the shaykhs. You can describe your shaykh's manners, but you can never understand him, because he is very high, very high... As high as you go, he is higher. Don't try to understand your shaykh: it is impossible. It is better to understand yourself than to look at your shaykh's behavior.

May Allah give us the power to understand our shaykh, Shaykh Muhammad Nazim al-Haqqani through him and by him, not through ourselves. It is impossible through ourselves. They do actions that cause people to wonder. In our eyes it is something, and in the eyes of the Prophet it is *qada'ullah*, the Decree of Allah.

SUBMIT TO YOUR HEART

This is a sacred word: Love. Everyone is trying to undo that word, trying to hurt others, trying to break the hearts of people. God never accepts that anyone break the heart of a believer, or a non-believer. Both believers and non-believers are the same to God, because they are His creation. Just as He created you, He created him, He created her. Judgment belongs to God, not to us. We have to look at everyone through our hearts, therefore, as the same. We cannot judge human beings. Allah has honored them. He gave them a secret in their heart to bring them to His Divine Presence, to love them more and more. He created them with His love.

You cannot run away from your Lord. Your Lord is Present everywhere as He said:

And He is with you wheresoever ye may be. And Allah sees well all that ye do.[134]

If you cannot see Him, there are people who can see. It is because of our weakness that we cannot see Him. God is present in everything. If we have open eyes, we can see Him everywhere. Look at all this creation; is God not there? He is everywhere, but look through your heart. Do not look through your mind. The mind never reaches anywhere. Hearts reach everywhere.

We need a peaceful life. We don't need a mad rush and a hard life. In order to get that peaceful life, you have to submit to your heart. Submit to your heart, don't submit to your ego.

---

[134] Suratu'l-Hadid, 57:4.

Anyone that submits to his ego will find that he is tired. Anyone who submits to his heart will never find himself tired. Always he will find himself living in peace and happiness. May Allah give us that happiness in our heart, and make us submit to our hearts.

Hearts Are All-Important

Hearts are everything in this life and in the other life. God did not create us for this life only. God has created us for this life, for a previous life, and for another life. Do you think that this is the only life that we are living here? There was a previous life before this life; and there is another life after this life; and there is continuity. The meaning of Creator is "One who creates continuously." There is no stopping. We were previously living, we are presently living, we will be living in the future. To God, past, present, and future are the same. There is no time. No one knows the beginning and no one knows the end. Don't underestimate your Lord's power. Your Lord's power cannot be estimated. The Creator is everywhere with His Knowledge.

God has sent us holy men, prophets and saints, to show us our path to Him, to say, "O My believers, O My servants, this is My path follow it." If you follow, you reach. If you don't follow, you are going to reach nevertheless; but not now. You will reach later. But later is not like now. It is more arduous. You will feel more beauty when you reach God sooner. You will feel that beauty and that happiness in you.

God is directing all of us in this world to reach the destination that He wants for us. This time is ending. This life is not going to last much longer; it is finishing. All holy men and saints are waiting for a big event that is going to happen on this earth, and it shall be happening very soon. For that reason we must prepare ourselves? How do we protect ourselves from being involved in what is coming in front of us? By keeping respect and love for God's creation. Allah did not create only humans. He created everything else all around us. We have to keep nature as we are keeping ourselves. If we can keep that, Allah will protect us in the midst of these events coming ahead of us.

All saints and holy men are praising God and asking Him to protect His servants, the true servants, the good believers, those who don't break the hearts of others. We must repeat what Shah Naqshband said, "If someone comes to us with all the sins of this world, it is easy for us to clean him from his sins. But if someone comes to us having broken the heart of another person, there is no way for that one to be cleaned."

Try, therefore, not to break the hearts of people. Try to help them. Try to respect them. Try to give them your hand. If you give them your hand, God will see you and give you His Hand. And when God gives you His Hand, what kinds of secrets will come to you, what lights, what powers, what love, what beauty, what mercy, what blessings, only He knows? Let Him reach you; don't disconnect yourself; don't put barriers between your heart and God. This barrier will go away with only one thing: by helping others. Help His creation; God will help you. If you don't help, God will never help you. At that time, you are egoistic; you only love yourself, you don't love God.

A father and mother love their children all the same. Why are we fighting each other? Are we not the same children of one father and mother? Are we not descendants of our parents Adam ﷺ and Eve? And who are Adam ﷺ and Eve? Are they not the creation of God? Did He not create them with His love? Why then are we struggling against each other and fighting in this confusion? We must give our hand to everyone that is in need for it.

The Purpose of Martial Arts

Why is our brother [points to a disciple] teaching swordsmanship? To help the students fight? No, but you are trying to give discipline with that teaching. You are going to help them be perfect human beings in society, to be disciplined, to have respect for others, to be humble. This sport teaches humbleness, respect. It teaches that the ego never wins. When you practice or play matches many times you may lose. If they lose, it means that pride is breaking up, ego is cut. Everything in this life, especially sports, and especially martial arts, teaches us to reach our Lord. For that reason the Prophet ﷺ said,

Teach your children swimming, swords and archery, and horse-riding.[135]

This disciplines us and causes us to know our Lord. When you play with swords, you concentrate, and it teaches you meditation. Meditating makes a connection between you and your Lord. You cannot simply go out and play with a sword. You must concentrate your mind, your heart, and all your feelings. You are then directing that light which is in your heart in a specific direction. That light one day is going to reach your Lord.

In a flashlight you may sometimes adjust the beam and make it narrower and more intense. That narrow beam will go very far. If you widen it, the angle of light will be bigger but the range very small. The narrow ray is very sharp. When you adjust your heart, that light in your heart which God granted to you can reach people quickly and adjust their own hearts. If you can use that power, you will adjust many and many hearts of God's creation. Many people will be attracted to you. And this is what God wants from us—to attract and help people through their hearts, to throw away the problems and difficulties from their hearts and to give them peace of mind, happiness and tranquillity. God has created us to help each other, to help those who are ill—

---

[135] Ibn Mindah, ad-Daylami, as-Suyuti.

and all of us are ill. Prophets and saints came to help us and take away our illness.

Carry Servants' Difficulties

A saint very near to God, Aba Yazid al-Bistami, once said to his Lord, "O my Lord, why are you sending illness to your people? Let me carry that illness and let them be free from it. I am ready to give my life and everything I have for the sake of those whom You have created. Let me carry this burden." God said, "O Aba Yazid, I am sending illness on them in order for them to sometimes remember Me. I created them and they are running away from Me. I love them and care for them. They are in My Divine Presence. They are My beloved creation. They are running away, and I am running after them. Never are they turning their face to Me, and I am patient, patient, patient, until I have to bring them back to their minds and hearts. So I send them illness to remind them of Me, and to make them say, 'There is a Creator who loves us and who created us.' Let them come back. I have provided them with everything. They are running after this life and its pleasure. They are not running after Me. For that reason they fall into difficulty; they are depressed."

When your students practice fencing they are not depressed, because at that time they are connecting their heart with their Creator. They are not thinking about anything other than that sword, and that sword will connect them. When they finish that one or two-hour play, however, they go back to this life which is full of difficulties. So they connect their heart another time, this time to this life. Then they are going to find themselves tired, depressed, finished and cut off from the love which Allah gave them in their hearts. Let us come back to God's love, and God will make us like shining stars. May God give us a spiritual sword. This physical sword is for play. It makes you happy to spend time practicing. Anyone that practices martial arts and sports is not wasting time. He is spending it usefully, because these activities give you power to concentrate on your heart and to meditate.

Allah never discriminated against anyone. Why are we making differences between brothers and sisters? He loves us without saying "This is good and this is bad." All of us are the same. No one is higher and lower. So come back to God by helping each other. This is what God wants from us.

God asked Moses ﷺ once, "O Moses, what are you doing for Me?" He said, "O my Lord, what can I do for You? I am worshipping You, praying for You, fasting for You, calling people to You." God said, "No, O Moses, this is something concerning you, not Me; I am not in need of your worship." People go to synagogues and pray there; they go to churches and pray there; they go to mosques and pray there; they go to temples and pray there. Allah does not need our prayers. He needs our love. He said, "O Moses, what you are doing is for you! What are you doing for Me? Give me a good answer." And Moses ﷺ was not able to give a good answer. He said, "O my Lord, what can I do? Teach me." God said, "O Moses, help those who ask for help. Help My servants. If you help My creation, at that time you are doing something for Me."

If you don't like to help, that is a sickness. If you cannot, that is not a sickness: you cannot do anything, so you try by praying. But if you can help someone overcome their difficulties, Allah will grant you rewards and lights and blessings in your heart as long as you are helping them. As long as you are helping people direct their hearts to the love of God, God is going to support you and give you more power. May Allah bless us and give us power and support. We are weak servants. We have nothing in our hands and God has everything.

O my Lord! We are coming to You, helpless, weak servants, and we are asking for Your generosity. O our Lord! Give us of Your generosity out of which You gave everyone so much that they drowned in it. Give us from that generosity that You gave to Your saints, prophets and holy men, those who were wise in their time. O our Lord, don't leave us to our ego. Don't leave us to devils and demons but lead us to Your hand, the Divine Hand of beauty and mercy, the Divine Hand of love and blessings, the Divine Hand of grace and generosity. There is no hand except Your hand, there is no love except Your love, there is no blessing except Your blessing. Bless us and give us support. We are weak and in need of that support. O our Lord! Don't look at our bad manners and bad characters. Give us from Your good manners and attributes. Dress us with the blessings of Your Divine Names, O our Lord.

May Allah in this holy night give us that happiness which all saints and holy men are feeling in their hearts. Hearts can contain this world: without making the world small and without making the heart big. What I am referring to by word is this entire universe which you see around you. Allah has created something in your heart, the secret of which no one can know nor fathom. As we said before, there are five levels in the heart. These are Sufi teachings, and we are ready to receive them because God is dressing us with the light of these teachings, the light of Sufi holy and wise men. May Allah make us enter their ranks! The first station of the heart is the Heart; the second is the Secret; the third is the Secret of the Secret; the fourth is the Hidden; the fifth is the Most Hidden.

Allah has given all of you the first level. One reaches it freely and goes in and out of it. That is why you sometimes have good inspirations and sometimes bad. The second, third, and fourth levels are in the hands of saints, prophets and holy men. If you can bring out the secrets of these levels, you will be granted everything in this life. The fifth level is in the Hand of God.

God has placed these levels in your heart to tell you to prepare yourself. Make yourself ready for these blessings and take them. We are asking our Lord to open, through His generosity, these five levels in our heart and let us know ourselves. *"Whoever knows himself, he will know his Lord."* If you do not know yourself, then, how are you going to know your Lord? There is no way. First, we have to know ourselves. Have we come to know ourselves yet? No. We are striving to know ourselves, but no one yet has reached the situation where one can say, "I know myself." That is why you are in depression.

If you want to get rid of depression, know yourself. As long as depression is stalking you, it means that you don't know yourself. Saints never suffer depression because they know themselves. When they know themselves they submit to God. They surrender to God: there is no will for them. Their will is God's Will. They are swimming in that Divine Will. They are not asking anything for their own benefit. They are asking everything for the benefit of human beings. If you can ask for human beings before asking for yourself, at that time you will be knowing yourself. As long as you want anything for yourself, you will never reach that level of self-knowledge. First, give your love to your people. Slowly, little by little, God will make you known to yourself.

May God accept our intentions from all of us and direct us to His path. Everyone of us has his own path. May God direct us towards His path, the path of reality. Our realities are there, always in His Divine Presence. Our realities are never found here. Here, we are but images and reflections of those realities. May God open that reality in our heart in order for us to know ourselves.

Knowledge of Allah's Names

Anything that comes under the heading of Allah is derived from His Names and Attributes. You can know Him through these Names and Attributes. Al-Karim, the Most Generous One, is an attribute. We say that Allah is the Most Generous One; but He is not "al-Karim"! That is, we say that He is the Generous One, but we say that as an attribute, not as His name. And Allah has a collection of attributes. When we say, "X is generous," it means that X is taking that generosity from that Ocean of Generosity, Allah's attribute, which is dressing X with the good manner of generosity. All these attributes, together with these His names, are indications of Him Whose name is Allah. It is the collection of the Names and Attributes that is Allah.

He taught Adam all the Names.[136]

Of human beings, so that he could know his Lord through them, because if I want to know someone, I know him through his name. I cannot know him through something else. Adam ﷺ knew Allah's greatness through the names of His creation. For that reason, in order to know our Lord, we have to know Him through His Names and Attributes. Everything on this world has a name, and that name points to that one Creator. If you can trace the name, you can reach your Lord. It is enough for a person to trace one name to find his Lord. That is the multitude of names that are meant in the hadith, "There are countless numbers of paths to God." Every name is a path, a complete spiritual ocean through which you can reach to your Lord.

---

[136] Suratu 'l-Baqara, 2:30

Saints' Ranks are on the Knowledg of Divine Names

The rank of saints is known by the number of names that they know. If a saint wants to know the power of another saint, he finds it out by the number of "Oceans of Names" that he knows. Every name is an ocean. There are saints that have reached two oceans only. Some, ten. Others, ninety-nine. Others, one thousand. And there are saints who have gotten to know God through countless numbers of names. Most saints know their Lord through two Names: *Tajalli 'l-Jalal wa 'l-Jamal*—Beauty and Majesty, because through His Beauty—meaning also through His Love—He created all this creation. All creation comes from no other than the Oceans of Beauty and Energy. One of the Names of Allah is , Al-Qadir, the Powerful, Who can say to anything "Be" and it will be. When Allah's will wants something to appear in creation, a power comes from the Ocean of Power or Energy, "*Bahru 'l-Qudrah*," and gives existence to that particular beauty. Creation, therefore, takes its power from two Oceans: Beauty and Energy. To appear, it needs power; to take shape, it needs form. It is empowered with existence through Energy and it is dressed with form through Beauty. Everything that we see is from these two oceans.

Where are the other oceans? Where are the ninety-nine oceans, the one thousand oceans, the countless oceans that some saints know? This is a hidden knowledge: it cannot appear except through Mahdi ﷺ. This is one of the secrets that the mind of human beings cannot accept.

The Power of Saints

Allah is great! He is higher than whatever you think of Him, and what you think is nothing. May Allah give us that power of understanding and knowledge which He is giving to the saints, and with which they are supporting and connecting the heart of every human being. Without anyone feeling it, they are reaching everyone through their hearts. Human beings are under the influence of drugs; they are under anesthesia. They do not feel what is going on in their hearts concerning the power of the saints. This is for all human beings. In these days, saints have thrown into hearts the power of *aas*, heedlessness, to make them unconscious while they are working on them.Saints are preparing hearts regardless of what you are doing in your daily life, and whether you are following a saint or not. The saint who is taking his power from God through the Prophet ﷺ, the greatest and highest in level, is reaching all human beings without leaving anyone out. He must reach. He has a station. He is always found there, and Allah is looking at him 70,000 times in every second of the day. Every time He looks at him, he dresses him with 70,000 blessings. These blessings have to be sent out and connected to all human beings. If God looked at human beings directly, they could not carry it. They would fall and be finished. They need something to lessen the weight of His gaze for them. That great saint is under Allah's gaze in order for His blessings to reach human beings.

Yesterday we went to a museum where we heard that in the world, every minute, there are 124 births. Who is reaching them? From where are their spirits coming to make this continuous creation? That saint must reach them with his blessings. If saints do not reach them, their creation would never come to pass. That saint is always one, in every century. We call him in Arabic, *"maqamu 'l-fardani,"* or *"fardu'l-'arsh."* That station is the Right of the Throne of God, although there is no "right" for God, but it is used for us to understand. In the same way the Prophet ﷺ explains to us, *"My Lord came to me in the most beautiful form."*[137]

---

[137] Tirmidhi, at-Tabarani, Ibn Kathir, Ahmad, Ibn Abi 'Asim, at-Tabari, Ibn Hibban, as-Suyuti.

And God says:

Whoever comes to Me walking, I come to him running![138]

This is for people to understand that Allah is not far away from you, He is coming to you—running, laughing, beautiful, like a human being.

Armchairs have two arms. The right arm is the *maqam* or position or station of the right, a unique station. That saint is always present on the right side of the Throne. He gets his blessings, and reaches everyone through the heart. If that power were not reaching us, no one could live but all would disappear from this life. When someone dies, it means that that power is no longer reaching him and he is now disconnected. They say the angel of death Azra'eel comes and takes back the spirit or soul; it is not true.

Who takes the spirit, according to what we know? The angel of death. There are people, however, whose spirit will be taken by saints. There are people whose spirit will be taken by the Prophet Muhammad ﷺ. And there are people whose spirit will be taken by Allah Himself. This depends on the position and station of each person.

No one has permission to take the soul of any person belonging to the Naqshbandi-Haqqani order, except *"Yadu 'l-qudrah,"* Allah's Hand of Power. When Allah wants you to bring His trust back to Him, a white light appears and that light accompanies you back. No one else is allowed to take your soul. This was granted to the Masters of the Golden Chain of the Naqshbandi order: that God Himself, by Himself, will take the soul of anyone connected with the Naqshbandi order.

---

[138] Bukhari, Muslim, Tirmidhi, Ibn Majah.

Die Before You Die

All saints have to go through an experience at least once in their life: to die before they die. The Prophet ﷺ said to the Sahabah ؓ, *"Whoever likes to see someone who passed away before he passed away, let him look at Abu Bakr as-Siddiq."* He killed his ego. When are all of us going to die? Allah may give us the power to kill our ego and make ourselves "die before we die."

I came back from Hajj (Pilgrimage) thirteen years ago, and some people came by to visit us. As soon as they entered, they brought a great burden with them. Because they were good disciples of Mawlana, he said to me, "Carry their burdens." At that point everything came onto my shoulders. It is very difficult to be a carrier of burdens. It will affect you immediately, because it is so heavy. As soon as I said, "Yes," I felt pain. It was a hernia, and I had to undergo an operation immediately. I flew back to Saudi Arabia the next day for that operation at the hands of my brother, who is a surgeon. I am giving this as an example for us to be ready. In the operating room, my brother put the anesthesia mask on me, told me to take a deep breath, and counted to three. I could still hear his voice counting "...Three!" when Grandshaykh appeared to me and said, "So, you came! You are coming to us now!"

He was laughing and said, "This was done to you on purpose, so that you would come to this station and let us check everything with you. You are now surrendering completely. You have nowhere to go. There is nothing to run away to; you cannot do anything. I am now taking your soul out of your body and making your body die."

"Look!" Grandshaykh said. I could see my body from afar. "They think that you have passed away. But your soul is in my hand. If I like, I can give it back; if I don't like, I am not giving it back. Look at what they are doing." I looked and I could see them apply electrostatic shock to my body; my brother looked extremely worried, but it was finished: there was no life. I could hear him say, "*Ya Mawlana Shaykh*! Where are you! *Madad*! Support!" He was afraid, because my mother would kill him! Moreover, doctors had to take an oath not to operate on their relatives, for fear of emotional distractions. "Don't they know," said Grandshaykh, "how easy it is for me to take you and bring you back?" As soon as he said this, he let the spirit go and I found myself entering back into the body. At that time I heard and saw them saying, "Good! Thank God! Everything is in order." They were happy, and Mawlana Grandshaykh was laughing. Then he said, "Now I am taking you back another time." After four or five minutes, he took me out again. He said, "Now, I'll leave them to do what they like, I don't care."

He said to me, "*Ya ahmaq*, O fool, how many times did I tell you to take initiation from my successor, Shaykh Nazim, and you have not done so until now?" Yet we had taken initiation. Even in Grandshaykh's time, our initiation was with Shaykh Nazim first, then to Grandshaykh. But this was a teaching for us. It meant that there was not yet 100% submission and surrender in that initiation. The ego was still playing. When you surrender 100%, at that time everything will be opened before your eyes. They will not veil anything anymore, and will not hide anything from you. Because you are surrendering, you can see through their lights.

He said, "They think that death is so deep. They are wrong. Now you are a dead body: look there: they are trying to revive you another time. But you are not dead. You passed from one room to another room. Why did you not give true initiation to Shaykh Nazim?" What was one to say? You cannot answer anything; this is proper *adab*, respect. You keep quiet. He said, "Now, you have to give true initiation, in my presence, and the Prophet's ﷺ presence, and Allah's presence." As soon as he said this, Mawlana Shaykh Nazim appeared, and the Prophet ﷺ appeared. Grandshaykh said, "I am going to bring your two brothers' spirits here." I saw my brothers coming, but as a reflection. This was the same way that Mawlana Shaykh Nazim and the Prophet ﷺ appeared. One cannot explain how they appeared and with what blessings. It is a secret and there is no permission to speak about it.

He said, "Give your hand to Shaykh Nazim." I and my two brothers put our hands on Shaykh Nazim's, Grandshaykh put his hand over all, and the Prophet ﷺ read by himself:

> **Those who receive initiation from you receive initiation from God; God's hand is over their hands; whoever takes back his initiation, he is going to lose; and whoever keeps the promise that he made to God, God will keep that person.**[139]

At that time we were under something like a shelter or a canopy. Grandshaykh said, "The previous one was the imitation of an initiation; this is a true initiation."

I was alone again with Grandshaykh, and he said, "Look at them, still trying to revive you, but now they have lost hope concerning you. Your soul is in my hand, and I can still bring you back. Now, I am going to review your life from your birth until now, see whatever sins you made, and judge you. I shall judge everything!" He did not say "what good you made." They don't look at the good. We have to know this: good is from them and bad is from us. This is *adab*.

> *Whoever finds good, let him praise God, and whoever finds otherwise, let him blame no one but himself.*[140]

---

[139] Suratu 'l-Fath, 48:10
[140] Muslim, #24 in Nawawi's Forty.

I was brought back through all my ages, as if I was living the same life a second time. One second of the man taking ablution near the river was seven years for the man standing next to him (see "Passing of the World Through the Needle's Eye" on page 231). This happened to me, except that one second for me was thirty-five years. I saw everything again from the beginning, as if I lived it another time. I was seeing, hearing, feeling, and living it completely.

These are saintly people. They do whatever they like. Allah has given them power. God's knowledge is so big, so extensive. No one knows Him. Not even the Prophet Muhammad ﷺ knows all that Allah has bestowed.

Say: "The Unseen is only for Allah (to know)."[141]

there is something unseen except by Allah, and even the Prophet ﷺ does not know it, although the Prophet ﷺ knows many of what is *ghayb*, many unseen things. Yet there is something reserved for Allah—or else the Prophet ﷺ would be a partner with Allah, and Allah has no partners! Yet Wahhabis—ignorant people—call us "associationists." Allah has no partner, but Allah gave many things to the Prophet ﷺ and to the saints. Do not underestimate the power Allah gave them.

Grandshaykh brought me back to the first hour my mother gave me birth, and I lived and saw everything again. Then he said, "I am sending you back for your operation, but I shall be taking you again another time." He disappeared for some time, I went back, and they did the operation. When they finished and tried to wake me up, he took my spirit back another time. He said, "Now, I am ordering you to keep everything right. Do not mess things up another time! You have some things left to do in this life and so I must send you back. But remember anytime that

---

[141] Surah Yunus, 10:20.

I want to, it is in our hand to take your life." He sent me back and I could hear my brother calling me, "Hisham, Hisham!"

Overwhelming Consciousness

For forty days I did not know what I was saying. Everyone who sat with me said, "That man is crazy." No one understood what I was saying. I was mad, but mad in the Sufi way, not as mentally sick people are. I was speaking about the knowledge of Sufis and their teaching.

They said, "He is crazy and does not know what he is saying." Yet I knew, but no one understood except Shaykh 'Adnan, my brother. I was dressed with that state for forty days: not sleeping, sitting always with Mawlana Grandshaykh, knowing. After forty days, they took that state away and threw it into the heart. When they put it in the heart, you come back to your normal station, but now you can speak through them. Before that time, all the particles in your body are speaking. I was feeling everything in my body saying something! What could one listen to? I heard everything at the same time, and every cell was saying something different. And you could hear all of their discourses without one overlapping the other. You could understand what all of them were saying.

This is the power of the saints. They can hear everyone at the same time. If millions speak at the same time through their heart, they can hear them. No one interferes with the other's channel. This is the nature of their connection, this is how they reach everyone. That state lasted for forty days. When it is generalized in your body, you are finished and people call you crazy. When it comes back to the heart, it reaches perfection.

May Allah give us the blessings of this day. May Allah show us the power of our shaykh, make him love us, and shelter us in his shelter, the shelter of the Prophet ﷺ, the shelter of our

God. Allah is the Creator. *Allahu Akbar, Allahu Akbar, Allahu Akbar*! God is great! No one knows how great.

☽

There Is Only One Main Station

In every association, we have to ask support from the main station. If there is no support, we cannot say anything. Without connection through the hearts, it will be difficult to speak. Inspirations are coming spontaneously. If they do not, they are not inspirations but are considered a composed lecture or book. Inspirations must come from the main station, and do not think there are many main stations. Allah has created only one, and you can never have two, or three, or more main stations. All saints, when they want to speak, have to connect themselves to that main station. If that main station does not support them and give them power to speak, then they are helpless and cannot say anything.

God sometimes causes one of His servants who is giving a talk not to receive support anymore, in order to tell him, "Do not be proud of yourself; if it were not for Us, you are nothing! We are giving that power to you; you are not gaining it through your progress. Whenever We want to take it away, We take it away and stop it. You must know that you are depending on Us. We are independent. I am not in need of anything: you are in need of Me. Therefore, when I want to disconnect you, I disconnect you. When I want to give you that power, I give it to you. Do not see it as coming from you. Surrender to Me! When you surrender, I give you all powers. When you surrender, I will be you, and you will be Me. I cannot be One and you Another. There must be One only, at all times."

If there are two, it means that you are "here" and He is "there"—then you cannot take any benefit. Allah has created us in a perfect way. He is the Creator (al-Khaliq) and there is His creation (al-'alam). What is in between? There is a great secret which we describe in a symbolic way as al-Barzakh, a bridge. What is that bridge?

We Are Images of Our Lord in This World

When Allah created human beings, how—through what power—did they appear in this world? He has created prophets and saints, and these prophets and saints stood one face towards God and one face towards creation. When you look into a mirror, you see yourselves. Can I say that the one in the mirror is not you? It is you, but not the perfect you. The perfect you is outside, the imperfect one is in the mirror: it does not see, it does not hear, it does not feel.

How did Allah create human beings? The Prophet ﷺ said:

God created Adam in His form.[142]

This is one of the greatest secrets. When you look at yourself in the mirror, you see yourself there—not any differently but with the same eyes, ears, hands, feet. Yet within that mirror your reflected self cannot see, cannot hear and cannot feel.

In this world, we are pictures of our Lord. God is All-Perfect, encompassing all creation. In every human being, He is manifesting; in every tree He is manifesting, and so forth. That is: you can see one of His images there, and that is the reason they appear. Whatever objects you see in this world are images—or attributes—showing you your Lord's Manifestation. For there is a mirror facing the Creator, and whatever you see reflects, according to the Attribute of His Face,[ix] through the mirror, causing these Attributes to manifest in this world. Accordingly God's appearance is in everyone, and

---

[142] Bukhari, Muslim, Ahmad, Humaydi, Ibn 'Asakir, Ibn Hajar, al-'Iraqi, Ibn Abi 'Asim, Bayhaqi from Jabir.

everyone must be considered as perfect as Allah's reflection and image.

That image cannot know everything but it knows itself. And God causes it to know precisely what He wants it to know, and no more. It is for that reason that the image cannot know God, for it knows only the limited knowledge that God wants it to know and no more. But the mirror facing the Creator, and through which creation is appearing, that mirror is a perfect one, and this is the perfect human being, al-Insanu'l-Kamil.

When a saint reaches perfection, he becomes a mirror of his Lord, and through him, God can manifest His appearance in this world. Without that intermediary, God will not manifest in this world. He has created 124,000 saints, and out of them 7,007 high saints, the Naqshbandi saints of our path, and out of them 313 higher in level, out of which forty are the highest, presided by five of them, out of whom there is the one for whom all stand in need and next to whom all are as nothing. No matter how many zeros you add to one it remains oe, and without it all else remains zero. Therefore nothing exists if that one is not there. That one is the mirror of God in every century.

In every century there must be one saint above all saints—that is the perfect one through whom all appearances come into this world, and by means of whom all appearances in this world are manifestations of God's Attributes. The saint who looks at all creation, therefore, respects all creation. If he does not respect it, he is disrespectful to his Lord and cannot remain at the station of perfection.

The Seven Powers of the Perfect Saint

Allah has dressed that saint with seven powers. These seven powers are in everyone, but the difference is that we were unable to use them and reach the station that he has reached. These seven powers are the seven essential attributes of God. God has ninety-nine Divine Names according to Scriptures; one thousand Divine Names according to some saints; and according to Naqshbandi saints an infinite number of Divine Names.

Every single object, including a simple tea-cup, is the manifestation of an attribute of God. If God's Power did not appear in the tea-cup, the tea-cup would never appear. It would never exist.

God gave human beings more than all creation. Unfortunately, human beings are not using those powers. He gave them a secret that no one understood except very few saints of this century. That secret was opened only recently, and permission was granted to speak openly about it. It was kept hidden until now.

Allah is the Ever-Living, al-Hayy, an essential attribute which Allah has given to everyone. He has given that secret to you, and you are living. You might or might not be generous: generosity is not, therefore, an essential attribute. As Allah has given of the attribute of the Ever-Living, He is asking you, "Why can you not be ever-living as I am ever-living?" This is the first power we have in ourselves.

Why did Allah give us seven essential attributes? Our saintly master, Shaykh Muhammad Nazim al-Haqqani, may God raise him ever higher, said:

> Everything is based on love. Because God loved human beings more than the rest of creation, He gave them more. The first step to understanding, therefore, is love. If there is no love, we cannot use these attributes which God has given to us.

And he recited:

If there is no love,

then you never wept at the sight of ruins;

nor at the thought of children

and country.

If there was no love,

I would never feel my Lover.[143]

The lover of saints is their Lord, and the lovers of God are His saints. Lovers and their Beloved are connected, as men and women who love each other connect themselves with a sacred bond. If they are breaking that bond easily, it means there is no love other than imitation. Love means that, if she says, "I have a pain here," he must feel that pain in himself; and if the husband says that he feels pain, she must feel it also. That is true love, and that love exists only with saints. Saints feel the miseries of every creature in creation. That is why they are full of love.

When God first created us, He loved us. When He loved us, He honored us with these seven essential attributes which He gave us but which He did not give to animals, the first attribute being: Ever-Living. Use that power! No one is using it, because we are running away from our Lover. How do we run away from the One to Whom we should throw ourselves and for Whom we should sacrifice ourselves in order to make Him happy? That is what saints and prophets did, and they are ever-living. For that reason one of the names of the Prophet ﷺ is ad-Da'im al-Baqi, the Everliving. This name is applied to all prophets and saints. They do not alter in their graves, even after hundreds and hundreds of years. This has been observed recently even in Singapore, an atheist country, where they could not open a highway over the grave of a saint who was buried near a small mosque. They took the grave apart and as soon as they opened the main coffin, light came from it, bystanders smelled a delicious fragrance and some fell unconscious. Others could see the saint lying intact and fresh,

---

[143] The Poem of the Cloak (*Qasidat al-Burdah*) of Imam Busayri.

as if he had been buried that day. I observed this phenomenon with another saint, in Lebanon, by the name of Sa'd ad-Din Hasan al-Jibawi.[144]

This happens because these persons are ever-living. If even the body is ever-living, what about the spirit? The spirit is everlasting. Allah has dressed everyone with that life and said, "This is My main attribute and I am sharing it with you." He is sharing it with you because He loves us. You share everything with your wife because you love her, and you don't ask her to pay you for it! You give her without asking.

Allah said:

My earth and my heaven contain Me not, but the heart of a believer contains Me.

Look at heavens and stars, and look at this small heart: how can it contain what the firmament cannot contain? This means that we are referring to knowledge and the true nature of the heart, in relation to which the galaxies, constellations, and billions of stars are nothing. If the Creator can be contained within the heart of a believer, what do you think of the power of this believer then, this saint? He can be anywhere and see anything. And this goes for everyone, but we are not trying to work with it. Surrender, and you will take this power; do not surrender, and you will never take it.

Allah is never going to leave those that left job, family, and everything in order to surrender. This is not a surrender to us or to our shaykh; when they accept such surrender, it means that those who surrendered are in reality surrendering to God. We are nothing: we are no higher than the dust on these shoes, because we are ignorant. As much as we go up there is more. What do

---

[144] See "Miracles in the Naqshbandi Way" in Book 1, page 64.

you know? You know nothing. But surrender comes after love. If there is not complete love and complete devotion to that person, it is not possible to surrender. Why did Romeo surrender to Juliet and Juliet surrender to Romeo? Because there was complete love and complete devotion. This is what is required.

THE SEVEN FOREMOST NAMES OF GOD

Obey God, obey the Prophet, and obey those in authority among you.[145]

As we said before about Allah's creation of human beings, Allah has created human beings and honored them; and when He honored them, He trusted them. When you honor someone, you trust them as a good person. When God created us, he honored us by saying:

We have honored the children of Adam.[146]

The children of Adam (as) means all human beings without discrimination. All human beings: red or yellow, white or black, different nationalities. In God's sight, there are no differences. All are the same.

When God created us and created heaven and earth, He created us to know him. Without that creation, we would never be able to know our Lord. Allah gave us two feet, two hands, two feet, two eyes—why two of all these and not one? There must be a secret there. Our master said, "The reason is to show us that God has created everything in pairs." Trees and flowers have only one stem or one trunk. But anything in creation endowed with a mind, Allah has created them with two hands, two feet, two eyes, two ears. Allah created solids without life. From His light, through the Ocean of Power, he caused inanimate objects to appear. He distinguished nature from stone and solids by adding

---

[145] Suratu 'n-Nisa, 4:59.
[146] Suratu 'l-Isra, 17:70.

life from the attribute al-Hayy (the Ever-Living) to that light from the Ocean of Power. Therefore nature has two powers: first, existence, since solids are existing; and secondly, above it, life, from the secret of the Ever-Living.

Human beings were even more honored, because they were given not only existence and life, but also mind and heart. As the Prophet ﷺ said:

God has created Adam ﷺ in His form.

Human beings are therefore pictures of God. You can see God through them. But not every human being—only those whom God has dressed with a power. Who are they and what is that power?

Seven Names or Attributes of God explain Him. The rest of the ninety-nine Names express a non-living quality, such as Generosity (al-Kareem), Patience (as-Sabur), Tolerance (al-Haleem), Providence (ar-Razzaq)... But God's essential Names are seven, and He has dressed human beings with those Names. As the Prophet ﷺ said in this hadith:

My servant (or slave) does not cease to approach me through voluntary worship or good manners, until I shall love him. And when I love him, I will be, at that time, the ears that he can hear with, the eyes that he can see with, the hand that he can feel with, the feet that he can walk with. If he asks Me, I give to him; if he seeks refuge in Me, I protect him.[147]

And the saying:

O My servant! I am the One who can say to a thing "Be!" and it will be. Obey Me and I will make you able to say to something,

---

[147] Bukhari.

"Be!" and it will be. I am the Ever-living who does not die. Obey Me and I will make you living, never dying.[148]

One of the foremost Names of God, therefore, is Love. In Arabic the term is Al-Hawa, but in the sense of *Al-hubb al-'udhri*, virginal love, innocent love, pure love. Thus saints consider that God is love, and that one of His names is Al-Hawa signifying Complete Love. The hadith says that when God loves someone, He gives him life. That life comes from the name al-Hayy, the Ever-Living. The first of the seven Names, therefore, is al-Hayy.

We also have life: Allah gave us from that ocean and from that secret. For that reason, if a person reaches perfection and sainthood, that person never dies but is always alive. They are alive even in the grave. That is why the Prophet ﷺ said, "I am fresh and alive in my grave!" And he said, *"All prophets are fresh and alive in their graves,"*[149] and so are all saints. When you reach perfection, how are you going to die? It is impossible. God has given you living power from the Name of al-Hayy, as mentioned in the saying.

After giving you love and life, He said: "I give you hearing." This is from the ocean of as-Sami', the All-Hearing. For:

Everything in this creation is praising God, but you cannot hear their praising.[150]

Why? Because we have not reached that level of hearing. You can reach it when you are dressed with hearing power from the Ever-Hearing, Who hears unceasingly.

These attributes are not like the other names such as the Generous. There is life in them and something of it also comes to

---

[148] An *athar* (narration) related by Ibn Taymiyya.
[149] *Majma'u 'z-Zawa'id* vol.8, pg. 211.
[150] Suratu 'l-Isra, 17:44.

human beings. You might not be generous or forbearing, but all human beings are endowed with hearing. Everyone is alive, but not everyone is a provider for people, not everyone is patient, not everyone has good manners. Yet the secret of al-Hayy is with you; why are you not using it? He gave you the power of life; He gave you the power of hearing. These attributes were given to every human being, whereas others were given less generally and more selectively.

God gave you vision from the Name al-Baseer, the All-Seeing. Then He gave you power from the Name al-Qadir, the All-Powerful. He gave power to human beings to subjugate nature completely, including the skies in heaven. al-Muqtadir, the Almighty, is another Name from that ocean of power. Then He gave you from the Name al-'Alim, the All-Knowing. By giving you the mind, He gave you the power to know and understand everything. Then He made you light from the ocean of an-Nur, the Light. He gave that to your heart. These are the seven attributes to which the hadith refers.

An-Nur, al-'Alim, al-Muqtadir, al-Qadir, al-Baseer, as-Sami', al-Hayy—The Light, The Knowing, The Mighty, the Powerful, the Seeing, the Hearing, the Living.

"I will be he." He did not say "We will be together," for that would be partnership and Allah has no partners. "I will be he" means that "this person has vanished and no longer exists in My Presence." It means, "he is nothing, and the only One appearing through him is I." The words *"hatta yakunu rabbaniyyan,"* do not mean, "until he becomes God," but they mean "until he becomes a representative of Me" so that "when he says to something 'Be!' it will be."

Our master said that when saints reach the level of these seven Names, they reach the level of perfection. God gave this perfection to everyone without exception. But we are still ignorant of everything. We know something or other, but we remain ignorant until we know everything and reach that level. The saints who reach the station of perfection entailed by that level vanish. They know that they are nothing and that these are God's Attributes they are carrying. When they carry them with ego, that causes them to appear separately from God; but when the ego vanishes, this light goes back to its origin. That is why they no longer see themselves, but see only God. There is no more X, Y and Z there. When they reach the station of perfection, there is only God in their eyes. Also, God appears through them: that is why they pull people to themselves through their heart: they are "appearances" of God on earth. Grandshaykh said, "At that time, the saint will be a mirror of God's reflection. He will be a mirror of God for human beings, and human beings can know their Lord through that person."

The saint has reached the level of the seven Names of God which God gave to all human beings, the Attributes of the name Allah, which encompass all other attributes because there is life and motion in them. We go back to the saying "God created Adam—meaning human beings—on His image" and that he gave us everyone of these organs of hearing, seeing, doing, and walking, in pairs. The meaning of this is that of all things there is always two sides: external and internal, material and spiritual. You cannot take one and leave the other, but you must take both. Just as you need two ears, two eyes, two hands, and two feet, you need internal knowledge-spirituality—and external knowledge—laws and obligations and good manners.

The Duality of Creation and Knowledge

You cannot come to God with external knowledge alone. You must have both types of knowledge. When you read God's word, the Holy Qur'an, you must not read the way ignorant people read, seeing only letters and words. This is not knowledge. You must read with meditation, *tafakkur*, because Allah gave the Prophet ﷺ the Qur'an through revelation coming to his heart, not written statements. It is not even inspiration, but revelation, *"manazil,"* meaning a descent into levels from one station to a lower station, until it reaches us at the lowest station of understanding. Scholars, when they read Qur'an, read it at the lowest station of understanding.

If you read Qur'an verse by verse through the heart and not through the tongue:

> ***Praise be to Allah, the God of human beings, or Lord of the worlds!***[151]

This is the ordinary meaning, is it not? This is the meaning that has reached us. But if you go through that verse with the hearing and the vision that He gave you, and with light from His Light, the meaning you understand will be completely different.

A saint is a representative of God. If God had not trusted him, He would never have made him a representative. God said:

> ***We have made human beings representatives and successors to Us on this earth.***[152]

Whoever can reach this level, he can represent God. For that reason, saints are representatives of God, and people can know their Lord through these saints. There are deeper meanings into which we cannot go: many people would not accept them, and they might listen and reject in their heart. One day, this knowledge will appear.

One day, God said to Moses ﷺ when he came to Mount Sinai:

---

[151] Suratu 'l-Fatihah,1:12. Arabic: *Al-hamdulillahi Rabbi 'l-'alameen.*
[152] cf. Suratu 'l-Baqarah, 2:30, Surah Sad, 38:26, Suratu 'l-An'am, 6:165, Surah Yunus, 10:14 and 73, Suratu 'l-Fatir, 35:39, Suratu 'l-A'raf, 7:69 and 74, Suratu 'n-Naml:27,62.

O Moses, I am your Lord, take off your shoes, you are in the sacred valley of Tuwa![153]

Why is Allah telling him to take off his shoes? How did he come to this valley? Was he flying or walking? When you want to reach your Lord you walk. When you walk, you use both legs. You cannot come on one leg alone. To saints, the two legs represent the two kinds of knowledges: external and internal. Moses ﷺ coming to God means Moses ﷺ reaching to the highest level of perfection, for no one can approach and meet his Lord if he did not reach the highest level. As Moses ﷺ was approaching through worship, externally and internally, he reached a level wherein he was able to talk with God—not seeing Him yet. When he reached that level, God told him, "Take away your shoes in My Presence."

These shoes are the shoes of ignorance and stupidity. When someone reaches God, he cannot reach him with ignorance and stupidity. That is the reason of His order, "Remove your shoes: Cast off ignorance." Understand that shoes are made of animal skin. In that time, they were using the skins of donkey to make shoes. Donkeys represent absolute ignorance and stupidity. "By wearing these shoes, you are coming to My presence carrying complete ignorance: if you want to reach the highmost station, take it away! If you take that ignorance away, I will open My vision to you." After God ordered Moses ﷺ to take off his shoes and Moses ﷺ was able to talk to God then:

When Moses came to the place appointed by Us, and his Lord addressed him, He said: "O my Lord!

---

[153] Surah Taha, 20:11-12

show (Thyself) to me, that I may look upon thee." [154]

He said, "O my Lord! Since I am talking to You, let me see You!" He said, "Let me see You" because there was no more ignorance at that point and he had reached perfection. But it is too late. You came to God still carrying ignorance with you— although he is a high prophet. When he asked God for a more advanced station—vision is more than hearing—God said, "O Moses ﷺ, you cannot see Me"—because you came with ignorance still—"but look at the mountain. If that mountain keeps its position after I look at it and does not disappear under My blessing, then you can see Me." That is, "Look at the mountain of your ego. Look at the biggest barrier between Me and you. Let that barrier melt like ice! Then you can see Me. As long as that barrier is there you cannot see Me." And when God looked at that mountain, Moses' ﷺ ego, Moses ﷺ fell down unconscious because of the vision and the power of the vision of God on his ego and his heart.

Moses ﷺ melted and disappeared. He was not able to raise his head. "*Sa'iqan*" is the word used in Arabic to denote death from electric shock. (Consider the foreshadowing in Holy Qur'an of a technical term used today. Everything is electricity and energy. All this creation, every single cell, consists of energy in the form of electrons moving at high speeds.) Moses ﷺ suffered an electric shock from that light—lightning rather than electricity—which God sent on his heart to break his ego down. It is not an ordinary death but a death from shock. Moses ﷺ was finished. He died completely, vanished in Him completely—there is no Moses ﷺ anymore, there is no human being anymore. When saints become immersed in the plenitude of that light, there is no

---

[154] Suratu 'l-A'araf, 7:143.

more X or Y or Z there. There is a *sa'iqan*, an electric shock, and in seclusion you are going to experience an electric shock. When a saint puts you in a seclusion, he is going to give you an electric shock to smash and kill your ego completely. When that ego is smashed, he gives you complete life again. "When he came back," or, "When Allah brought him back to himself," meaning, "After I gave him existence through My existence—now he knows there is no Moses ﷺ, there is only I—he became a mirror for Me, a true representative of Mine, he became Me," as in the aforementioned hadith, *"until he says to something 'Be!' and it will be."*

He woke up another time, now in a different station. He went from the station of ego and ignorance, coming to God through external and internal knowledge. When external knowledge is not pure, it brings a lot of ignorance with it. That is why Allah said to him, "You have reached Me through your ignorance, but why did you not remove it before coming to Me? Remove it now. But you cannot see Me unless I give that electric shock to the ego represented by the mountain."

The mountain is the ego—not, as they say in ordinary explanation, a mere mountain at which God is looking. God looked at Moses' ﷺ heart and broke it into pieces. When Moses ﷺ was broken down into pieces, he woke up in God. After he woke up in God, Allah sent him to his people. Only after that time did Moses ﷺ get his commandments, as a true representative of God. Anyone who looked at Moses ﷺ then saw the manifestation of God.

Anyone who looked at Jesus ﷺ saw the manifestation of God. That is what confused Christians. Anyone who looked at the Prophet Muhammad ﷺ saw the manifestation of God. For that he said:

Whoever saw me saw me the Truth (al-Haqq).[155]

Anyone who looks at saints sees God. Because Jesus ﷺ came to God differently than Moses ﷺ, more powerfully and without ignorance, he was able to reflect God more directly, and that confused the people. When Muhammad ﷺ came, he came in a higher and more perfect state: at the same time that he was with God, he was with the people completely. That is the highest level. That is why he said:

I have a time with my Lord and a time with creation.

And again:

I have two sides: one facing my Lord, and one facing creation.[156]

This is a state of most high perfection.

May Allah make us know and understand these secrets of high Sufi knowledge and inspirations that our shaykh is sending to us and instructing us to explain. *Insha'-Allah* this knowledge is going to be spread far and wide in a very short time with the support of Mahdi ﷺ and the help of his spiritual power. May Allah bless us with these inspirations and bestow more and more to our hearts. May Allah raise our saint—our shaykh—higher and higher in his levels and stations.

---

[155] *Musnad* Ahmad, 11096.
[156] Qushayri.

PASSING OF THE WORLD THROUGH THE NEEDLE'S EYE

When the Prophet ﷺ went in the night of Ascension (Laylat al-Isra' wal-Mi'raj) and was approaching his Lord, he reached a place where Archangel Gabriel ؑ (the Holy Spirit) said, "I cannot go any further. This is my limit."ˣ The Prophet ﷺ proceeded to leave our time and penetrate into Allah's "time." He went through five stations or levels. When they asked him about those levels, he said:

> *There are five hundred of Allah's years between each station of paradise,*[157]

And Allah said:

> **a Day the length whereof will be [like] a thousand years of your reckoning.**[158]

In human time, the Prophet's ﷺ journey took him five times five hundred times three hundred and fifty times one thousand years!

Was he going through empty space? Was there no creation there, only a void? There are creations, and he was penetrating through their time. In one night, he was the Prophet for all these stations. How long did he live there? With every creation through which he passed, he lived a complete life. To us, in one second he penetrated everything. But Allah stretched that second and made

---

[157] as-Suyuti, Ibn Kathir, Ibn Qayyim.
[158] Suratu 's-Sajdah, 32:5.

it so immense as to enable him to live 500 of Allah's years. In a short time, he lived through a very long time.

God can make the camel go through the eye of a needle without making the universe smaller and without making the eye of the needle larger.[159] How will you understand that? And how to explain it?

Power of the Shaykh

One day two disciples of Sayyidina 'Ubaydullah al-Ahrar, one of the saints of the Golden Chain, were making ablution at the river-shore. One of them was saying, "*Subhanallah*, God is great, and our shaykh is great! Allah has said in his Holy Book that He can make the camel go through the eye of a needle without making the universe smaller and without making the eye of the needle larger. And our shaykh has this power! He can do this." The other one was not yet a good disciple. He mumbled, "For Allah, fine, we can understand; but for our shaykh...?" As soon as he said this, he slipped into the river and found himself in a completely deserted place. He started walking until he reached a village and asked where he was. He was told that he was seven months away from his original spot. At that time there were no cars or other such means of transportation. Who put him there?

That was the power of the shaykh. The disciple had been thrown there: be careful not to be thrown! In the village, he found a blacksmith. He asked for some food and the blacksmith said, "Yes, but you have to work for me." He used him for one year and found him a very trustworthy person, so he gave him his daughter in marriage. After seven years, he found himself with five children. He was reflecting after all that time how he got there, and said, "*Subhanallah*, all this because I made a mistake with my shaykh."

---

[159] C.f. Suratu 'l-A'araf, 7:40.

Don't make any mistake with your shaykh! If they say that he can make this earth pass through the eye of a needle, say "Yes!" What are you going to lose? Nothing. Why then say no? If he says, "This is black," say "it is black"; "this is white," say "it is white." What is going to happen? Nothing. You will be raised. It is better than to stay in your level. Better to be in higher levels than in lower. So say, "Yes, *Na'am! Sadaqta ya sayyidee*," as Sayyidina Abu Bakr as-Siddiq ؓ kept saying to the Prophet ﷺ, "Yes! You have said the truth, O Prophet ﷺ!" But no; they want you to fight your shaykh. They want you to say that they are wrong and you are right. Right about what? You are full with ego, you are sitting in your own waste, and you dare ask, "From where is that bad smell coming?"

Do not dare to speak about your shaykh? Whatever the shaykh does or says, say, "*Amanna wa sadaqna*—we believe and we bear witness to the truth." This will give you more power. But it is hard for someone to say "Yes, you are right," for the ego whispers to you to say, "No, he is wrong and you know better than him. His age is eighty and your age is thirty: you know better! How can you say yes?"

When Shaykh 'Ubaydullah saw that his disciple understood and accepted, he appeared to him and told him: your doubt cost you seven years and five children! I am bringing all of your family back so that people will believe. In one second he found himself back in the water into which he had slipped seven years before, but only one second of his life had elapsed. He came back home and saw his family and five children running towards him.

The shaykh can reach anywhere in space and time without impediment. If you give him complete trust and complete faith, your faith will effect the miracle. If you don't have faith, and if you have any doubt, it will not lead to the best result. Complete faith in the shaykh will get you whatever you like.

The Last Seven Breaths

"When you are giving away your seven last breaths, Allah can elongate them," our shaykh said, "up to 137 years. He will never send you away from this world except with complete and perfected worship." In our eyes your last breath may take one second, but in the eyes of saints and the Prophet ﷺ and Allah, it can go up to 137 years of complete and perfect worship.

We were asking whether the Prophet ﷺ was travelling through empty spaces or spaces full of creation. When he was moving with the speed that traverses 500 years of Allah's reckoning, he covered immense space. When the Prophet ﷺ was passing through those spaces, Allah at that time brought their creation into being. The Prophet ﷺ, therefore, was the key for that creation. The Prophet's ﷺ passing through time and space is like the code that effects creation within it. Such is the creation of this earth from nothing to "Be!" and it was.

Allah is so great that no one can reach His Greatness, even the Prophet Muhammad ﷺ. Allah is great above everything. This is to clarify the understanding of what I am going to say next. For the Prophet ﷺ was as manifesting the Attributes of God for this creation. Such is the wisdom with which Allah sent him to His presence.

> *Say, "O my servants who have transgressed against themselves, do not despair of the mercy of Allah!"*[160]

Allah said, "***Say: O my servants!***" He did not say, "Say: O Allah's servants!" He is talking to the Prophet ﷺ. Yet later in the verse, he speaks of Himself in the third person, "***Do not despair of the mercy of Allah.***" Why did He not use the third person for

---

[160] Suratu 'z-Zumar, 39:53.

"my servants" also? And why did He not say, "Do not despair of My mercy?" This means, "O Prophet ﷺ, these are your servants. Tell them not to be disappointed in Allah's Mercy." There are two subjects, one here, one there. The sense is therefore, "O Prophet, tell your servants not to despair of Allah's Mercy." If Allah wanted to refer these servants to Himself, He would say to the Prophet ﷺ, "O Prophet, tell My servants not to despair of My Mercy." We are, therefore, servants of the Prophet ﷺ.

A saint came to Madinah one day. Everyone was praying towards *qiblah*. He was praying in the direction of the grave of the Prophet ﷺ. They came to him and said, "You have to pray towards the Ka'bah, are you praying to the Prophet ﷺ?" He said, "Of course I am praying towards the direction of the Prophet ﷺ!" He continued: "If not for the Prophet ﷺ, how would I know about the Ka'bah! The Prophet will pray towards the Ka'bah, and I shall pray towards him! It will reach. But if I myself pray towards Ka'bah, where will it reach?"

It means "I am directing myself towards the one whom I know. He will direct himself towards his Lord."

Earth, Moon and Sun

The moon represents, in Sufi teachings, the saint who is always facing the Prophet ﷺ, never swerving from his presence. The sun is the Seal of Prophets ﷺ and the Seal of Saints is the moon. They always face each other. Without the Seal of Prophets, there are no reflections on this earth. And without the Seal of Saints, there are no reflections on earth. Reflections follow a route from God to the Prophet ﷺ—as the Prophet ﷺ is the mirror of God, the Other Face of God—and from the Prophet ﷺ to the Seal of Saints. What is "the Other Face"? Just as we can see only one side of the moon, the bright side, while the other side is dark, similarly we can only see the manifestation of God: that is the

Prophet ﷺ. What we see of God's manifestation is the Prophet ﷺ! No one can see God Himself.

The side that is reflecting God's light towards us, then, is the Prophet ﷺ. But even that reflected light cannot shine upon us directly: no one can behold it. It is reflected yet another time, therefore, to the other mirror which is the Seal of Saints. Having descended from God to the mirror of the Prophet ﷺ, the light of God then goes from the Prophet ﷺ to the mirror of the Seal of Saints.

The five poles, *qutbs*, or great saints, are responsible for providing the knowledge and carrying the burden of *shafa'a*, intercession. The Prophet ﷺ is "distributing" himself into them as into five points or powers. Every power represents a part of him in every century. This is the secret of the meaning of:

It must be known to you that the Prophet is among you at all times.[161]

It is in this sense also that the Prophet ﷺ said in hadith, "*I have one hour with my Lord and one hour with creation,*"[xi] and, "*I have one side facing my Lord, and one side facing creation.*"

Records of human history begin, at the earliest, seven thousand years ago. But they have discovered some bones now, and they say, human beings existed millions of years ago. If so, where are the records of their civilization? Were they so dumb as not to leave a scrap of their passage over millions of years, when only in one hundred years we are capable of such a civilization as ours? Allah has brought people and removed them.

When we read Fatiha, we read:

Owner of the Day of Judgment.[162]

---

[161] Suratu 'l-Hujurat, 49:7.

We have to know which judgment. Has Allah only one Day of Judgment? That is the common understanding. Allah's Words mean continuity! They are never stopping. As His creation never stops, so it is with His Day of Judgment. Every second there is a Day of Judgment. Every moment, Allah is creating and He is judging. This is God's Greatness: He creates on one side and He judges on the other—unceasingly.

When Sayyidina Khidr ؑ asked Archangel Gabriel ؑ, "O Gabriel ؑ, do you know when Allah sent Adam ؑ?" Archangel Gabriel ؑ said, "Which Adam ؑ are you talking about?" Khidr ؑ said, "Is there any Adam ؑ other than this Adam ؑ?" Archangel Gabriel ؑ said, "I know of 124,000 Adams ؑ. They came, they had their creation, they had their Judgment Day, and they left. The Adam ؑ you are referring to is the last Adam ؑ. Before him, 123,999 Adams ؑ came. This is what I know: I saw their creation and I saw their judgment. I asked my Lord one day and said, 'O my Lord, can you show me Your creation since the beginning, and can you show me where it ends?' And Allah opened to me an ocean of which there is no beginning and of which there is no end! An ocean like a desert, all full of grains like sand, and each grain of sand was in itself a complete universe such as the one you see, made of heaven and earth, suns and stars as far as the eye can see. What you consider a universe is a grain of sand in relation to the ocean of Allah's creation!"

"A green bird alights there every day and his food is one grain of sand of that creation. As soon as the bird puts one grain of sand in his mouth, Allah creates a creation by saying 'Be!' and it will be. This whole universe is but a grain of sand to this green bird, which he takes into his mouth. That bird is the Prophet Muhammad ﷺ, and every grain of sand he puts in his mouth is a

---

Continued from previous page ...
[162] Suratu 'l-Fatiha, 1:4.

complete creation with its beginning, its end, and its judgment day. What then are you asking me about?"

No one knows the secret of *"**Maliki yawmi 'd-deen— Owner of the Day of Judgment.**"* Allah is continuously creating and continuously taking back everything back to its origin. In relation to what we know and think, we are still babies. Our knowledge is nothing compared to the knowledge of saints of the Golden Chain, or to the knowledge of the Prophet , or to the knowledge of God.

May Allah open for us the way to our hearts and give us from the wisdom of this knowledge, and bless us.

"He Is Closer to You than Your Jugular Vein"

The question of God's Essential Attributes opens a large ocean in which saints drown and out of which they cannot come back once they enter it. Once, our shaykh was concentrating on one of God's Names, as-Sabur, the last of the attributes according to tradition. In every century since the beginning of creation until now, God has sent His blessings through His Attributes. On this earth, only ninety-nine Attributes were sent. Above the station of this worldly life, there are endless numbers of Attributes. If this world were to carry more than ninety-nine Names it would vanish. That is why saints, after reaching the ocean of these Attributes and entering it, try to go above and reach the ocean of endless Attributes.

Our shaykh had entered the ocean of all ninety-eight Attributes, and he was trying now to enter the ocean of the ninety-ninth. When you "enter," it is understood that you must see, and hear, and feel, and taste. If you do not, then you are still in the imitative life, in the life of images and not in the real life yet, although Allah has given everyone the power to be connected with His reality. As soon as our shaykh took the first step into that ocean through the meditation of his heart, he heard God addressing Him, saying, "O my servant, if you enter that Name, you will never go back to your life in this world. Leave that Name. It is not the time."

Some saints, when they try to enter these oceans, accept that God take their life and make them pass into the next life, because this body cannot carry that light, just as a 120-volt lamp will burn if you give it 360 volts. Our body cannot carry deep knowledge except when you prepare it through seclusion and training. At that time, if you can see something which Allah is showing you, you can carry it.

As I said before, the seven Names are the essential, basic Names of God. Al-Hayy: the Ever-Living One. Since He loves us, He gave us life and He let us share in this Attribute. It does not mean partnership. He dressed us with this Attribute that is essential to him. It is essential because it is part of everyone's creation, unlike, as we said, generosity, patience, and so forth. The attribute of the Ever-Living, as its name indicates, points to life with God and not just in this life. When one vanishes to this world, destroys oneself, surrender and submit to His will, at that time one is "*la 'aynuhu wa la ghayruhu*—neither He nor another." You cannot say about that servant whether he is still human or not. He is His Lord's image in a perfect mirror. God has dressed him with His Attributes. That is why you cannot take your gaze away when you look at a saint. You no longer see them.

One night after midnight, I woke up and I went to make ablution. It is an obligation, if you open your eyes at night while in seclusion, to get up and do ablution immediately; even if it kills you, you must get up and, if you must, die in ablution. I got up and I passed by Grandshaykh's room. His door was open and he was making *dhikr*...

Some saints have a power to go wherever their mind likes them to go. They can travel a billion light-years' distance in a single instant. In that state, if your mind thinks of the seventh heaven, you will be there in body as well, at the same moment. As for the heart, there is no limit: hearts will go to the Divine Presence. Everything we know about heaven and earth and the universe is limited. What is unseen to the eyes, however, is seen to the heart. There are saints, therefore, that can penetrate through time and space in one second. With that speed, Aba Yazid al-Bistami ق entered the Divine Presence.

He reached a place where Buddhists end. That is where the Naqshbandi order begins. They say that, when they enter complete emptiness, they reach perfection. This is not true. Aba Yazid Bistami reached that place. It is complete darkness to us, but it is light to the saints. When he entered there, he heard a voice coming to him, saying... HU. He tried to spend all his power looking at what he knew of creation. Allah gave saints a power in the heart that enables them to count, in five minutes, all that Allah has created in this world, each thing by its name, and every person by their name, without missing anyone. They can reach everyone, because Allah said in the Holy Qur'an—as it is found in other holy Scripture—that:

He is closer to you than your jugular vein.[163]

With that power, the saint is able to reach everyone's heart at the same time.

Aba Yazid spent all his power and counted all human beings and all creation on this earth again and again, for twenty four hours, to find out who were the created beings making that recitation, "HUUUU..." Yet he was unable to find out who they were. At that time this came to his heart, "O Aba Yazid, what are you doing in a place where you do not belong? Don't you know this is special to me? Those are *ad-dhakirun Allah wadh-dhakirat*— the men and women reciters of Holy Names whom Allah created, and no one knows their number." The reciters were under the control of Shah Naqshband, our Master, and followed his teachings. Anyone that is present in any of our associations in the Naqshbandi order was present at that time and reciting, when Aba Yazid entered that ocean. Everyone of us here was present

---

[163] Surah Qaf, 50:16.

there. But no one knows how many, because that number includes this earth and other creations as well.

The site of this meeting was beyond the complete emptiness which Buddhists take for the last and highest point of realization. After that, there are hundreds and thousands of stations! Aba Yazid was afraid that Shah Naqshband, under whose power those spirits had been placed, would chide him for interfering with him. He quickly retreated, and said, "O my Lord, I know my limit. I will not go there."

When I passed by Grandshaykh's door, it came to my heart not to look, but he, Grandshaykh, made me look. As soon as I looked, I saw this. From his two eyes, two lights were coming out. These two lights were reaching the Throne of God, and if you looked with these lights, that is what you were able to see. Anyone that looked into the light that came out of his eyes could see at that time, as in an opening through space. That cannot be described. It is for the heart to know and cannot be spoken on the tongue. As soon as the Throne appeared, Grandshaykh disappeared. As soon as he disappeared, everything around us also disappeared: the house, the stars, the sky. And everywhere I looked I could only see Grandshaykh. His head and his legs did not appear, only his body up to his neck and down to his knees. The beginning and the end was missing because they were out of the reach of understanding and vision, for:

Above every knower there is a greater knower.[164]

For forty days after that, I was unable to speak. I was mentally rapt and my mind was gone. When these saints enter into one of the oceans of God's Attributes, everything vanishes, and through them you can see.

---

[164] Surah Yusuf, 12:76.

You cannot do anything through yourself. You can do everything through your shaykh. If you surrender completely through your shaykh, he can take you, with the power that God gave him, to the presence of the Prophet ﷺ and to the presence of God. Short of that, what then can one say about the Essential Attributes of God that others can understand? What can you understand? We will be happy if they give us some kind of knowledge; but where is taste? Where is vision, where is hearing?

The Three Stations of Certainty (*Yaqeen*)

There are two sets of parallel stations in Sufism. The first step in this path is love—love (or presence in the heart) of the shaykh, love of the Prophet ﷺ, and love of God. This is the first station, and parallel to it, in the other set, there is *'Ilmu 'l-Yaqeen*, the Knowledge of Certainty. "Certainty" means that there is absolute certitude in your knowledge without falsehood. From love you go to presence: many people have that presence in their heart. They are always asking: where is my shaykh? How can I reach him and be with him? Their hearts are burning with love of the shaykh. If the shaykh sends more of that love to the hearts of people, they will burn. For that reason, he sometimes veils it a little bit, taking it away. At that time that person can work and think; otherwise he will be entranced with the love of God, of the Prophet ﷺ, and of the shaykh.

After knowing, you go to vision '*Aynu 'l-Yaqeen*, the Eye of Certainty. Wherever you look, at that stage, you are going to see your shaykh, you are going to see the Prophet ﷺ, and you are going to see God. You no longer see yourself. When the Prophet ﷺ approached his Lord, God asked him, "Who are you?" He answered, "You, O my Lord." There is no Prophet ﷺ there anymore.

The higher level is to vanish and surrender to the shaykh completely. Then the shaykh takes you to the Prophet ﷺ and the

Prophet ﷺ takes you to God. This is *Haqqu 'l-Yaqeen*, the Certainty of Truth. You are swimming in the Reality of the Divine Presence. At that time you can see, hear, feel, taste, and know. At that time, you are dressed with the seven Divine Attributes that we have mentioned.

OBEDIENCE IS THE TEST OF LOVE

bey! Teachers know that God's Order is upon every human being. No one can say, "I am not under that Order." It is a loving order. We are saying:

Obey God, and obey the Prophet, and obey your (spiritual) leaders. [165]

Love never comes without obedience. If you love someone, you have to obey them. If you don't love, you don't obey. That is why the *pir*, the shaykh, the saint, knows whether his disciple loves him or not, by sending him an order: will he complain or not? Will he accept or not accept? Will he give excuses or not? Will he say, "I cannot do this, it is wrong"? This is how he checks his love. He does not check it for himself: he knows; but he wants you to know, for you don't know. He makes you know by giving you an order.

The shaykh never tells you, "Do that!" Instead he says, "Can you do that?" Because if he says "do that," or "don't do it," it becomes very difficult for you and a disconnection might follow. For if you don't accept a firm order, it is going to be a big problem for you. That is why he does not like to give a firm order, but he gives it in an indirect way, and looks at your heart. He tries you by giving orders, but not firm orders. If you accept, it will be easy.

If there is no love, how to obey? Check yourself and see if there is love. This is your scale: are you obedient or disobedient?

---

[165] Suratu 'n-Nisa, 4:59.

When love is in the heart, love dominates the heart. That is why, as we said, all saints and *pirs* wrote poems describing their love to God in terms of love for a woman. This is the easiest way for the mind to approach the subject. How will the man devote his love to the woman or she to him? Similarly *pirs*, when they look at the complete love and beauty of God, they find that it is dominating and controlling their heart. If it is controlling their heart and when God orders that saint something, he has to do it.

When Aba Yazid Bistami ق approached the door of God through love, he reached the station where he spoke to God as Moses عليه السلام did. When he reached that station, he said, "O my Lord! Open Your door for me," the same request that Moses عليه السلام made. God said, "I cannot open My door before I test your love. This is not in order for Me to know—I already know the love that is in your heart—but for you to realize whether you are loving Me correctly or not, or whether there is still one percent or one-billionth of one percent of your love missing." God never accepts even such a small amount of love to be missing. He only accepts complete love for Him. He told Aba Yazid, "Go back and be a dumping ground for My servants; sacrifice yourself for them; if you love Me, love them; accept their burdens and then come to Me. Express your love to My servants as you express love to Me. If you love Me, you have to love everything related to Me."

In our countries, if a man loves a girl, he loves her entire family. Gifts come for the mother, the father, the brothers and sisters, in order to approach that girl. If you marry the girl, it is as if you are marrying the whole family. You have to keep their love in your heart. If they are upset, she is going to be upset. That means there is no love for her: so you have to keep all her family happy in order for her to be happy.

We saw President Bush on television running to the helicopter, and always two are dogs following after him. All his bodyguards took care of the dogs. Why? Because in that way they show respect to President Bush. What about God's creation? If you love your Lord, you must love His servants. This is the difference between saints and ordinary people. Saints must love everyone as they love God. If they don't show everyone respect, they cannot be considered saints.

Saints never accept for anyone to be upset. Everyone must feel loved. They give permission for people to say whatever they like. God said to Aba Yazid, "If you love My creation as much as you love Me, at that time I accept for you to see Me. At that time I accept for your heart to contain Me." This is according to God's words reported by the Prophet ﷺ:

Heaven and earth contain Me not, but the heart of My believing servant contains Me.

This means, "Love Me, and I shall send that light to you."

How could Aba Yazid become a dump for people's sins? He had to cause confusion in the city in order for people to be upset with him and to throw everything at him: curse him, reject him and swear at him. Then he would check his own heart: am I changing or not? Love cannot be tested when you are in harmony with people. It is easy to feel love when there is harmony and understanding with each other. Love is love when there is no harmony. If your shaykh curses you in front of people, you must not allow your love for him to change. If you do, this is not a true love. True love continues no mattter what happens. Aba Yazid went to a public spot and said, "O my people! You are praying and making prostration to a wall. There is nothing there but a wall. Do you want your prostration to be accepted? Make it for me." That meant, "Make me God, because when you prostrate before someone, it means that you consider him as God."

Most of the people ran to him and said, "You are a heretic and a hypocrite, a corrupted person trying to change the belief of people!" and they left him. Seven hundred of them made prostration. As soon as they made prostration, he opened the light of the heart that God had given him and he showed it to them. He showed them what they were really worshipping, Whom they were worshipping. None of us can see what we are worshipping except if we meditate and close our eyes: only then do we see, hear and feel. At that time they saw. Four hundred of them fell unconscious. He left them, and the remaining three hundred followed him. The biggest test was coming. He wanted to see who was going to stay with him and who was going to run!

He took them to a narrow street. From one of the adjacent streets, a very beautiful lady in make-up appeared. He hugged and kissed her, entered a house with her, and shut the door. At that point the people said, "First he made himself God and we accepted; now, what is he doing? He must be a bad person after all." And they all left except one. Look at the teachings of love by the shaykhs to the hearts of their followers. They teach and test them, teach and test them to the end. Then they open to them that power. What did that disciple do? He said to himself: "It is not my business. He does what he does, it is between him and his Lord. I know him. Even if he sleeps with a hundred women, this is not my business. My love never changes."

What does the shaykh need after sleeping with a woman? To take a shower. There was no running water at that time, so the disciple quickly brought water, heated it, brought a towel and soap, and waited outside the door for his shaykh to come out and ask for water. After some time, the shaykh opened the door. He found his disciple waiting with respect, connecting his heart to his master. The disciple did not sit. When people wait for the shaykh in other places, they sit and talk nonsense and rubbish. *Adab* (etiquette) demands that one stand with respect and wait for the shaykh to appear. This comes from love.

Love makes miracles. Everything depends on love. Without love, God would never create us. How do you think that

He is going to send you to hell? Does He send those He loves to hell? One saint said, "If one of us blows on God's hell a breath from the love that is in his heart, he will bring hell down and there will be no more hell." God is the Source of love: therefore love everyone and keep the love of your shaykh in your heart.

The shaykh opened the door and gave him another test, "My son, you are here?" He said, "As you see, my shaykh." He did not say, "Yes, I am here!" for perhaps he is there but his heart is not. He was not proud of himself. The shaykh said, "Where are your brothers and sisters?" The disciple did not say "They ran away and said you were a corrupted person," or "They ran away because they had doubts." If he said that, it would mean, "They are bad and I am good" and that also is pride. He said, "O my shaykh, I don't know, I am only looking after my business." He said, "And what is your business?" He said, "My job: water, towel, and soap here and ready." He said, "You don't know where they went?" He said, "Allah knows and you know."

The shaykh must know everything. If a *pir* does not know everything, then he is not a *pir*. He must know hearts. Even if the disciple is not present, he can reach him even if he is 20,000 miles away. He can reach him in one second through his heart from America all the way to China.

The shaykh said, "O my son, since you don't know where they are, come inside." If he had said, "I know," he would have passed the first two tests and failed the last one. He would have had to repeat everything from the beginning. When you fail one you have to start from the beginning. He made him enter and said, "This is my sister. I am marrying you together." He gave him his trust and opened the light of his heart for him. He said, "Now you represent me. After this incident, everyone thinks that I am a corrupt person and they are going to hang me." When he said these words, knocks were heard at the door. Police had come to take him because he had done two things that were not acceptable.

Instead of hanging him, they said, "He has to suffer more. Put him in the city square and stone him until he dies." This was the punishment they used against him. Where was his heart at that time? His heart was with his Lord, he did not care. With the love of God in his heart, he did not feel anything. He did what God had ordered him, "Carry the burdens of My servants, My people." How to carry them? He had to cause confusion. He caused confusion, so they cursed him and had to throw him out. They brought him to the city square and they brought all the people they could find to throw stones at him. Young and old, children and women came and stoned Aba Yazid al-Bistami, one of the greatest saints.

How much do saints suffer to reach sainthood! It is not easy. You see scholars of our day who sit in mosques or churches, giving talks on television, speaking so emotionally. What is the value of such talks? If they are not trained as saints are trained, they cannot reach anyone.

They stoned him until he fell unconscious. Blood was streaming from his body. They came near him and found that he did not breathe anymore. He was not dead, but they thought that he had died. They ordered the children to pull him by the legs and throw him in the city dump. What God had ordered him was being fulfilled. He was thrown there. For seven days, he was not able to move and he was meditating. When you are sick, your connection with your Lord is more powerful than when you are not sick. Sometimes, they send sickness on some people to make them connect themselves more.

When Aba Yazid was bleeding, the connection was stronger. He said, "O my Lord! Anyone who threw even the smallest stone at me, I accept taking all his sins and burdens and giving him the favors and the rewards You gave to me." He meditated on this for seven days. He said to saints—for when they meditate, all saints are connected to each other's heart—"If they knew the favors and good tidings I was going to give them in return for their actions, they would have wished to kill me and make me alive again and kill me another time, uninterruptedly. For as much as they beat and kill me, I am going to reward them in return."

This is the love of saints for God's creation. After seven days, he regained some power and started looking through the garbage for some rotten food to eat. As for us, we throw food away after leaving it in the fridge one day—it is not even rotten. For another seven days, he got stronger and stronger.

This is how God checks your love to see whether you love Him or not. He knows, but He wants to make you sure that you love Him or not. When a shaykh gives you an order, therefore, he is telling you, "This order will show you to what extent you love me, depending on whether you accept it or not."

If Pir Vilayat Khan tells anyone of his followers, "Do this," they will do it without using their mind, because their love for him is so powerful. This is what is needed from saints and their followers. That love must be in the heart, and without it you cannot build paths and *tariqah*. This is the only way.

God is asking from you that same love that He put in the hearts of saints and *pirs*. "I am not asking you to worship Me, because I am not in need of your worship. Worship is for you; but love is Mine. I created you with love; I want that love reciprocated. You have to love Me, and to love Me is to love My creation, My people." And all of us are creations of our Lord, servants of our Lord.

God tested Bayazid, because he had come to His door, the first time by virtue of his worship. God sent him back and said to him, "Come to Me another time with love, and I will open My door." Love, therefore, is most important for us to learn in this life. Unfortunately, love between people is no longer to be found. It is finished. There is no connection. Show me one family that lives with love. After the child turns fifteen or sixteen he leaves and is not seen anymore. Wives leave husbands, husbands leave wives.

Where are family ties? In our countries, they are the most sacred ties. Why do people keep genealogical records and descriptions of ancestors and their actions? Because there is love of the family there, and it is very important. We lost this in this century. Intellectuals and scholars do not have love in their hearts. Only spiritual people do. Anyone that has spirituality in his heart likes to bring people to love each other. Yet misunderstanding always comes between couples. No one says, "I will keep my anger down and my love up."

Saints, therefore, check the love of their followers by giving them orders. That is the meaning of that verse which we quote time and again, **"Obey God, obey the Prophet, and obey your spiritual leaders."** Everything is based on obedience, and obedience comes from love. In order to show you the extent of your love, saints order you, "Do that." If this is white and they tell you it is black, obey; say, "Yes, it is black." They are checking your heart: are you accepting or not? If you accept, they will give you all freedom, because they know that they can trust you. They will connect their heart with your heart. You will be connected and there will be harmony all your life.

Keep the love of God's servants and love each other without any discrimination nor differences in the heart. And may God bless everyone that loves human beings, and loves nature, and loves what God loves.

The Precious Knowledge

Saints do not like to use miraculous powers because these powers also lie in the hands of demons and devils. Saints prefer to use knowledge. They like to spread knowledge and wisdom in the hearts of people. This is the most important thing we have to learn concerning saints.

About this life Allah has told all His prophets and messengers according to narrations which have reached us from the Prophet ﷺ:

Ask for knowledge even as far as China.[166]

That means "seek knowledge as far as you can. Run after it. Study and learn." When you study and learn, you can teach yourself how to behave and practice good manners.

The teaching and studying we are talking about is not about technology. People study technology for their daily life. "Knowledge" is knowledge of the heart, God's knowledge, learning how to be His servant, the knowledge that He gave to His angels, to His saints, to His prophets. The knowledge of the wise: that is the important knowledge. That is the knowledge we have to run after and ask for.

Allah has sent such knowledge to the hearts of His servants through inspiration or through revelation. All saints, all prophets, all holy men have to sit by themselves and meditate on their Lord in order for their Lord to send them this precious knowledge.

---

[166] Ibn Hajar, al-'Iraqi, Zubaydi, al-Khatib, Bayhaqi.

We spoke before of a great saint of one of the Mediterranean countries by the name of Ahmad al-Badawi, who tried his best to memorize the Old Testament, the New Testament, the Holy Qur'an, and all books of wisdom that had been written. He was progressing through this hard labor and finally asked, "O my Lord, open Your door of knowledge for me." Every saint asks his Lord in a different manner. The connection of the heart is different for every wise man.

Every one is a holy person. Allah did not discriminate in His creation. He did not say, "I create this one a holy person and that one a bad person." Allah created people to be saintly. As the Prophet ﷺ said:

Every child is born in innocence and purity.[167]

All of us were born as such children, with purity equally, and with that same light in the heart. Some used that power, some did not. Those who used that power became holy men. Those that did not, stayed what they were.

Aba Yazid al-Bistami was asking for love. Ahmad al-Badawi was asking for knowledge. He journeyed to the door of al-'Alim, the All-Knowing, until he said, "O my Lord, give me the key to that door." As he was asking, another holy man passed by the place where he was praying, and said, "O Ahmad al-Badawi! I have that key you are asking for. If you need it and would like to take it, I shall give it to you." He said, "No, I will not take that key from another person—like you—but from the Keymaker Himself. I am not in need for your key."

You are free men and women. Do you want that key? Take it. You do not want that key? You are free. It is up to you. Ahmad al-Badawi refused the key from that man. He said, "I

---

[167] Bukhari, Muslim, Ahmad, *Muwatta Malik*, at-Tirmidhi,

shall take the key from the Keymaker." If you can take the key from the Keymaker, go ahead and take it—if you find it! Why can't you find it? He is near us:

We are nearer to you than your jugular vein.[168]

but you cannot see Him. Why? Because there are veils of darkness covering your heart! Blocking the sight of our Lord!

He refused to take the key and went back and prayed more, asking for the key, until God spoke to him in those terms, "O My servant, I have created this earth through cause and effect and for everything there is a cause. You cannot come to Me without a cause. My Wisdom, My Justice and My Will have made that person who spoke to you the keeper of your key. Go and take your key from him. You cannot come to Me directly. You are short-sighted. You need a guide to guide you to My door. You cannot come to Me with your ignorance and your ego. You have to follow a guide that lets you take your ego away and lift the veils of darkness from your heart. In this way you can approach Me."

Now, Ahmad al-Badawi heard it directly from His Lord and there was no doubt about it. He started looking for that person who had come to him before, but he had disappeared. For six months, he ran to every corner in the city asking about that person but no one knew him. That saint was watching him and veiling himself all the time. Finally, he took off his veil and appeared to him. Ahmad al-Badawi said, "O my master! Please give me the key." He said, "Now you want the key? I came to you and offered it freely but you refused. This time, you have to pay a price." Ahmad said, "Take whatever you like of my possessions and myself." He said, "We are not after your things. You have to give yourself to me. Surrender to me. I shall clean you and return

---

[168] Surah Qaf, 50:16.

you clean. I must do this in order for you to get your key. Do you accept?" He accepted immediately.

The saint looked into the eyes of Ahmad al-Badawi. Whatever Ahmad had gained through studying books and schools, and all kinds of knowledge, was flushed out and emptied from his heart completely. He said:

> **Which then is best? - he that layeth his foundation on piety to Allah and His good pleasure? - or he that layeth his foundation on an undermined sand-cliff ready to crumble to pieces?**[169]

The knowledge you have learned was learned through the ego, and spiritual knowledge cannot be built on top of ego. You have to empty your heart from this knowledge you have learned through books."

Books never give you correct knowledge, because the writer who wrote that book only wrote what he knows. It might not be for you. Every person has a path. God gave to every person a different way to reach Him. That is why He said:

> **Each one is swimming in his orbit.**[170]

You cannot swim in my orbit and I cannot swim in yours. The Prophet ﷺ and all Messengers and saints said, "The ways to God are as numerous as the breaths of human beings." How then are all of us going to learn only from So-and-so's book? That writer did not sit with you to see what kind of disease you have in your heart in order to address it. Who wrote these books? Some of them passed away; some of them you did not know before;

---

[169] Suratu 't-Tawbah, 9:109.
[170] Surah Yasin, 36:40.

none of them knew your diseases. How are they going to affect your spirituality?

Spirituality consists in a living saint sitting with you, diagnosing your spiritual sickness, and then giving you the correct medicine. When you go to a hospital, you go to different kinds of specialists. You cannot go to one doctor for all things. Even if you do visit a General Practicioner, he will give you red tablets and give someone else yellow tablets. For X, antibiotics, and for Y, Tylenol. Everyone needs something different. Not everyone has the same disease and gets the same treatment.

The writer wrote the book derived from his experience with his community, not from his experience with you. How are you going to benefit? It is a misunderstanding and an incorrect assumption that makes people run after bookish knowledge and read. You can learn something, but it is not spirituality. It is something without taste. You read it and enjoy it, and then it will leave you and it is finished. You cannot live what you are reading about. With a living saint, you can live, feel, and learn. He will take your sickness away from your heart and direct you after you take initiation from him and say, "I am following you and trusting you to guide me to the path of my Lord."

Saints do not want anything from you, but they want you to find your love; to find your knowledge; to find your reality; to find your Lord. They are not after you for your money; they are not after you for a certain reason. They are after you to direct your heart. For God ordered everyone, "Try to direct the heart of my servants to Me; to love Me as I love them, and to know Me." To know God means to know with His knowledge. Know your Lord. How will you know Him? Try to know Him until you know, you feel, you taste, you see and you love. May Allah give us this power and make us know Him and love Him through revelation and inspiration through our hearts.

Ahmad al-Badawi was the most knowledgeable scholar in Egypt at the time. If there were problems that needed a judge in matters of church, synagogue, and mosque, people went to him. The saint took all of Ahmad al-Badawi's knowledge out of his heart and left him as empty as a young child not knowing even how to read and write. The people started saying, "Ahmad al-Badawi has become mentally ill." He did not tell them what had happened, and so they did not know the secret of his state. All they knew was that from the big scholar that he was he had changed into nothing.

When you are nothing, you are everything. When you are non-existing, Allah will give you existence in His existence. But when you are appearing in front of God saying, "You are there, I am here; You are You, I am I," it cannot be. We have to know that there is nothing except God. We are His reflections. We are His manifestations: He created us because He loves us, and when He wants us back, He takes us.

For six months, Ahmad al-Badawi remained in that state. Children were running after him in the street and mocking him. People said, "What a fool he has become." God was testing him, "Is he going to keep his love for Me or not? Is He going to keep asking for this knowledge or not?" Where could he go after everything had been taken from him? Had he listened from the beginning, he would not have suffered in this way.

This is the difference between listening from the first order and rejecting the first order. If you reject the first order, you are going to suffer later. If you love Allah, you obey from the first order. If you love your shaykh, you obey from the first order, whatever he says to you, even though it may be a great burden to you. Do it, and you will not suffer. This is an example.

Ahmad al-Badawi suffered. He said he did not need a guide. Everyone needs a guide. You cannot go to your Lord without a guide. What does that guide want? Only to clean him.

If he had listened to him from the beginning, he would not have imposed all this suffering on him. He would have given him the key and sent him to his Lord. Because he said no, the saint wants to break that pride in him and not let him reject his orders. Therefore, do not reject orders coming to you from God or from saints. Listen, and you will succeed. If you do not listen you will fail. Do not say, "This is too much; I cannot do it." Do it. What is going to happen?

After six other months, the saint appeared to Ahmad al-Badawi again. He said, "O my son, I know that you have waited for me for six months. I was beside you, but you could not see me because of the veil of your ego. Now, my son, look into my eyes." Ahmad looked into his eyes. Ahmad looked into his eyes, and the saint gave him the knowledge of true spirituality which God had revealed to his heart, the knowledge that God wants His servant to know.

This is knowledge that you can build on, not knowledge of books. Your faith is built on such knowledge and so is your path to your Lord. He filled him with knowledge with which he became able to treat other people and give them the keys to their ways. May Allah not cause us to suffer but may He cause us to listen to our master from the first order, and by listening to succeed.

As soon as Ahmad received that light it began to glow from his eyes. Anyone that looked into his eyes at that time fainted, so he wore a veil or *burku'* to cover his eyes. Such a light is a treasure which God has given His servants because He loves us. When someone loves you, He gives you everything and He cares for you. Allah loves all His creation, and He cares for everyone. He is asking you, "Come to Me, and I shall give you all your treasures. I shall give you Divine light and put you in My Divine Presence. I shall put you with My saints and My prophets. But come to Me." Everything must have a cause and an effect.

You must make the intention, and Allah will give. If you do not, He will not give. Not in this life, at any rate, but He will give you later.

May Allah accept our intention from us and make us true servants for Him and His beloved saints and holy people. May Allah keep our hearts together as one unit and one group, brothers and sisters, without differences and without discrimination.

A time is coming on this world, a time of peace and harmony when everyone on the earth will say *"La ilaha ill-Allah,"* and see it with the heart, not say it only with the tongue. It is very soon. Saints are waiting: will it be tonight or tomorrow? Do not think it is too far. Saints are not sitting idle. If you knew what they do! After everyone goes to sleep, they sit by themselves and meditate in their heart and pray in prostration and multiply prayers. What they ask their Lord shakes the Throne of their Lord! They are not sitting idle. That One is coming very soon to bring peace to all this world. We are asking our Lord to extend our lives in order for us to see him. We do not know when He will take us back. May the Lord of heaven and of everything else accept our request. Call him by whatever name you wish, yet everyone must know that there is someone with the power of creation in His hand, and He is the Creator.

My shaykh once said, may Allah bless him and raise him ever higher in his stations, "Even if you worship a stone as the idol-worshippers of old, to worship it with correct understanding is tantamount to worshipping God, because it takes God to originate that stone. How else is this stone appearing: by itself? Or by that light through which God has ordered that element to appear? It is appearing with a name of God, as everything on earth appears with one of the different names of God, which makes this different from that. Hence there are countless names of God, and no one can know His Names! It is impossible to count

His Names! Everything that appears on this earth, from stones in caves to people, animals, trees, and bacteria: everyone is appearing with a name. That name is the Ever-Living."

Everyone is a Worshipper

My shaykh said, "Every person on this earth, therefore, is a worshipper. No one exists except as a worshipper according to their understanding. For that reason, Allah is not going to punish anyone." If more is said on this issue, all people are going to be confused! This news makes people shake. Everyone has different beliefs: when they hear this, they are finished. But this is reality. Reality cannot be given just like that. This is the knowledge that Ahmad al-Badawi was running after. You cannot find this knowledge in books. This is the knowledge of hearts and heavenly inspiration.

Every second there is inspiration according to the station the saints are putting you in. There is inspiration! There is power! There is knowledge! There is light! There is Divine Presence! There is God in every station they put you in! You have to take from that. But because of these eyes we have, because of this ego we are carrying, it enters from here and leaves from there... Nothing comes to the heart. If saints opened what is in their hearts, they would make people dance with love for their Lord. If they gave permission to speak, one saint can make people cease prostrating to God! One saint can stop people from worshipping, because if he opens what is in the heart concerning the mercy that God is going to bestow on His servants, no one is going to worship anymore, and no one is going to come to the Lord: they will all run, because they will know that He is going to bring them to His arms and hug them in the end.

When the one who will appear appears, he is going to appear with that kind of knowledge. Saints are waiting. May Allah bring it to pass very soon. A week ago, one saint said, "O my Lord, if you are not going to give permission for that one to appear, I am going to break all the barriers between him and his appearance on his earth!" Heaven and earth shook from the power of that speech. God has appointed a day for saints: saints now know the day when he is going to appear, but there is no permission to speak about it. It is very soon.

May Allah show us that day and make us see that golden time. It is the best time, the lovely time of peace and harmony on this earth, without boundaries between countries. You are going to hear beautiful singing and chanting through all this earth, day and night, "*La ilaha illa-Allah*" in all different types of languages. This music they call Beethoven and Mozart will pale like dust on the shoes of angels in comparison to the music of the angels in the heart of a believer! If one could only hear it. When that music appears for everyone in the golden age, people are going to be drunk from hearing it. They will be dancing and feel ecstatic. They will be moulded over with that lovely music.

ENDNOTES

[i] This hadith is related with reference to Hjiaz in place of Najd in Bukhari and Muslim.

[ii] Imam Isma'il ash-Shafi'i al-'Ajluni relates from Mullah al-Qari, in *Kashf al-Khafa wa mazid al-albas*, "Though al-Saghani says this is *mawdu* (forged) even so I say its meaning is *sahih* (authentic) even if it is not a hadith."

Ibn Taymiyya said in his book *al-qaida al-jalila fi 't-tawwasali wa 'l-wasila*, "...and like that is the hadith ...from 'Umar ibn al-Khaṭṭab ؓ *marfu'an* and *mawqufan 'alayh*, that when Adam ؑ has committed the sin, he said, 'O Lord! I ask you for the sake of Muhammad [*bi haqqi Muhammad*] to forgive me.' He ﷻ said, 'How did you know Muhammad?' He said, 'because when You created me with Your Hands and blew into me from Your Spirit, I raised my head and I saw on the legs of Your Throne written, '*la ilaha ill-Allah Muhammadun Rasulullah*' so I knew You would not put next to Your Name except the one who is the most beloved to You.' He said, 'you have said the truth, O Adam, and if it were not for Muhammad, I would not have created you.'" [*law la Muhammadan maa khalaqtuk*].

"And this hadith is narrated by al-Hakim in his *Mustadrak*, from the hadith of 'Abdillah bin Muslim al-Fihri, from Isma'il bin Salama. And Hakim said, 'and it is the first hadith I have mentioned from 'Abdur-Rahman in this book. And Hakim says that it is *sahih*. And it is related by Shaykh Abu Bakr al-Ajuri, in the book *ash-Shari'ah mawqufan* on 'Umar from hadith 'Abdillah bin Isma'il bin Abi Maryam *mawqufan* from 'Abdur Rahman bin Zayd bin Aslam."

[iii] Hadith mentioned in *Ruh al-Bayan*, commentary on Surat al-'Asr. In another version the Prophet ﷺ said, "If my Community keeps on the right, it is going to enjoy an age of one day, and if it becomes corrupt, it will have an age of half a day." Al-Munawi cites it in *Fayd al-Qadir* from Shaykh Muhyi al-Din Ibn 'Arabi.

iv Quoted in Misri's *Reliance of the Traveller*, (ed. and trans. Nuh Ha Mim Keller, Dubai: 1991) p. 862 and from Ibn 'Ajibah's *Commentary on Ibn 'Ata Ailah, ¬qazu 'l-himam fi sharhi 'l-Hikam* (Cairo: 1972), p. 6. See also Abu Bakr al-Warraq's saying quoted by al-Bayhaqi in Branch 18 of *The Seventy-Seven Branches of Faith*, trans. 'Abdal Hakim Murad (Quilliam Press: 1990) p. 14.

v Ibn 'Abbas ❧ said, "Meditation for one hour is better than standing the night in prayer." Al-Qurtubi.

Anas ❧ said, "Meditation upon the difference between night and day is better the worship of eighty years." Ad-Daylami.

vi The authenticity of this hadith is disputed, however, the hadith scholars like Imam an-Nawawi says the meaning of it is true. It is backed by the hadith reported from al-Hafiz as-Suyuti in his *Hawi* from our Mother'Ayesha that when the Messenger of Allah ﷺ was asked:"Who is the one who the most knowledgeable of his Lord? He said, "Those who are most knowledgeable about themselves."

vii Abul-Fath ibn Abi Fawaris in his *Amalee* from al-Hasan (*mursalan*). Related by ad-Daylami and others from Anas (*marfu'an*) and Abi Shaykh from Abu Hurayrah and Abu Sa'eed (*marfu'an*) with the wording, 'Verily the month of Ramadan is the month of my Nation.' However Ibn al-Jawzi in his *Mawdu'at* (Forgeries) related it through many different ways, as did al-Hafiz Ibn Hajar in *Kitab tabayyin al-'ajab feema warada fee rajab*.

viii Al-Ghazali mentioned it in his *Revival of the Religious Sciences*. It is similar to the Israelite tradition Ahmad has related in *al-Zuhd* from Wahb bin Munabbih who said that God opened the heavens for Ezekiel until he saw the Throne, so Ezekiel said, "How Perfect are You! How Mighty are You, O Lord!" So God said, "Truly, the heavens and the earth were too weak to contain Me, but the soft, humble heart of my believing slave contains Me."

ix Sayyidina 'Ali ❧ said, "Allah's Face is the Truth (*al-Haqq*); Mujahid said, "It is He Himself." Ad-Dahhak said, "Everything perishes except Allah, Paradise and the Fire." Ibn Kaysan said, "It is His sovereignty." It was reported in Bukhari's *Sahih* from Abu Salamah that Abu Hurayrah ❧ said, "The Prophet of Allah ﷺ said, "The truest word of a poet was the saying of Labid, 'indeed everything except Allah is false.'"

ˣ *"Farafadanee Jibreel"* in Ibn Abi Hatim and Ibn Kathir's *Tafsir*s, while al-Salihi in *Subul al-Huda* (3:129) has *"Fata'akhkhara Jibreel"* – both meaning "he left me and stayed back."

ˣⁱ Similar to a saying reported by al-Qushayri in his *Epistles*, and similar to a hadith related by Tirmidhi in his *Shama'il*, reported by Sayyidina 'Ali ؓ where he said, "The Prophet ﷺ when he entered his home would divide his time in portions, one portion for Allah, one portion for his family and one portion for himself, and the later he divided between himself and the people." And this is reported by La'ali.

www.ingramcontent.com/pod-product-compliance
Lightning Source LLC
Chambersburg PA
CBHW030311080526
44584CB00012B/529